D0231670

Caught by the river

A COLLECTION OF WORDS ON WATER

KILPHEDERIR BURN

ALNESS

FORTH

IRVINE

COQUET

PENKILN
BURN   ANNAN   WEAR

OUSE

DOUGLAS

MERSEY   TRENT
PORTER
& DON

NORE

SEVERN   CAM

TEIFI

LOUGHOR   LEA

AVON

OGMORE   UPPER
            THAMES   MOLE   CRAY
KENNET   THAMES
& AVON   WANDLE

CARY   ROTHER
        STOUR

VALENCY   WELLSBOURNE
TREGASEAL   TAMAR
STREAM   TIDDY   DART

HELFORD

Caught by the river

A COLLECTION OF WORDS ON WATER

COMPILED AND EDITED BY JEFF BARRETT,
ROBIN TURNER AND ANDREW WALSH

Caught By The River would like to thank: Simon Benham, Mathew Clayton, Steve Phillips, Chris Yates for setting the ball rolling, Paul Kelly, Lora Findlay, John Richardson, Laura Price, Simon Ward & all at Cassell Illustrated. Special mention to all at Heavenly Recordings for putting up with us. Massive, heartfelt thanks to everyone who has contributed to this book and to the website.

The Illustrators

Robert Gibbings (1889-1958), artist, book-designer, and travel writer. Born in Cork, he was educated at UCC and served at Gallipoli. He came under the influence of the artist Eric Gill, running the Golden Cockerel Press from 1924 to 1933. Besides a series of books on rivers – including Caught By The River fave, *Sweet Thames Run Softly* (1940) – he wrote about the South Seas in *Coconut Island* (1936). Illustrations reproduced with thanks to the Heather Chalcroft Literary Agency and the estate of Robert Gibbings.

John Richardson studied graphic design at Newcastle College Art where he met his wife Sue. They have two children, Katherine and Michael. John worked in Advertising and Graphic Design then in 1993 he decided upon a career change and joined Buckinghamshire New University where he built up a thriving BA Illustration course before becoming Head of 2D Design and running MA courses in Illustration and Printmaking. In 2006 he retired to pursue his love of printmaking having purchased a fine Victorian Albion press, www.thetwoterrierspress.com.

A Cassell Book

An Hachette Livre UK Company

First published in the UK 2009 by Cassell Illustrated,
a division of Octopus Publishing Group Ltd.
2–4 Heron Quays,
London E14 4JP

A CIP catalogue record for this book is available from the British Library.

ISBN-13: 978-1-84403-667-7

10 9 8 7 6 5 4 3 2 1

Commissioning Editor: Laura Price
Cover artwork: Paul Kelly
Illustrations: Robert Gibbings
Maps: John Richardson
Design: Paul Kelly and Lora Findlay
Production: Caroline Alberti

Printed in Great Britain by CPI Antony Rowe, Chippenham, Wiltshire

CONTENTS

FOREWORD

————•◦•————

Januarry 2009. Attempting to write an introduction to a book about rivers isn't exactly familiar territory for us. Having spent a fair portion of our lives in the music industry, even our close friends and families aren't really sure how we got here.

It happened like this. In 2007, we had the idea to start a website. We gave it a name – Caught By The River. Originally, we just had the vague notion that it would document the odd fishing trip whilst also allowing us to enthuse about our passions. It transpired that these were books, music, films, booze and sometimes even cake recipes. Not written about in the cynical all-new-stuff-is-cool, buy-me-please way that we're used to in our line of work. We just wanted to extol the virtues of things we care about.

The theme that joined these disparate passions was taking time out, having a breather and escaping from life's modern forms of slavery – BlackBerrys, mobiles and the like. As the website grew we came into contact with people who shared our views – writers, musicians, anglers, drinkers. Opinions were usually exchanged over a pint or three.

Last year, buoyed by the success of the website, we took what was rapidly becoming our obsession a stage further and decided to piece together a book of writings on British rivers. We wanted the book to get across all aspects of life on the river – the pace and the sounds; Childhood memories and life-long reminiscences; stories about angling, stories about canoing, stories about sitting idly with a beer in your hand staring at the water.

We approached the challenge in the same way we'd put together a compilation album. We managed to secure our first 'key song' when Britain's leading angling writer Chris Yates agreed to write a piece for the book on the Dorset Stour. With that in place the ball was rolling and before long we'd amassed 400 pages worth of wonderful musings on the rivers of the United Kingdom (and one in Ireland). Some of the writers are household names, others of them will be before too long. We've interspersed this exemplary collection of essays and poems with with etchings by the late, great Robert Gibbings alongside specially commissioned beautifully handcrafted maps by John Richardson.

Somehow it's all come together. We're delighted. We hope you enjoy.

Cheers!

Andrew, Jeff & Robin, Caught By The River

The Language
Of Rivers

—•◆•—

BY
SUE CLIFFORD & ANGELA KING

At the turn of the river the language changes,
A different babble, even a different name for the same river...

River, Carol Ann Duffy

—•◆•—

The richness of our long cultural relationship with rivers is evident in the names we know them by and the clues which linger in our place names. We have all but forgotten that many old languages jostle with modern English. Avon is still recognisable as the Welsh word – *afon* – and has persisted as a proper name where the newcomers did not understand that the word simply meant river in the old language.

We have many words for streams. *Sike* or *sick*, a name used in the north of England for a runnel or trickle of water has its equivalent *sitch* in the south. *Beck* and *gill* (from Old

Norse) are north country words for brook which tend to be used most in Cumbria and Lancashire, whereas *burns,* prevalent in Scotland also flow eastward down from the Cheviots and the moors across Northumberland. The winterbournes of Wiltshire and Dorset are known in the Yorkshire Wolds as *gipseys*, as *nailbournes* in Kent and *lavants* in Hampshire. Rhynes are the names given to ditches made to drain the Somerset Levels, in west Sussex they are called *rifes*.

Waterfalls are called *forces* in Yorkshire, elsewhere they may be described as falls, steps, cascades, gorges, cataracts, spouts, rapids and eas.

Our ancestors described significance and captured meaning in names. Many place names show the importance of water – springs (Fonthill, Teffont – fontana, a fountain or spring), wells (Sadler's Wells, Southwell, Chigwell); fords – the most numerous descriptive name relating to water (Oxford, Fordingbridge, Belfast – sandbank ford); bridges (Trowbridge – tree bridge, Bristol – meeting place at the bridge, Bridgenorth, or simply Brigg); weirs (Ware – place by a weir, Edgware – Ecgi's weir); ferrys (Rock Ferry, North and South Ferriby); places by mill streams (Melbourne, Millom) and by waterfalls (Moness).

Many of the names of rivers themselves are descriptive: Thames – dark; Cam, Croome, Wellow – winding; Aire, Taw, Tern – strong/swift; Stour – strong/powerful; Leadon, Lydden – broad; Kyle, Coly – narrow; Cray – pure, clear; Derwent, Darent, Dart – oaklined; Iwerne – yew-lined, and so on. The discipline of etymology has learnt much since Ekwall produced *River Names* in 1928 but this book is still the

exciting starting point for further speculations, as well as the county volumes of the English Place Name Society.

In Northamptonshire, somewhere between Thrapston and Wellingborough, the River Nene changes its pronunciation – to the south it is the nen or nairn, to the north the neen, this identifies further particularity.

The Tarrant, a small tributary of the Stour, has stamped identity onto the villages in its catchment: it gives its name to a number of Dorset villages the Tarrants – Gunville, Hinton, Launceston, Monkton, Rawston, Rushton, Keynston. This stream, a winterbourne in its upper reaches, owns the valley. It is thought that its name means trespasser – it wanders into the road, after prolonged rain, sometimes for half a mile, but the road was not there first....

Along the stretch of the Thames through the City, the new Tate or Millenium Bridge continues the accumulation of names

– Old Swan Pier, Nicholson's Steam Packet Wharf, Irongate Stair, Limehouse Reach, Cast Iron Wharf, Puddle Dock, Pickle Herring Stair, Old Jamaica Wharf.

Pub names carry references to previous customs or events. 'The Fountain' at the northern base of Shaftesbury's steep greensand hill recollects the dependence which the hilltop town had on the village of Enmore Green the source of its pure water and the basis of the strange Byzant Ceremony, a ritual of exchange.

In Sutton Poyntz, south Dorset, the pub sign for 'The Springhead' shows horses hauling a giant pipe. It transpires that when the Great Eastern, Brunel's first ocean liner, was broken up around 1890 the Weymouth Water Company bought one of its five huge funnels and installed it in the spring above the village, where it still collects millions of gallons a day.

Sue Clifford and Angela King are the authors of England in Particular *and co-founders of the arts and environmental charity* Common Ground *www.commonground.org.uk*

THE
RIVER
ALNESS

BY
JON BERRY

Rivers run through men as surely as they run through the landscape. Geologists and topographers and those whose souls have not been flooded by water speak of springs, of sources, of uplands and lowlands, of estuaries and tributaries. To them, a river is a physical entity, a geographic reality, and can be reduced to a line on a map or, worse still, a description in a ramblers' guidebook. I wouldn't question their scientific integrity or adherence to the material facts, but rivers run other courses that cannot be charted so clinically. Those who have lost hours and days knee-deep in moving water, who have let the current pulse through them rather than around, will know this. Rivers can, when allowed, flow through a man's dreams and beneath his skin, in to his blood and straight to the dark core of his heart. Rivers are not a mere act of geology. They are viral.

The best men I have known have all been consumed by a river. Some have been fishermen, others poets, a few have been writers, and one a kayaker with a philosopher's disposition. All had a river that pulsed within them, and none could do anything about it.

I have spent a lifetime staring in to water, attempting to conjure fish from the depths. In four decades, I have fallen headlong for more than a dozen rivers, sleeping beside them, drinking tea from them, bathing in them and fishing them. All have flirted back, but as is the way with these things, it was the first one that got me. It is almost forty years since I surrendered to the Black River.

That, of course, is not its real name. To the locals in the Highland Town through which it runs, it is the Alness River.

Those who wish to nod towards its ancient past use its Gaelic
name, the Averon. I use both, but think always of its deep
pools, its dark bubbling waters, its time-hewn boulders and of
the canopies of trees that shade it along much of its ten miles.
In truth its colours run from peaty brown to a post-glacial grey
that characterises much of that part of the Highlands, but when
I first saw the river as a small child, water had never looked so
malevolent. It frightened me, and before long, it owned me.

———•◦•———

The river flows from the south-east point of Loch Morie, high
in the mountains of Easter Ross, to its end on the northerly
shore of the Cromarty Firth. Its Gaelic name translates as
'small river', and the ancient Celts were right; the river is
neither particularly long nor overly wide. Only at its estuary
does it broaden to any degree, and its final miles lie quietly
in the shadow of Cnoc Fyrish. Much of the upper river passes
through land owned by the Munro-Fergusons of the Novar
Estate, but it becomes the property of the people upon enter-
ing the town that gives its name, where it marks the division
between the parishes of Alness and Rosskeen. And yet, such
notions of ownership seem ridiculous when applied to a river,
and when I stand beside it or in it, I know that it is also mine,
and that it owns me too.

Our first encounter was captured through the lens of a box
brownie. As I look at the photograph now, it shows only two
young boys – my twin and I – leaning over the metal rail above
the Stick Pool, a deep funnelling lie for running salmon, as a

summer sun warms the brooding and turbulent water. Days earlier we had become fishermen; cousin Ricky had taken us both to Bodle's Burn, a typical Highland stream that ran westward off the main river, past the Manse and through the graveyard in to a small dammed pool. There, bamboo pole and worm had fooled a small brown trout, and Ricky had decided we were ready to see the river itself.

The Stick Pool, with its concrete flood barrier on the westerly bank and seemingly bottomless glide beneath, is a consequence of the actions of The Blind Captain, Hugh Munro, who was given the job of diverting the river after disastrous flooding in 1844. It was here too that our cousin had landed giant sea trout and the largest spring salmon of the year, and so we already knew of its magic. Later that week we would cast in to it, clumsily with flies, as the light fell and the monsters woke. We caught thumb-printed parr and tiny brown trout that hid behind rocks, but both Ricky and the river knew we were not ready for more. I have yet to take a salmon from the Stick Pool, but it was there on a later summer holiday that I inhaled my first cigarette, and where one of the poachers plucked bottles from a bankside cave and gave Chris and me our first taste of whisky. My brother and I were ten.

During term-time, in Hampshire, the river seemed so much further away than its six-hundred miles, and it was difficult to distinguish between Ricky and the river itself. Both haunted us, and were inseparable. We talked of little else, and planned new adventures with our cousin and the downfall of the river's finny inhabitants for weeks before each school holiday. Of course, being impatient, we fished the local ponds and

rivers for carp, perch, eels and tench, but our thoughts always returned to the river, and to Ricky.

It wasn't just Ricky in whom the river lived. It maintained a fluid hold on other members of my mother's family – there were poachers and hunters, Inca the labrador-alsation cross who would steal its quivering bounty in his jaws, and an uncle who was dragged, drunk but alive, from its shallows before abandoning it and disappearing with a band of travellers. My grandfather passed over the river, marching to war – and five years in a prisoner of war camp – in 1939, and back over it when he returned, a more embittered man. It was in this river's valley that my mother played as a small girl, and there too where she was later courted by my father. As a young man it was where I took every girlfriend, and it was in one of its pools, years later, that I accepted the failure of my own marriage. Ricky was with me, enjoying the grilse run, but it was the water's persistent flow and soft unending voice that told me it was time to move on.

———•◦•———

In later school holidays we explored upstream. There was the Douglas Pool, a boiling froth below a cliff face where fly-fishing was impossible but worms were legitimate, and the exclusive waters of the Novar Estates where only a Spey-cast fly was permitted. Now in his late-teens, Ricky was a respected ghillie and could secure us days and nights on these otherwise forbidden waters. Our favourite place though was at the river's source, high in Easter Ross. Loch Morie is now overlooked by the incongruous propellers of a wind farm, but in my childhood the only evidence of humanity was the abandoned boat house and Kildermorie Lodge at the far end of the water, two miles north-west. We camped there, caught and cooked trout on its shores, and battled the evening midgie hatches with ointments and cigarette smoke.

Morie is like so many of the large ice-age lochs of the Highlands, a long, narrow and moody body with depths over three-hundred feet. Brown Trout, Ferox Trout and Arctic Char live beneath its surface, and many of the river's salmon are born there, returning only to die. Where the loch shallows and forms the head of the river, a circle of rocks breaks the surface forming a natural sepulchre for the returning fish. My own ashes will be there one day.

Ten miles downstream the river joins the Cromarty Firth in a large estuary. We explored there, too, as boys. The land was waterlogged, dotted with pools and lochans and overrun with rabbits and ducks. Animal carcasses, snares tied to crude fences and unearthed artefacts from early settlers could all be found with little effort among the ditches and heather. To young senses, it seemed neither land nor water but an ominous purgatory between them. Ricky took us hunting in this coastal wilderness, but we were always pulled back in to the flow.

The river here is proletarian water, cheaper than the town water to fish and more tolerant of irregular methods. It was here that I hooked, and lost, my first salmon. The landscape is flatter, and the river less animated; the ferocity of the middle river gives way to slower glides and riffles, and when the tide rises and questions the natural flow, it can seem to briefly stand still. Only a long stare out to sea, towards the illuminated oil rigs at Nigg and the distant lights of Cullicudden and Balblair confirm that a populated world is still out there, turning.

My river will always seem black to me, but its heart is less malevolent than many I have known since, and its spirit is benign. Three-quarters or more of its bank has yet to be settled by man, and this matters – in spite of the flood banks, the Teaninich Distillery, the new industrial estate and the road bridges, the river runs freely and unfettered, and nature remains its dominant influence. Only a river so mercifully unmolested can truly steal a man's soul. Living so far away, I have spent more hours by other waterways, but none has captured me with such permanence. I was able to walk away from the Kennet's pastoral, garden-lawn banks with barely a backward glance, while the Bristol Avon – my local river – amused but did not possess. The currents of the Hampshire Avon, Teme, Severn and Loddon all permeated, but did not stay.

Only the Thames came close to supplanting the Black River in my veins. It was the river's history that enthralled me, its place at the arterial heart of England which enlivened every visit. I see it every day in its infant form, beneath the rumble of the Cirencester Road near Castle Eaton, but it is the mature water downstream that draws me. It isn't the fish – there are too few of them to hold my attention when closer waters are so munificent – but the ancient footsteps in which the modern Thames visitor treads which appeal.

Once, when researching a book, I was obliged to know the capital's river a little better, and every plunge below its surface revealed a new scandal. The waters of the Thames are as dark as any. There were the bloody invasions of the Danes, whose raiding parties in long boats pushed the locals upstream and extended the Danelaw, and the inhumanity of the floating prison hulks a millennium later. There was the bloodless coup of Runnymede where Magna Carta was signed, and the countless fist fights of Victorian Thames Professionals, a 400-strong band of men who vied for the custom of visiting anglers with bare knuckles and skulduggery. Murder, piracy, rape and regicidal treachery have all visited its banks, while even the community-minded frost fairs of the 1700s were outraged by the prostitutes who plied their wares on ice. Perhaps these are the reasons the Thames did not possess me – I offered myself to it, but it was simply too busy with the souls of others.

Exorcising the Black River would have been futile, and if I had succeeded it would have been disloyal to let the memory of a cholera-infested Thames replace it. When a river takes hold, it shapes a man inexorably, and my river suits me. I return infrequently now. Ricky is still there, and so are the salmon, but the virus in me has abated sufficiently to allow me the freedom to work and fish and love in southern England. And yet, if I close my eyes, I can see and smell the Stick Pool, the Douglas Pool and the Estuary beat, and feel their rhythms pulsing. I can touch the smooth rocks in the shallows and sense the current on the backs of my legs with every step in to the black.

I have the left the river, but it has not left me.

Jon is a member of the infamous Golden Scale Club and is the author of the critically acclaimed A Can of Worms *for The Medlar Press. His second book,* A Train to Catch, *will be published in 2009.*

There Is
Nothing
In The
Water

BY
FRANK COTTRELL
BOYCE

I spent the first part of my childhood on the bank of a river, though I didn't realise it at the time. The Mersey flowed by, just a few hundred yards from the block of flats where we lived, but it was hidden away behind a monumental dock wall and a tangle of streets in what was then one of Europe's most densely populated districts. Once, standing out on the balcony, I saw something amazing – unmistakably the funnel of a ship, out of all proportion in size and in the intensity of its colour, shovelling steam into the sky, cruising along between the terraced rooftops. Even this vision didn't make me think of the river. Instead, I imagined some weird road, down in the next parish, where they did everything differently, where – for all I knew – ships instead of bread vans went clattering over the cobbles. It was the sea, not the river, that called to me then. There was a cabinet in the corner of the living room, full of the treasures my Grandad had brought back from his travels – dainty China tea services, medals and inexplicable ornaments. There were photos of him and of my uncles in dress uniforms of angelic white. There were vague stories of sea battles, of a birth caul that would give him immunity from drowning, of him jumping ship and the ship later going down with all hands. One day I too would run away to sea.

The first river to take hold of my imagination was a fictitious one – the Say in Philippa Pearce's *Minnow on the Say*. The book opens with one of the most inviting scenes in literature. Adam's house backs onto the river. One morning, after heavy rain, he discovers a canoe – the Minnow – washed up at the bottom of the garden. He decides that he has to paddle back upstream and try to return it to the owner, a boy called

David. And so begins a magical Summer of treasure hunting, code breaking, friendship and loss. I could see right away that canoeing had certain serious advantages over running away to sea. Run away to sea and you're on your own for a good long while. Climb into a canoe and you can be back by teatime. The big danger in on the banks of the Say was a dodgy estate agent. At sea, my grandfather was burnt to death in an onboard explosion long before I was born. Take me to the river.

Of course the Mersey is not a Say kind of river. It's more of a vast muddy lagoon. If you were going to wander around it the way that David and Adam did on the Say, you wouldn't get far in an old kayak – you'd need a tug boat and a crew of bristly old salts at the very least. And where would you end up? Stockport.

———•◦•———

I was a grown man, a Dad, by the time I saw the Annan, but I recognised it straight away. The river strolls into the Solway Firth round the back of Annan Town. In these lower reaches it's a good-natured municipal resource. There's a "trim trail" along the bank for the cardiovascular benefit of the ratepayers. Its last bend encloses the town football pitches. There's a neat pathway for dog-walkers that leads up to the footbridge, where, in the season, everyone gathers to watch the salmon running. All the way over the footbridge, you're in Trumpton. But beyond that point, the path gets muddier and more overgrown, the river louder and more turbulent. Near Warmanbie, a river island forces the main current into two accelerated streams that meet on the other side in a confluence so riotous you can't hear yourself think. The banks gets steeper and more densely wooded. That's where I saw my first otter. By the time I've walked the couple of miles to Brydekirk, where the Annan roars through caves of leaves and over a reef of rocks, I feel like *Aguirre Wrath of God* at the head of the Orinoco. Even though I know that the Gretna Outlet Village is selling designer labels at high-street prices ten minutes from here.

That's what appealed to me about the river trip – adventure without renunciation. The freedom to battle upstream into the unknown and then drift back home again afterwards. Freedom – the Annan begins and ends with freedom. It rises in "The Devil's Beeftub" – a sheltered depression formed by four interlocking glacial spurs, or, as Walter Scott put it, "a d_d, black, blackguard-looking abyss of a hole". At the rim of the Tub is a monument that marks the spot where John Hunter was killed, defending his religious freedom. He was a Covenanter shot dead by pursuing Dragoons during the "Killing Times"

of the mid 1680s. The Beeftub gets its name from the fact that Border Reivers used it as a hiding place for stolen cattle. This area was part of the "Debatable Land" – an ill-defined No-Man's Zone between England and Scotland where a rough and read "Border Law" was upheld by feuding families whose core business was cattle-rustling and kidnapping. It's from the Reivers that we get the word "bereaved". The area is full of legends of one-horse daring, like the tale of "Kinmont Willie", rescued from Carlisle Castle by a mounted posse of his outlaw friends. According to legend, the head of a border family would be served a "dish of spurs" when the cupboard was bare – the spurs being a hint that it was time for him to lead out the "hot trod" and go and nick some food. Until the seventeenth century, this was Britain's Wild West. It was pretty much free from the laws of either nation.

I always use the area as an example of another kind of free-dom. Whenever some prat tells me that anything – anything at all – whether its the Troubles in Ireland, or the Exuberance of Cuban Music – can be explained by reference to genetic fatal-ism – to something in the blood, or in the water or whatever – I always recommend they take themselves to Moffat. The citizens are separated from their bloodthirsty past by a handful of well-documented generations. Many of them still bear noto-rious Reiver surnames – Armstrong, Bell, Johnstone, Nixon. But now these people would not steal a cow now if it was made by Haribo and sitting in the Pick-n-Mix. There is not a more law-abiding, house-proud, civic-minded people on the whole face of this Earth. Or off it. After all, the first man on the Moon was an Armstrong (family from Langholm) and the President

he rang was a Nixon. There is nothing in the water. We build our own destinies.

After Moffat, the river passes close to the Corncockle quarry where in the nineteenth century a group of workmen found some fossilised dinosaur footprints and showed them to the Reverend Doctor Duncan, who got his naturalist friend Frank Buckland to come up from Oxford and explain them. He covered the Reverend's kitchen table in pastry and make a model of the feet to show how – from the evidence of the footprints – he could deduce the size and shape of the dinosaur. Doctor Duncan was a paleontologist who also invented savings banks and excavated the Ruthwell cross. Doctor Duncan, an unfettered mind, the Annandale Da Vinci.

The river flows out into the Solway round the back of Annan town. Until the nineteen thirties, there was another great monument to freedom at this end of the river. Namely, the disused viaduct, which originally carried the Solway Junction Railway over the firth to Bowness on Solway. The railway itself was closed in 1921 but, until it was demolished in 1934, the bridge was used by pedestrians, mostly on a Sunday afternoon, when Scotland was legally dry but you could still get a pint in England.

The story of the bridge has something to say about messing with the freedom of water. It was built to carry cargo to and from Port Carlisle, but the metal spans changed the direction of the currents, causing Port Carlisle itself to silt up and in a whirlpool of causality, rendering the iron bridge useless.

All these freedoms – legal, historic, genetic, alcoholic – seemed to sparkle on the Annan water as I walked its banks. But none of them was as intoxicating, as immediate as the simple freedom that Adam and David enjoyed – the freedom to go off with a mate, a bottle of pop and a couple of hardboiled eggs, and adventure till bedtime, the freedom to come home just as it was getting dark, no questions asked. That kind of freedom didn't exist where I lived, if it existed anywhere. And it's not the kind of freedom you can buy as compensation for a prosperous middle-aged bloke, because the real freedom they were relishing in the Minnow was the freedom from all sense of their own mortality. It's the kind of freedom that everyone says that even children are denied now, thanks to health and safety and child protection. But I was going to be a different kind of Dad. I was going to give my children exactly that freedom. I was going to give them the Annan. And this is where the story gets darker.

I spent a lot of time on the riverbank with my two oldest boys, hoping that the whole river-freedom metaphor would sink in. We went out at dusk looking for bats and otters. We saw kingfishers up near Hoddom. I took the eldest one fly-fishing at Warmanbie and he dutifully transcribed the size of his fish and what kind of fly he used in the hotel catch book there. I read them Minnow on the Say a couple of times, just in case the river wasn't explaining itself clearly enough. I threw in A River At Greene Knowe and Wind in the Willows, too. And then I bought them the dinghy. We went out together in it a couple of times. There's a shingle beach just below the weir. If you launched it there, the force of the waterfall would send it skeetering over the shallows like a freeform log flume. We screamed. We got wet. We drank hot chocolate. But they were still with me. Dad was still on board. Nice for me. But defeating the whole object for them.

So one day I drove them way upstream. I found a little tributary burn, wriggling through a muddy rhododendron wood, under a bridge before joining the river. It didn't look too fast, or too deep. The banks were overgrown, which was great. The burn would take them somewhere they could never walk. And half a mile or so downstream, I'd be waiting for them under the bridge. I'd catch them before they hit the river. It'd be a real adventure but only ten minutes long. They were ten and eight years old at the time.

I sat them in the boat. I saluted. I pushed them into the stream, scrambled up the bank and ran like the clappers, the half-mile or so to the bridge. And waited. And waited.

And as I was waiting I began to notice the noise of the river itself. That merry watery chuckle, what causes that? Fast, cold water running over bloody sharp rocks, that's what.

What if I hadn't run fast enough? What if they'd already passed the bridge and were out there in the river now, being swept towards the weir, and on and out to sea? It couldn't be. I'd run so fast and the burn was quite slow. Yeah but I'd had to scramble up the bank first. And they had paddles with them, what if they'd just really rowed hard? I walked downstream a bit further and peered out into the river. Couldn't see anything. Which is good. Unless it means they've sunk.

I slogged back up to the bridge and yelled their names. What if they'd capsized up there? I had to go back up the path and try and find them. But what if they shot past me while I was retracing their steps? I couldn't do nothing. I ran back up the path, watching the water. But there was a point at which the path and the burn diverged. The water hid behind an impenetrable screen of brambles, fifty yards thick. I yelled their names.

"Dad!" they answered.

No punch, no kiss has ever landed on me with such visceral force as that syllable. Relief poured into my bloodstream like whisky.

"You OK?" I was trying to sound cool.

"We're stuck."

And even though I now knew they were alive, there was something eerie and unnerving about yelling into the brambles and hearing their ghostly voices wafting back towards me.

"I'm coming just wait there."

"I've told him he should get out and push ..."

"No, no. Don't do that. Just wait there."

I went back up to the bridge. I waded happily through the

water towards them. The banks were cloaked in nettles. The bottom was a slime of mud. When I was dragging them back downstream, the only way to get any purchase was to grab handfuls of the nettles and pull. My arms, my legs, my face, were all covered in stings. It felt like penance. It felt heroic. I dragged them out of the stream, numb with pain, covered in mud and weeds like some river god. I felt like I had brought them back to life. I said, "There. You're safe now" and waited for them to thank me.

"You just nearly killed us," said the elder boy.

I had completely forgotten that it was me who shoved them into the burn in the first place.

"You. Are. Not. Wise," said my son and then he said, "Come on" to his little brother and led him off to the car, while I tried to get rid of the worst of the mud from my clothes.

I watched them walk away. It's taken me till today to realise that maybe they gained a different freedom there. The freedom you get from realising that your Dad is not all that after all.

The thing is you can have your own ideas about freedom. But you can't make other people share them. I should have known that already of course. Because somewhere up this river is another tidy little town, a town with a memorial garden. A town called Lockerbie.

Frank Cottrell Boyce is a British screenwriter, novelist and actor.

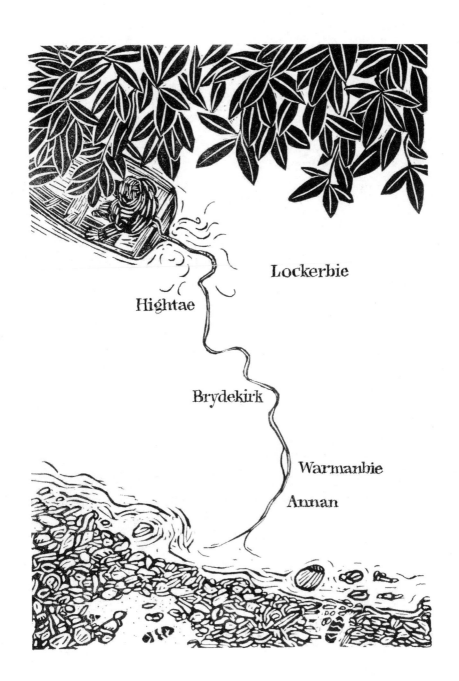

Lockerbie

Hightae

Brydekirk

Warmanbie

Annan

THE
RIVER
CARY

BY
GAVIN PRETOR-PINNEY

The morning of our departure arrived chilly and foggy. As we walked down to the river across the field next to our house, the grass was heavy with dew and cobwebs that stretched between the blades hung with beads of moisture. These looked like tiny strings of light bulbs. It was as if the spiders had hung out illuminations to see us off on our voyage. The oak trees in the field, only half-there in the fog, stood watching our departure like enormous ghosts. My wife Liz and I hacked through the nettles along the river's edge, and eased our brand new canoe into the inky water of the river Cary. Two days of *Swallows and Amazons*-style adventure awaited us. Or so we hoped.

I've always loved the sensation of walking through the fog, but it is not nearly as much fun as canoeing through it. Overhanging boughs emerged only once we were almost entangled in them. The only noise, somehow magnified by the lack of visibility, was the gentle gurgle and drip of paddle through water: a sound that is at once restful and charged with the anticipation of going somewhere.

A few bends on, we came to a tangle of willow-tree limbs and exposed roots piled up on the bank. They resembled some sort of horrific car crash – but one that just involved trees. The willow had clearly grown top-heavy, its limbs splitting from the trunk and pulling it down into the river. The gnarled wood must have been lifted out of the water and shoved back onto the bank when the river was last dredged.

The willow trees along this stretch used to be pollarded for their shoots. Now that they're left un-pruned, their limbs grow weightily from the stubby trunks, until they fall and split the springy timber into deep, bowed crevices. Such neglect seems tragic when you consider that, aside from the oak, willow trees support more insects than any other British tree. But it is the rotting wood of their split and fallen limbs that makes the best habitat. This was no willow car crash. It was a luxury insect high-rise or, if you're a bat or a bird, a multi-story restaurant.

A kingfisher darted out from the reeds with a flash of turquoise and disappeared downriver. The church bells in town were ringing off the hook. Their muffled peals added to the atmospheric delights of the fog, which was now beginning to lift and give definition to a pale disc of a Sun.

We had to get out and wade to get through the shallow water under Somerton Door Bridge. Two boy-racers cut the engines of their L-plated mopeds, to stare down from the small bridge

"We came to a tangle of willow-tree limbs and exposed roots piled up on the bank. They resembled some sort of horrific car crash"

and follow our geriatric progress. We picked our way between the stones, until it was deep enough to climb back in.

'Let's race them,' we heard one say to the other, as we paddled on sedately.

A particularly species-rich stretch led us to our lunch spot. A flotilla of foot-long chub sneaked by, flanked by the distinctive stripes of a couple of perch. A school of tiny fish darted and weaved through the water ahead of us, ushered along by our advancing hull. These tiny water sprites seemed like some local equivalent of the playful dolphins tourists watch cavorting through the bow wave of their ship as they cruise across the crystal waters of the Pacific.

—◆—

The Cary has not always enjoyed such abundant wildlife. Before we left, a friend told me about an incident in the late 60s that killed every living thing along this stretch of the water.

'The day before had been torrential rain,' he remembered, 'and it was still raining quite hard, as we went out fishing.' The effect of all the surface water running from across the wide valley and into the river was to cause the water level to rise rapidly. 'In the space of an hour and a half, as we sat there, the river rose by three feet.' It was soon after this that the first fish began rising to the surface.

'My uncle came down to where we were sitting. He'd been fishing further upriver, and said that the fish were dying there too.' His uncle ran to alert the farmer to keep his livestock away from the cattle drink at the river's edge.

The river was polluted all the way from past our house on the eastern edge of Somerton to the sluice gates at Henley Bridge, seven miles down river, where we were planning to spend the night. Everything died. The fish were wiped out, as were the water voles and moorhens. At the S-bend before the viaduct, the water surface became covered with a stinking mass of dead fish. The eels too, of which there used to be large numbers, were as good as wiped out.

The cause of the incident was never identified.

———•◦•———

Park Bridge, the next that we came to, had a more elegant appearance than any we'd passed so far. It had turf over the top of it and presumably served as a tractor crossing point. Rising in a steep arch, it is known locally as 'hunchback'. Just past the bridge we reached our first major obstacle. Some wire was stretched back and forth across the river and around a couple of wooden posts sticking out of the water near the opposite bank.

We would have to go under, limbo-canoe-style, I told Liz, who began fretting that the fence might be electric. Of course it wasn't electric, I declared, touching the wire with my bare hand to prove it.

'Are you sure that it's not electric?' persisted Liz. She was carrying our unborn child, she reminded me, and we wouldn't want to spark it to a frazzle before it had drawn its first breath.

'Look,' I sighed, 'if it'll make you feel better, I'll hold onto the wire as we go under.' Anyway, were we not in a boat made of plastic? Even if it were electrified, the current wouldn't run through us unless we stuck our other hands into the water. There was no way for the electricity to get to earth.

I gripped the wire and lay back into the canoe, as I began to pull us under. A strong pulse of electricity shot up my arm, spazzing every muscle in my body. We went into emergency-reverse-limbo mode, frantically paddling backwards to free ourselves of the wire. The first time I had touched it had been between pulses. Thankfully, we freed ourselves before the next one arrived.

Given the height of the banks here, the only way we could get past this peril was to climb out of the canoe onto the hoof-pocked mud of the cattle drink. Liz left her wellies stuck fast in the middle of the quagmire, as she stepped up onto the grass verge in her socks. Using branches to ease the canoe under the wires, we guided it downriver until we could re-embark. We were on our way once more, causing some confusion amongst the tiny water-skating insects as the ripples from our bow swept through the shadows of an overhanging tree.

I had called up the farmer in advance to ask if we could pitch our tent in his field next to Henley Bridge. We hauled the canoe up onto the bank and made camp. Liz assembled tent rods, while I pumped up the inflatable mattress. Black silage bails, peppering the field around us, cast long, mauve shadows in the setting sun. A flutter of tiny fish leapt in unison from the surface of the water. No doubt, some hungry perch was in hot pursuit.

I fiddled around with twigs and bits of cardboard as I tried to get the Kelly kettle boiling. It is a fantastic invention, in which the heat from the little fire in the aluminium base fills the funnelled chimney that runs up the centre of the kettle. This heats the water so efficiently that the weediest fire is enough to boil water in no time. You can even cook in a little pan that sits on an attachment at the top of the chimney. I have always been very proud to tell people I own a Kelly kettle. But, to tell the truth, I've always been pretty rubbish at getting it to work right. I seem to get through about two boxes of matches and several Sunday newspapers each time I try to make tea.

As we sat and ate our food in the dying light, a pair of swans performed a low-altitude fly-by, heading down the course of the river towards Sedgemoor, which we would be crossing the next day. As they beat their wings, they let out rhythmical, almost musical, wheezing sounds. Though they look extremely graceful as they sweep by, they sound like a pair of forty-a-day smokers on an ill-fated jog round the park.

As we zipped up the tent, we congratulated ourselves on a successful first day. Having paddled nine miles, we'd made it half way from the point where the Cary passes our house to the river Parrett – our intended destination the next day. Best of all, we were still talking.

———·•·———

The morning had been forecast to be foggy again, but no more than the odd wisp of mist hung amongst the cattle in the field opposite. I set about making a fire in the Kelly kettle. A few boxes of matches later, we feasted on bacon baps and tea.

The sluice gate at Henley Bridge produces a 4ft drop in water level. This is where the nature of the river changes dramatically. Here is where the medieval monks of Glastonbury Abbey diverted the course of the Cary in an effort to reduce the flooding of the Levels onto which it discharged. And it is also here where, in 1798, the river's gentle flow was redirected back across the fenland in the managed form of the newly-constructed King's Sedgemoor Drain. The transition from natural to man-made watercourse could hardly be more apparent.

The serpentine curves of the previous day's river, which had been flanked by gently undulating hills, now gave way to a dead-straight channel, heading off across the heart of the reclaimed pastures of Sedgemoor. Examining the map, we discovered that throughout the ten miles from there to our destination at Dunball Wharf, there were no more than three slight bends in the unwavering line of the King's Sedgemoor Drain. Already nostalgic for the *Wind in the Willows*-vibes of the previous day, we paddled out into the 135 square miles of the largest remaining area of lowland wetland and wet grasslands in Britain.

Somewhere along the Drain – there were now precious few landmarks against which to plot our progress – we came across a huge digger parked on the north bank, with an over-sized arm attached to a wire scoop, resembling some sort of giant colander. This was the river-dredging machine. And, as it happened, the dredger himself was just turning up to work as we paddled by.

He told us he'd been dredging the Cary and the King's Sedgemoor Drain 'for 48 years and 9 months'. The reason for dredging is to lower the level of the water, thereby increasing the channel's ability to drain water from the surrounding pastures and withy beds during the wet months. 'Where the reeds build up, they hold water back, like' he explained. 'Once we take out all the vegetation and stuff, the water level can drop by two feet.'

Decades ago, the dredging was far more intensive, and included cutting all growth on the banks to no more than 4 inches so that the water would run into the Drain more easily. 'They don't want that now, of course,' he said with a slight roll of the eyes, 'because of the butterflies and voles and that stuff.'

We asked what had changed during all the time that he had been working on the river. 'The main change has been the eels,' he said without hesitation. 'And, do you know what, that is actually not our fault. It's the elvermen that have killed that. I might see one eel now in weeks and weeks. Years ago, every bucketful would be eels and eels.'

The elvermen fish the young eels with large nets on the nearby River Parrett, catching them on the incoming tides. They used to fish them to eat them, but now they sell them to Japan: 'a kilo of elvers – about 3000 of them – is worth £400 these days.'

He explained how, when he'd scoop out the dead vegetation on wet days, the eels would wriggle and slither their way across the grass to find their way back into the water. 'We used to get some big ones then – about 3 ½ pounds – now we might just see the occasional bootlace.'

After Cradle Bridge, the water seemed particularly still. Reflections of the cumulus clouds danced lazily over the glassy surface. The channel widened to some 50 feet across. We had, for some time now, been herding swans. Whenever we approached a pair loitering in the reeds to the side, they would start to paddle downriver ahead of us. Each time we came across another bunch, they would join the increasing herd, which by now had grown to as many as thirty. Liz worried that if we ushered them too far from their 'hood, they might turn on us. Can't a swan can break a man's leg with the beat of its wings? I felt sure that they only get aggressive when protecting their cygnets. Every few minutes, one of the bolder swans would lose patience and, with the usual hullabaloo of wing-flapping and water-treading, would start an exodus back upriver. This would clear the blockage until the swans built up again.

A breeze was picking up as we reached Greylake Bridge. We could see on the map that there was a sluice gate just after it but, with the bridge in the way, our view of the sluice was obscured.

On the bank before the bridge, an angler watched our approach with a look of disapproval. Liz wanted to ask him if it was safe to go under the bridge. I told her that we'd look like a couple of idiots with no idea what we were doing and, anyway, on the other side there was lots of space between the bridge and sluice to pull in. 'It's not the space,' she argued. 'It's how fast the current is going.'

She proposed to get out before the bridge and carry the canoe over the road and around the sluice. This was ridiculous, I insisted. The road was busy and it was so much easier to get out on the other side, just before the sluice.

We were trying to keep our voices down, as it was a bit embarrassing arguing in front of the stony-faced angler. No doubt, we were scaring off his fish with our dithering and our bad vibes.

'Excuse me,' Liz called out to him, 'is it safe for us to go under the bridge? Will we be OK?'

I was mortified. We were already pissing him off with shilly-shallying about, and now we looked like a couple of tits, with no idea what we were doing. While it may have been the case that we'd no idea what we were doing, but there was no point in broadcasting it.

'Actually, I don't think you should really be on the water here at all,' he replied.

Bickering under our breaths, we pulled in across from him, just before the bridge. Liz got out so that she could walk across the road, and meet me at the other side. I paddled under, avoiding eye contact with the angler, and the two at the other side of the bridge, though I got the feeling they were more amused than annoyed. Of course, there was plenty of bank before the sluice gate itself on which to pull up and get out. The King's Sedgemoor Drain is wide here, though – some 60 feet across – and so the sluice itself was somewhat scarier than the little ones we'd grown used to. It was also one that rotates automatically, and can rise or fall without warning.

We carried the canoe around and, once back in the water, our passive-aggressive post-tiff tension was soon lost to the sound of the poplar trees rustling in the breeze.

In fact, it was becoming more than just a breeze. The wind was starting to pick up now. Out here in the flat expanse of the Levels, there's nothing to obstruct the wind. Soon, it wasn't schools of minnows or sticklebacks that we watched dance across the water, but the little diamond-shaped ripples, known as 'cats' paws', which followed the capricious gusts of the wind. Suddenly, these gusts corralled and combined into a coordinated flow.

This was just the sort of thing that you wanted to have behind you to help propel you along, Hawaii-Five-O style. The problem was, it wasn't behind us. It was blowing right in our faces. As the clouds gathered, the paddling suddenly started becoming hard work.

——————•·•·•——————

By now, we were in the heart of Sedgemoor, approaching the village of Westonzoyland. It was a mournful spot, famous as the battlefield where 1,300 farm labourers and artisans support-ing the Protestant Duke of Monmouth, were slaughtered by the troops of the Catholic King James II in 1685. Unarmed and untrained, the locals stood no chance against the King's profes-sional troops. Their bodies were piled high in the very rhynes that now spilled from the banks beside us.

With its high concentration of Protestants, the West Country was a natural place for Monmouth to land and march on London. But he got a bit of a shock when the promises of a large Protestant army and unbridled support that had been assured by his supporters in Holland turned out to have been wildly optimistic.

When he first landed in Lyme Regis, in Dorset, he only managed to muster some 300 supporters. Figuring that the march on London could wait, he took them north into Somerset, where he toured the area, skirmishing with Royalist troops, and drumming up support from the locals. A couple of weeks after landing, by the time he had made his way to Taunton, his following had swelled to over 6,000 largely agricultural workers and artisans, though they were armed with nothing more than farm tools and a determination that England should retain its Protestant monarchy.

Then it all started going downhill for Monmouth. When the King's forces turned them back at Trowbridge, many of the Dukes supporters began deserting him. Far from reaching London, they were pushed back to the Somerset Levels, where the Royalists gathered around them on the plain of Sedgemoor.

The battle took place in the middle of summer, a short distance onto the moors from Westonzoyland. Monmouth attempted to surprise the Royal army by attacking in the dead of night. A local herdsman, who knew the area like the back of his hand, offered to lead the way across Sedgemoor. The only problem was, it became so foggy that he lost his bearings, and missed the vital crossing point over Langmoor Rhyne. The noise and confusion raised the alarm of the Royalists.

Without the advantage of surprise, the untrained pitchfork army didn't stand a chance. Labourers, miners and craftsmen were shot down in their hundreds, though they fought on long after Monmouth fled. The dead were buried out on the moor where they lay, by a small stream known as the Bussex Rhyne – now a ditch that feeds into the King Sedgemoor Drain. That night, 500 of the survivors, many badly wounded, were locked up in the church at Westonzoyland, while their comrades were forced to build gibbets for the hangings.

After eating lunch amongst a group of trees on the bank past Westonzoyland, we returned to the canoe with sense of fatigue. The wind in our faces was a strong as ever and, by now, we'd worked out that canoes are rubbish boats when it is windy.

The problem is their lack of keels. Heading out from the reeds into the middle of the waterway, the wind would catch us on our flank and proceeded to blow us across to the opposite bank. Both of us would paddle on the same side of the canoe to try and counter the force of the wind, and stay in the centre of the channel, but this proved to be extremely hard work.

The only way we could progress on a reasonably straight course was to have our bows pointing directly into the wind. So that it was unable to gain purchase on either side of us. Only the slightest deviation from windward would let the air current catch our side, and start to push us back across the waterway. Needless-to-say, whoever was paddling on the side we were

being blown towards would start shouting, 'Paddle on my side, for God's sake, paddle on my side!' 'I am, I am!' the other would cry. And we would both battle as hard as we could to stay in the middle of the water but, without a keel to counter our sideways drift, would inevitably slip across into the reeds once more.

Fighting against the air like this, and proceeding at a tortuous pace, we eventually reached a major landmark in the course of the King's Sedgemoor Drain: a slight bend to the right. Clearly drawn to this outstanding feature, a few anglers were spread along the southern bank. We must have looked a sorry sight, weaving from side to side, as we fought our way towards them.

Once we turned the slight bend, the new angle of the wind meant that we were immediately swept into the reeds. The anglers stared impassively from the opposite bank. Once again, tensions rose aboard the canoe.

Liz had had enough. She said that we should call my dad to bring the car with the roof racks and pick us up from here rather than Dunball Wharf.

We couldn't just stop here, I scowled. We'd come all this way. In a few more miles we'd reach the Parrett. It was crazy to just give up now. And anyway, how could Dad get us from here? What are we going to say to him – 'We're out in the middle of the Levels, near some anglers, can you come and get us?'

'Well, the anglers have clearly driven here,' she argued, pointing out the car that was parked on the track running down the side of the waterway.

'We've no idea which gate to tell him to take from the road. Even if we had, we can't just ask him to drive along the edge of

people's fields. This is the anglers' patch. They have an arrangement to fish here. They know where to drive to get here.'

I couldn't bear the thought that we might not reach our
destination. At least, I said, we should go as far as the next road
bridge, where we can think about what to do. Liz thought this
idea stupid, and told me that if I wanted to go to the next bridge
so much, I could paddle there myself. She would walk along the
bank. Which she did.

The anglers watched as I battled single-handed against
the elements. Was that one shaking his head at me? I was sure
I saw him shaking his head...
but, as I used all my might to
shove myself off from the reeds
once more into the windswept
central channel, I didn't give
a toss what he thought. I have
as much of a right to enjoy
the bloody King's Sedgemoor
Drain as he, I ranted to myself,
half crazed by my exertion. Yes,
I may be disturbing his fish. But

"Fighting against the
air ... and proceeding
at a torturous pace, we
eventually reached a
major landmark in the
course... a slight bend
to the right."

at least I'm not giving them bloody lip ache by yanking them
out with a hook.

I battled as hard as I could to stop myself from being blown
over towards their fishing lines. Even I accepted that actually tangling myself up in their lines would not be good river
etiquette.

Liz looked back at me from downriver, pausing from her
leisurely stroll to give me time to catch up. I avoided the

anglers' lines, but continued to weave from bank to bank like some steroid-fuelled outward-bounds instructor.

And this is how our river adventure ended. On finally reaching the road bridge, Liz helped me pull the canoe up onto the bank. The cats' paws were still prancing like crazy over the water's surface. My sense of defeat in the face of the wind felt all the more keen by the need to be rescued by Dad.

With the canoe up on the roof rack, we asked if we could make a stop-off on our way home. Walking along the edge of Bussex Rhyne from the gate where we parked the car, we reached a small brass plaque set into a blue lias plinth. There, in the middle of the windswept fields, with nothing around it but four carved straddle stones, it commemorated 'all those who, doing the right thing as they gave it, fell in the Battle of Sedgemoor and lay buried in this field.'

I apologised to Liz for my crazed 'lock-on' about reaching the river's end. The motivation for our journey had been a simple curiosity to see where the water passing our house would lead. No matter how far we had gone, it would always be moving on.

Gavin Pretor-Pinney is the author of the The Cloudspotter's Guide *and the co-founder of* The Idler *magazine.*

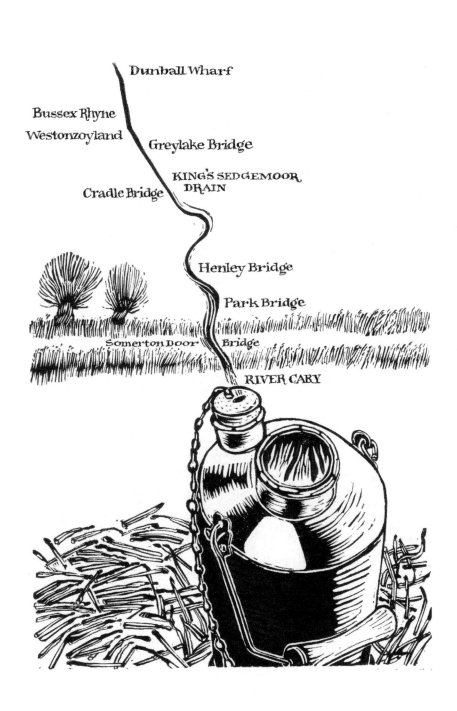

Dunball Wharf

Bussex Rhyne

Westonzoyland

Greylake Bridge

KING'S SEDGEMOOR DRAIN

Cradle Bridge

Henley Bridge

Park Bridge

Somerton Door Bridge

RIVER CARY

THE RIVER COQUET

BY
CHRIS WATSON

Murder Cleugh, Bloodybush Edge and Foulplay Head are fearful place names that belie a now tranquil landscape. Standing in north Northumberland way up in the Cheviot Hills, I'm clutching Ordnance Survey Outdoor Leisure Map 16 and gazing across a landscape littered with these disturbing-sounding locations. Rough grasslands, marsh and moor set amongst an undulating pattern of soft low hills which in turn form a mosaic with wind-bent copses and dark coniferous plantations. I've been walking off-road for the past hour and due west along the Border County Ride and I've not seen any other person and very few signs of occupied habitation, yet this place is full of life, wildlife. It's late May and high above, out of my sight, a skylark pours out its aerial song, a stream of silver notes cascading out of the white flecked sky. Meadow pipits squeak and dash between broken fence posts and tufts of sedge grass, raven voices croak and crack, their huge black wings overhead flashing semaphore style between the rolling, rounded hills. Wandering a couple of hundred meters further west, a sinking feeling confirms my position. Tiny bubbles pop and fizz as rings of acid brown water ooze from the sphagnum moss around my boots and I squelch a few more steps up on to a dry slope. This firmer ground is across an invisible boundary and I look back into my recent footsteps which are now full of water and realise that I've arrived at Coquet Head, the source of my favourite English river, and I'm looking at it from Scotland.

The spring weather here might be calm and mild however this is still a dangerous place as my map clearly indicates to me in red ink 'Danger Area'. This is the edge of the Otterburn

Army Ranges now, however the area is nowhere near as dangerous as it was in the distant past. The Roman Army built Chew Green Fortlet here, a remote and exposed outpost on Dere Street and many leagues to the north of Hadrian's Wall which was the notional northern geographical limit of the Roman Empire. Perhaps the clean head waters of the River Coquet was a reason to site a camp here, certainly it must have influenced the later settlement of the medieval village of Kemylpethe, the irregular shape of which lies alongside the square Roman outlines. The real danger here however was between the 13th and 17th centuries, when most of the foreboding place names on the map were set in stone and blood. During this period the local clans and families became known collectively as the Border Reivers. Peaceful and pastoral farmers they were not. Kidnap, murder, arson and cattle-stealing occupied much of their time; this was serious business, and it was theirs. Laws made in London did not trouble those in these lands; they made their own and argued their case with strength in numbers, sheer aggression and the sword. The ancestors of the ravens above me here would have had more than just the odd sheep carcass to feed them, as the carrion of battlefield and reiver skirmish would have sustained significant numbers of these highly-intelligent and opportunistic birds. The human population then was relatively high and casualties of the times were frequent and often bloody, after all, if you were visited by the Border Reivers, you were bereaved.

I assume that weaponry and wounds are far less frequently washed in the emergent bubbling waters of the Coquet these days despite the evidence of soldiers' recent activity. Discarded ration packs, used smoke grenade canisters and empty bullet clips are piled in small ceremonial mounds marking temporary camps and all within easy reach of the clean water supply I am now following. However, most of the resident human population has passed into history leaving only their marks on the map. Today I'm watching an oystercatcher probe the green edges of the gathering flow. This large black and white wading bird has a powerful orange bill, which has evolved for opening shellfish and as such appears out of place up here in the Cheviot Hills more than 40km from the seashore. A few pairs of these birds migrate up the River Coquet to find a suitable nest site amidst the tall rushes and wet pasture well away from the higher densities of birds and competition for food down on the coast. "Kleep, Kleep, Kleep, Kleep, Kleep": a pair flash past following the silvery water trail oozing web-like through the juncus grass. On the ground, I'm starting a much longer and winding journey east but still going with the flow.

Where Catcleugh melts into the Coquet, I stop and crouch by the water's edge. For the first time I listen to the sound of this river and it appears to me now as a real flow, just over two meters across and with a shallow bed of exposed stones, gravel and scrapes, it gurgles, bobbles and turns. There is a dialect at least if not a voice yet. Further beyond me, the hint of a distant overheard conversation as Blindburn joins in from over the border to the north, so not an English stream, yet. I'm still within sight of where I guess the border is, but the boundaries here are still vague and largely irrelevant. I let the water pass before my eyes, left to right, and listen. This is one of the few places left in England where you can actually open your ears and listen. Everyday we are bombarded by sound and noise, we hear almost everything, but so rarely have the opportunity of really listening. In order to simply communicate and carry out our day-to-day activities we have to filter out most of the acoustic mess that fills our ears and brain. Shops, banks, transport and all forms of electronic communication play noise and 'music' at us creating a form of sensory overload, which inevitably clouds our thoughts and imagination. We need a space between our ears and brain to focus, a place of respite to relax, consider and create. As the writer and poet Roger Deakin said: "this is not just some artistic whim or fanciful notion, the sense of tranquility created by quietness is important for our general health and wellbeing." At Kateshaw Crag I back away

a few meters from the riverbank to balance the sound of flowing water with the surrounding ambience so I can really open my ears to this environment. The resulting mix is a wonderful blend of quietness upon which I can rest my imagination. In the distance there is the song of a grey wagtail, a migrant bird from the lowlands, probably recently arrived and now establishing a waterside territory into which to attract a mate, build a nest and raise a family. The short bursts of song modulate perfectly with the rippling sounds of distant water, yet cut through quite distinctly. These are waterside birds that feed upon insects and build their nests in streams and riverbanks.

Another skylark bursts from a patch of sedge grass, hovers momentarily, and then ascends whilst engaging its song flight. I listen and watch the bird's soaring perspective until it reaches a vanishing point high above. Perspective and dynamic range are the two most important component parts of this valuable soundscape, not the absence of sound. Silence is not golden, silence is a form of sensory deprivation and other than in a vacuum is usually an artificial construct. Several years ago I had the opportunity of experiencing silence inside an anechoic chamber at the University of Mississippi in the United States. This is an acoustically-damped room approximately 4m x 5m with a suspended wire mesh floor and surrounded on the walls and ceiling by large acoustically-absorbent foam wedges. Once inside, I was left alone and the door was closed with a low 'clunk'. The door was also lined on the inside with the same wedges, so at once disappeared into the fabric of the wall. There were no reflections and no reverberation. Sound sank into the lining and was absorbed, never to be heard again. My ears and brain searched for a reference sound, a foundation, something to latch on to. If I made any sound or moved the result would just die in that instant. There was nothing, no sound. After a few moments I began to search inside my head and discovered the internal vibrations of my own body, pumping blood and a steam-like rushing from the middle of my head; it was dreadful. My experience of silence lasted about one minute before I asked to be released.

———————·•◦•·———————

In the real world we can walk away and back off from the source of a sound: this will increase the sense of perspective and reduce the dynamic range relative to the surroundings. Understanding our ability to do this is one of the first stages of taking control of our own acoustic environment. Listening in this way is an active and creative function and is also one of the best ways to engage with that environment. Nearby the village of Holystone, the Coquet starts to meander through a more open and softer landscape. Farms, ancient patterned field systems and way marked footpaths. I walk up a trail from the river that follows Dovecrag Burn, a narrow, twisting and secretive waterway more often heard rather than seen as it gurgles deep down around the huge sedge clump islands. These mounds are difficult to negotiate and were no doubt created by the burn when swelled with rain running off Dove and Harbottle Crags to the west.

A gloomy wall of Sitka spruce trees almost block my passage trying to follow the burn into the evergreen darkness, but I know my way. Within a couple of hundred meters the plantation gives way to a real woodland, oak woodland and one of my most treasured sites in Northumberland. Lady's Well is here and must once have been a spring, which watered an early Pagan settlement. St Paulinus apparently baptised 3,000 people here in AD 627, but the atmosphere around this now gently-manicured site is pre-history. The Lady of the Well may have originally been a Naiad, a water spirit who lived beneath the surface and one who was worshipped as an essential to fertility and life. The water held within the soil of this woodland certainly sustains an ancient population of oak trees, which in turn support an enormous community of insects, flora, mammals and birdlife. In late May, the dawn chorus of bird-song in these oak woodlands around Holystone is a remarkable sonic experience. On a clear calm night from around 3 am the first song will be heard, most likely a redstart, in the broad leaf canopy high above, a simple solo penetrating through the blue-grey forest light. These notes spark competitive song battles across adjacent territories, which in turn awaken all the other woodland birds. Soon the individual songs of robins, wrens, woodpigeon, song thrush and blackbird collaborate and coalesce into the event of a dawn chorus with chaffinch and wood warbler contributing to a finale around 5 am. Soon after this, the urgency subsides, the intensity declines and the chorus melts into the contemporary sounds of that day. Heard from the perspective of High Farnham on the far bank of the Coquet, the chorus appears as an ambient silver glow across the river, a Phil Spector style mono block of sound, which rolls out and fades into the early morning mist that drapes the pebble-dashed bank side. Like a great film, this is the perfect collaboration of sound and image.

I follow the clicking flight calls and whirring wing beats of a dipper as it flashes brown and white low across the water's surface. This is a remarkable bird of upland rivers which gathers insect larvae and fresh-water shrimps by wading into and even under the surface of the water, disappearing into a torrent of silver and white only to re-emerge with a beak full of food. For years the song has eluded my attempts at record-ing. Dippers will sing on the River Coquet from mid-January usually from a favourite perch on a mid stream rock or over-hanging branch. The song is a series of piercing notes sound-

"The chorus appears as an ambient silver glow across the river, a Phil Spector style mono block of sound which rolls out and fades into the early morning mist"

ing rather like small shards of broken glass strung out into long phrases, the pitch of which is high above the fundamental frequency of a fast-flowing stream and a wonderful example of a song that has evolved alongside running water. A few minutes later I watch as this bird returns up stream darting past my position still calling and clearly on a mission with a beak full of Caddisfly larvae to feed newly-hatched young. The nest will be hidden somewhere in a bank-side overhang or even at a long-established site under the supports of one of the small stone bridges, which span sections of the river. In a secure site such as this, dippers may use the same nest for generations. I take note of a couple of guano-splashed rocks midstream promising myself to return before the spring thaw early next year to fix a couple of weather-proofed microphones alongside and wait. For now, I'm just pleased to watch and listen to these birds because their presence here is a good indication of healthy water quality.

——————·•◉•·——————

To the south and east of Hepple, the Coquet thins out and scatters across the landscape with skeletal fingers twisting around layers of shallow sand and gravel. Then slowly and much more quietly, the water wells up into glass-thin patterns which slide over bumps and ridges into the man-made pools of Caistron quarry, a scene for many of my location-recording experiments. Over the years, the commercial extraction of sand and gravel has created pits, which in turn have become occupied by the water from the river Coquet and Bickerton Burn. The quarry is a low-intensity industrial site, which out of hours has that magical sense of anticipated calm often found by stretches of open water. I was last here in early March with my hydrophones, lurking in the weed-fringed margins of a small pool on the edge of the site. Hydrophones are special underwater microphones and I have been excitedly listening below the surface of many places since first trying them out in the deep Pacific Ocean currents off the Galapagos Islands several years ago. Sound travels through water over four times faster than

through air, and in March I was here at Caistron Quarry to record a very particular sound through both mediums simultaneously. Common frogs gather in the secluded clear pools in early spring for their mating and spawning sessions. The males arrive first and try to attract a female by making a soft purring croak as they sit or perch half-submerged in the shallows. Advertising themselves in this way is a risky strategy so most activity takes place after dark and out of site of predators such as herons. The frogs are also very sensitive to movement and disturbance, so during the late afternoon I suspended a couple of small microphones on a wire coat hanger 10 centimetres over the pond edge and fixed my hydrophones in the mud a few centimetres under the surface.

My recording position gets cabled back 20 metres to a site where I can sit and wait. This is one of my favourite times when recording as I settle back into an environment and simply let things happen all around whilst remaining sonically fixed on the anticipated events from another place, rather like fishing for sound. The ambience sinks into a rhythm where elements come and go and carry the narrative of sunset and the onset of the night. A heron passes across the sky, right to left, huge wings scooping up the air until, out of sight, it calls with one explosive "craak" which I hear echo off the coniferous wall of a distant plantation. As the light level falls my hearing seems to get more focused, the river's muted murmuring on the other side of a ridge, which was inaudible in daylight, I now hear clearly. Then "plop", "bubble" and "fizz" as the first frog surfaces around my rig. He immediately launches into his love song, the loudness of which surprises me and I drop the recording levels accordingly which in turn creates a very low and intimate background ambience. This is a powerful solo performance of rich, deep notes, which twist and roll their way into my headphones. This sound and its vibrations cause other frogs to join in and, after several minutes, there is an amphibian chorus in a wide arc ranging around the pool's edge. I switch to the hydrophones and the scene changes instantly. Gone are the topside velvety tones as below the surface the croaks are percussive and sharp revealing instant and powerful messaging. Paradoxically, the frogs are so close to the hydrophones that the recording has no ambience and appears disembodied from its source and the sound reminds me of the alien voices from Tim Burton's *Mars Attacks!* The changeover is spectacular, particularly as it's the same sound simply heard through different mediums.

————◦—————

Now in May the frogs have dispersed but below the surface of the same pool I can see plenty of activity. Beetles, water spiders and larvae flick and spin, an ancient gathering of both predatory and mating rituals playing in front of my eyes but in another world. Lowering the hydrophones into the soft silt, I let the murk and weed settle before listening. Mechanical scratching, pitch-shifting clicks and whirrs that combine into thin clockwork rhythms. This still water is alive with the most delicate music. The visual displays I see and the performances I hear are also not synchronised and appear rather like a piece of contemporary and transient ballet. However, I can only record for three minutes before the roaring of an Tornado GR4 fighter jet tearing across the adjacent Simonside Hills wipes out any further audio activity as hydrophones, rather like aquatic insects, are sensitive to all forms of vibrations.

Meandering back and forth over countless millennia, the River Coquet has shaped the open spaces of Coquetdale just before its controlled rush and thrum as the river is funnelled through the town of Rothury. To the east, the water emerges from the town deeper and darker, as if conveying a covert spirit beneath the surface, and it seems that contemporary human resources are also trying to guard this passage with notices suggesting; 'Private Woodland', 'No Access to River' and 'No Fishing – By Order'. I'm suspicious.

Pathway and waterway eventually converge again nearby a site where the function of the signs has long passed into history, nevertheless they endure and continue to fascinate. The Cup and Ring marks at Morwick are between four to five thousand years old and their significance cannot be fathomed by current archeology. These beautifully simple engravings describe cup shaped carvings in particular rocks, which also have concentric circles or semi circles carved alongside or around. The marks are in a quiet deciduous woodland location and are best viewed from a boat as they are inscribed in a sandstone wall, which rises vertically out from the riverbed. Tracing my fingers around the rough grooves is a wonderful way to connect not only with the stone but also helps in creating a virtual land-scape within my imagination whilst being lulled by the sound of the river's flow.

The piercing electric burst of a wren song drags my atten-tion back to the current time. Over forty notes in eight seconds is an incredible rate of delivery and appear to my ears like a burst of elaborated data, which, of course, it really is. This tiny bird weighing around 10 grams communicates messages about its territorial boundaries and sexual status in these few brief moments with a speed of resolution that is beyond our under-standing as the individual notes smear into a rolling trill. I'm also here seeking unheard frequencies because this stretch of the Coquet is the hunting ground for some very successful nocturnal mammals. Throughout spring and summer, bats hawk for insects in the woodlands and along the surface of the river. Visible only briefly as the sunset light fades they are best moni-tored by sound, but as their echo-location sounds are of such a high frequency, a special device is required for us to tune into them. A bat detector can pick up these ultra-sonic sounds and reproduce a version of them in our audio domain. At the appointed hour of 10 pm it's very dark by the river underneath the tree canopy, and above there is an uneasy whispering in the leaves as a light breeze through the oaks and beeches rattles and hisses. The speaker in my bat detector pulses with exciting bursts and irregular techno-sounding rhythms, which are pitched down from around 45KHz and rapidly modulated as these bats, common Pipistrelles, home in on their airborne insect targets. An hour later I hear a machine gun burst of sounds around the same frequency which are produced by a Daubenton's bat as it skims the River Coquet trawling a few centimeters above the smooth surface for insects. In this darkness the air is full of sounds I can't hear but this device is giving me an amazing acoustic window into an unseen, unheard parallel world.

Daylight reveals the northern bank, its undergrowth half concealing a dank medieval hermitage which is almost under the shadow of Warkworth Castle, the massive 12th-century walls and keep, constructed within a tight clockwise loop of the river as it makes one final twist before heading to the coast. Down and on past the weir, herons patrol the muddy tidal edges, mallards and mute swans glide across the river's surface whilst redshank and oystercatchers mingle and probe at every opportunity. There's a change in the air, I can smell the sea, and my walking pace accelerates crunching on the tarmac path bordering the A1068.

Warkworth Harbour is actually in the coastal town of Amble, and I stand portside gazing out past the fishing boats to the long strands of pale dunes and marram grass across the broad river mouth. The tide has turned and slowly, slowly a band of freshwater from way up in the Cheviot Hills melts into the turgid waters of the North Sea and passes out beyond Pan Rocks to, perhaps, make one last contact with a place that bears the river's name. Coquet Island lies less than 2 km off the coast and holds a special place in my memory and audio files as not only the endpoint of my journey, but the starting point of a great bird migration. This is a summer island of terns, in particular the Arctic tern or sea swallow, a bird with a sharp percussive voice that is best summed up with the onomatopoeic Icelandic name of "Kria". These graceful birds fly for a living and, after fledging from the island in July and learning to plunge dive for sand eels in the waters around Coquet Mouth, they move south in August in a big way by migrating to the Antarctic. Flying via Western Europe and West Africa or across to the east coast of South America, they return to Coquet Island the following year after a round trip of approximately 40,000 km whilst experiencing more daylight than any other animal on earth. I stand and watch and admire these beautiful birds with their piercing voices dance and wave in the air over Coquet Mouth. It is believed that they carry an aerial map in their memory of the place where they hatched in order to accurately navigate their return, and for these island birds that must include an avian image of the River Coquet greeting the sea.

Chris Watson is the UK's leading sound recordist specialising in wildlife. In a previous life he was in the band Cabaret Voltaire.

Bloody Moss   Coquet Head   Murder Cleugh

Holystone

"...this is not just some artistic whim or fanciful notion, the sense of tranquillity created by quietness is important for our general health and wellbeing."

Rothbury

Amble   Warkworth

Coquet
Island

Lazy Cray-sy Days Of Summer

BY
KEVIN PEARCE

Down on the Dartford delta. Where the modern world began. From whence the Rolling Stones and the Pretty Things sprang snarling from the shadows. Where Dave Godin first heard his beloved soul music, and subsequently started his Tamla Motown Appreciation Society. The Dartford delta. A mythical enclave bordered by three rivers. The Thames, flowing down past Erith Reach, the Darent, and its Cray twin. The River Cray. Goes back to the year dot. The name means pure or clear. A name close to my heart.

The heart of sweet and sour suburbia. Subtopia. The outer limits of your *A to Z*. The same as anywhere. Poverty and plenty. Good and evil. And the River Cray runs through it. Nine miles long, and nothing to write home about. But it is ours.

Hours by the river. Doing what people do by a river. Walking dogs and pushing buggies. Kicking balls and throwing stones. Flying model planes and angling for Cray fish. Bird-watching and wild-flower spotting. Confessing and confiding.

The nefarious and the law abiding. The flytippers and the conservationists. At loggerheads. The joggers putting on a show and the pettifoggers in full flow.

Follow the flow of the river far enough and you'll come to Hall Place. A grand old manor house and grounds. Free for all. Stately with a small 's'. Nevertheless Ian Nairn called it "an astonishing place to find a few yards from the Dartford by-pass and right beside a busy road, full of industrial traffic. On the South side, there is a mad topiary garden that is like an exhibition of modern sculpture gone vegetable. There it all is, snoozing away as though the twentieth century had never happened."

That was forty odd years ago. Little has changed. Thank goodness. It's near enough and far away enough to escape to. My place of refuge and retreat. Particularly in the summer. When most people are off shopping or working. A time and place for reflection. For watching the squirrels scavenge for buried treasure, while the traffic rumbles in the distance. Laughing at the ducks waddling in rhythm. Smiling at the absurdity of the moorhen's plates of meat. Wondering whether there really are pike in these here waters. The gregarious geese gobbling down dry bread like there's no tomorrow. The lovers walking hand in hand. The kids playing football, if only dad would relinquish the ball once and for all. Nothing very mystical, but there are moments when ...

Like one sunny summer's day, sitting by the River Cray, whiling away the time, busy doing nothing, happy doing nothing. No music, no books, no mobile, no demands on my time. Just important things to wonder about like, "how old is that willow tree?" and "how many passing trains will I see?"

Screwing my eyes up against the glare of the sun, humming that Brenton Wood song about giving me just a little sign. Turning just in time to see two bright green parrots swoop out of the old oak tree, and soar away downriver. A young boy squeals in delight at the sight, and points after the birds. "Look mum, green parrots!" Only to be told not to be so daft. The boy stops. Shakes his head. Looks up to the skies again, then back along the riverbank, catching my eye in the process, challenging. I nod. Yes. He smiles. Skips off to catch up with his mum. Ah, but we know don't we. And we'll dream won't we.

Kevin Pearce has created the series of Hungry Beat *fanzines; the Esurient Communications record label; and the study of obsessives and outsiders in pop,* Something Beginning With O. *More recently he has started a free 'zine called* Your Heart Out *to share enthusiasms.*

13

---◆---

BY
LAURA BARTON

It has six legs, a triangular head, and a yellow and brown body that moves upside down like a rowing boat. This is how you recognise the water boatman. With our jam jars and fact sheets and grazed knees, we crouched down low, spied him swimming along by the towpath. Two hind legs, oaring great strokes, propelling his little silvery body. The sun was high, and we lay on our bellies in the grass by the edge, watching his steady journey westward through the dark water of the canal.

The northwest is a region ruled by canals: the Bridgewater Canal, the Manchester Ship Canal, the Rochdale Canal. Bold and broad and straight they run, across the landscape of Liverpool, Lancashire and Greater Manchester. They stand as a monument to the great Industrial North, to an age when the North was the shirehorse of this nation, our great strength harnessed for mills and mines and manufacturing. To a time when everything in this region was made to run in straight lines: pit shafts and production lines, warps and wefts, trains and terraces. And the canals themselves – as if even the counties' waterways had been tamed, as if they have been combed and set straight, smoothed down with a little spittle.

We grew up in thrall to the Leeds-Liverpool canal. One hundred and twenty-seven miles long, a spectacular feat of engineering, begun in 1770, and completed in 1816, at a cost of more than £1 million, it ferried coal, cotton, dust, ash, pigeon dung, rags, soap, bricks, lime and clay to-and-fro between Yorkshire and Lancashire. By the time I was born, it was barely still in active service, having retired into a destination for school trips and silent Sunday fishermen. It was here that we learned about sticklebacks and water boatmen, coots and moorhens, about coal barges and collieries, and all the things that made us Northern.

Amid it all, amid all the glory and the grandeur of the canal, we almost forgot about the River Douglas. The Douglas ran nearby, a tributary of the River Ribble, it covered thirty-five miles across the countryside and out to the sea, where, for its final ten miles, it is tidal. I think of the river now, viewed from a bridge near my childhood home: a small curve hurrying off towards the cabbage fields. Its banks grown wild with bind-weed and Indian balsam. I think back to its tributaries – Tarra Carr Gutter, Strine Brook, Centre Drain, Roaring Lum, The Sluice, Wham Ditch – names that feel rough and familiar to the tongue, like the morning roll-call at school, like the kick of vinegar and pea-wet at Gaskell's chippy. They are words that carry me home, somehow, like the stations passed on the train back to Lancashire.

And when I think of the River Douglas now, it seems to represent to me the true spirit of the North, running a route that was not cleaved from the Earth, straight and man-made, but forged by nature's own willfulness. And I think, too, of how her path is somehow mingled with the freedom and the wild-ness of my own youth, how her 35-mile territory matches the stomping ground of my own teenage years.

Up on Winter Hill she begins, on the West Pennine Moors, where the land is gorsy and windswept, and where the TV and radio masts stand. "Live from the tower of power on Winter Hill!", the local radio jingle used to run, and, on cold days, you can only just make it out – a crisp white line against a hard, white sky. Such a strange, dark hill, a place of plane crashes and UFO sightings, murders, disappearances, electrical drones. From here on Winter Hill, fifteen hundred feet up, on a fine day you can see as far as Jodrell Bank and Blackpool Tower, to the Isle of Man, Snowdonia, Cumbria, the sea.

We used to drive up here when we were teenagers, just to look down across the county, to look out at all the streetlights and the roundabouts, at all the things we were desperate to flee. We went driving its looping roads with the windows down and the stereo up, the taste of brandy and wet air on our lips. We drove wildly and too fast, drove with no particular destination, and though we never thought of it then, I like to think of us driving the same course as the Douglas – broken free, now, from the Ribble, as if our path were somehow divined by the river running along beside us.

The Douglas feeds Worthington Lakes, the reservoirs that supply Wigan and the surrounding area. In the mid-1800s, the river was diverted for this purpose, ducking out of sight, disappearing into a tunnel for about half a mile, before emerging back out into the open air, blinking in the light. There's a park around Worthington Lakes now, 50 acres of nature reserves and footpaths and an Environmental Education Centre.

We called them the "The Resies". Hard 's'. It was where people hung out after school. Where they drank cheap cider, kissed with tongues, had sex. It was where boys had fights and girls got love bites. Even in the daytime I used to believe there was something a little seedy about the Reservoirs. And when I pass by them now, I always think of how the River Douglas got diverted here, in the same way so many young people seemed

to get diverted here too – thrown off course by all the boys and the booze, but, unlike the Douglas, they rarely found their way back again.

Through Wigan, the River Douglas runs, and on she goes to Gathurst, a small, glowering village best known back then for being the first stop where you could get a Rail Ranger ticket, which would take you all over the county, as far as Oldham

Mumps and back again, for £3.60. You can see the river from the train window, dancing and rearing and tumbling.

We would walk down to Parbold to catch the train, and, on the way, you crossed first the river and then the canal. The canal looked so sedate and mild-mannered now, with the old mill turned into a fancy dress shop, and a little car park built for dog-walkers and fishermen to leave their vehicles while they head to the towpath. By comparison the river still seemed so scrawly and unkempt, crossed by a strange green metal bridge, underfoot its panels revealing glimpses of the water beneath, while overhead stretched painted metal bars that boys would jump up and swing from, as if going branch to branch, to impress the girls. And sometimes it worked; sometimes, on this little bridge, out of sight from the road, we would twine ourselves together for kisses that tasted of nervous passion and warm beer. And below us, the river churned and spiraled and knotted itself around its banks.

———◆———

The River Douglas does not run quite as nature intended. You can still plot its original course on old maps and along the parish boundaries, but, in the eighteenth century, as industry expanded, it underwent a process of canalisation. I think of this as the river's Caliban moment; the point at which this mooncalf, this freckled whelp was tamed, made civil and learned a language.

In 1712, a Liverpudlian named Thomas Steers surveyed the River Douglas and advised that its waters be made navigable to ships, so that coal from the fields surrounding Wigan might be transported along to the Ribble and on to Preston. In the original application it was argued that the navigation would be "very beneficial to trade, advantageous to the poor, and convenient for the carriage of coals, cannel, stone, slate and other goods and merchandise." Authorised in 1720, it ran from the junction with the Ribble to Mirey Lane End, and opened in 1742. They called this the Douglas Navigation.

It required the construction of thirteen locks. Today the records relating to the navigation's construction make for strangely affecting reading, a reminder of the raw materials and sheer brute strength needed to alter the course of a river, not to mention the chaos caused by flooding and the shifting of silt and soil: "2 Jan 1740: [1741] Paid Timothy Fairhurst for Damages in his Meadow by Carting Stones to Dean Lock and Dam 10s-6d" states one entry. "25 Apr 1741: Pd Daniel Kannan for Opening the Old River Along Crook Meadow £7-5s-0d" reads another.

There were two types of boats that sailed the navigation: small, open vessels known as flats, carrying a cargo of some 20 tonnes, and that ran along the navigation or the Ribble estuary only, and then the boats, which were larger, about fourteen feet wide and sixty feet long, with covered hatches, able to carry larger cargos, and which could also make short coastal passages.

Records hold that, in the earlier days of the Navigation, there were three flats, named the Resolution, the Dispatch and the Speedwell, staffed usually by four men and a boy. By 1747 this number had increased to five flats, named Success, Assistance, Supply, Tender and Pink, and there were seven decked or covered flats, each capable of carrying around 40 tonnes, and named Resolution, Dispatch, Speedwell, Concord, Three Sisters, Three Brothers and Laurel. Another documented vessel named the Pleasure Boat is thought to have been an inspection boat of sorts. The decked boats remained near the coast while the flats journeyed further up the Navigation and over to Preston. It cost 2 and 6d per tonne of cargo to travel the Navigation, though local land-owners could use it for free for the purposes of transporting manure.

By the 1770s, there were several flat-owners working the Navigation, but times were changing. In 1770, an Act of Parliament had authorised the Leeds and Liverpool Canal, a project so costly and prone to alteration that it had to be conducted in sections. The Wigan-to-Liverpool section opened in 1777, and to obtain a water supply the Canal Company sought to purchase the Douglas Navigation. In 1772, they bought 28 of the original 36 shares. In 1783 a further Act of Parliament gave the company the authority to purchase the remaining shares and for the Leeds and Liverpool Canal company and the Douglas Navigation company to merge.

After the merger, the canal was extended onwards to Wigan in a parallel route. They then built the Rufford Branch of the canal, leaving the main route at Burscough, descending through eight locks to Tarleton. Those final two miles follow the old course of the River Douglas, and the branch ended where River Lock joined the canal to the river. When this branch opened, it meant that all trade moved to the canal, and only the lower portion remained in use, from Tarleton to the confluence with the Ribble. By this time the navigation was in a state of disrepair — riverbanks had collapsed around Bank Bridge and Rufford, causing sand and silt banks and flooding, and it was leaking badly onto the surrounding land. An estimated £7000 was needed in repairs, with further costs inevitable. In 1801, the River Douglas Navigation was abandoned.

At first the Canal had travelled from Liverpool and ended at Newburgh, and for some while from there vessels used the Upper Douglas Navigation to reach Wigan. This was, Joseph Priestley explained in his Historical Account of the Navigable Rivers, Canals and Railways of Great Britain, "A distance of seven miles in which there is a fall to Newburgh of 30 feet."

"This is the place where the straight-laced Leeds-Liverpool canal once became entangled with the River Douglas, as if falling in with a bad crowd"

This is where I grew up, in the village of Newburgh, seven miles and 30 feet below Wigan, right where the canal met the river. It is a small village, sloping down towards the River Douglas in the north and the east, and to one of her tributaries to the southeast. These days, it is famed only for its prettiness, for its summer fair and its strawberry fields. Historically it was a farming community, but with the Navigation and the Canal, a little prosperity came to the village – quarries, rope-works, coal-shafts, but the collieries and the wharves have disappeared now, and all that remains is a couple of old miners' cottages, a track to the water and a large depression in the earth.

Still, I like to think that this is the place where the straight-laced Leeds-Liverpool canal once became entangled with the River Douglas, as if falling in with a bad crowd, and running a little wild. It was here we played out our mild rebellions too. On weekend afternoons and school holidays, we would often drift down to the water, my best friend and I. No longer staring face down at water boatmen in the canal, but lying on our backs now, in the long grass by the river, talking about boys. Or walking through the fields, along its banks, sipping sweet wine. Or climbing up into the branches of the tall trees that overhang the current, sitting with our legs dangling, shelling peas, feeling the rough bark against bare skin, breathing the heavy smell of summer, listening to the music of the river.

On Friday nights we would journey those seven miles, climb those 30 feet up to Wigan. On Saturdays we followed the river out to the sea. On school mornings we walked together to the bus stop and watched the mist hanging heavy over the Douglas Valley, waiting for the bus to come glinting down the hill, over the canal, over the river and hiss to a halt before us.

You don't realise how much a river has got under your skin until you leave it. It is more than a decade since I left the River Douglas, and since then I have encountered many more, I've fallen for the Nile and the Jordan, for the Isis and the Cherwell, the Seine, the Menai Straits, the Mississippi, I've crossed the Columbia, the Willamette, the Hudson. And I have settled in London, somewhere between the River Thames and the Regent's Canal.

But there is something about the Douglas, still, that makes my insides twist. It's there in the deep, rich green of its banks and the dour grey of its water; it's there in the way its hardness turns so giddy and flushed in the sudden sunshine. It is the soft, sad warmth of its familiarity, the face of your first love, caught across a crowded bar.

Over 200 years since it was abandoned, traces of the Douglas Navigation can still be seen: a hole in a field at Douglas Chapel; at Gathurst, a lock-keeper's cottage facing the river, rather than the canal; a navigation weir at Dean. They stand largely unnoticed of course; they exist as reminders only for those who go looking. But I go looking, and they seem to me now reminders of all the things I left behind, the things left unsaid, the half-recollections, fragments from a time before we grew so straight and narrow. I look at these fields, at the land where the river once wrapped itself around the canal, and I feel the wild, restless pull of the Douglas. I swim backwards, through the dark water.

Laura Barton writes for The Guardian. *Her first novel is published in 2010.*

WHEN FENLANDS
FINEST RACED WITH

JACK
FROST

BY
ROGER DEAKIN

As you approach Grantchester Meadows on the path out of Cambridge, your eye is attracted to a sheltered water-meadow curiously dotted about with the rusting stalks of antique gas street lamps. It is a puzzling sight until you discover that they once illuminated a natural skating rink. When the north wind blew across the fens in the first months, the shallow flood would freeze readily, and night-time has always been favoured by ice-skaters because the ice is harder, faster, and more romantic.

Fenland skating is one of the last great hidden subcultures in our land. And it goes back well past the Middle Ages. It is mostly hidden because the conditions for its open expression only occur from time to time, but all across the fens, pairs of cobwebbed skates still hang optimistically in sheds and attics waiting for the next big freeze. And in the isolated pubs strung out along the big horizons of the Hundred Foot River and the Ouse Washes, the oldies still sit and tell stories of the fen skaters and their rivalry beneath photographs of some of the legendary races.

——————

I first became aware of the strength and importance of the fen skating tradition as an undergraduate at Cambridge in the exceptionally cold winter of 1963. It was the winter of the death of Sylvia Plath, perpetual grey. Had it not been for the endless clouds, it would have been even colder. All through January and February we crouched around our gas fires and awoke beside stone-cold hot-water bottles. On January 23 there were 20 degrees of frost and by then the Cam and Granta rivers were already frozen solid. I used to hasten down Mill Street each morning and sit on the bank lacing up my skates amongst dozens of others busy declaring their shared secret passion for the ice.

The atmosphere was memorably festive and good-humoured, even anarchic, like a Bruegel painting. The ice drew us all to it, and the river became the main thoroughfare. People skated, strolled, made slides, played ice hockey, pulled sledges, rode bicycles, even motorbikes. A gang of us skated to Grantchester and back, the professionals whizzing past us streamlined in body stockings and balaclavas, heads down, hands clasped behind their backs like high-speed penguins. I showed off my trick of throwing jelly babies into the air and catching them in my mouth like a performing seal while skating at full speed. The river was full of shouts and the swish of skates, the ice engraved and criss-crossed in sugared lines.

Someone even drove a Mini along the frozen Ouse from Ely to Littleport. Some of the older skaters pushed brooms before them to steady themselves, and the cardboard boxes of old skates that had languished in the corner of every junk shop in the city suddenly walked.

The miracle was in the spontaneity of the occasion: the sudden transformation of the landscape and the physical laws of nature that enabled us to walk on water. Reincarnated by the frost, the fen people, normally sedentary and earthbound, toiling in their potato fields or allotments, mysteriously emerged like swallowtails or dragonflies from their larvae, skimming about the frozen fens with all the urgency of Cinderella at the ball. The great fenland sport is as evanescent as the ice itself.

As soon as there is ice thick enough, the normally deserted Ouse Washes from Welney to Earith can still wake up to a sudden throng of skaters and spectators, and word goes round somehow that the Fenland Championships are on: held whenever, and wherever, the weather permits.

In the Fens, where, until as recently as the 1930s there were few roads, people stayed close to home with potterings to the village pub and occasional outings to the market in Ely. You made your own amusements, swimming or skating according to the season. The coming of frost brought with it a sudden, dramatic increase in mobility. When the temperature dropped below zero, the skaters emerged on to the liberating highways of ice, no longer earthbound but moving with all the fluidity of the water itself, or the eels they understood and trapped.

The fact that the land, too, would become too iron-hard to work meant that this was a kind of enforced (and unpaid) holiday, and the farmworkers would skate from pub to pub, often racing each other. It was working men's sport, and many of the races were originally for prizes of desperately needed food put up by the farmers: a leg of lamb, or a ham. In the sluggish world of the fens (my favourite river is the Snail), it must have been doubly exhilarating to glide at speed over miles of ice. Literally hundreds of miles of it would suddenly open up with the coming of the cold. Around Ely alone, there are some 580 miles of rivers and dykes.

The earliest fen skaters were almost certainly Flemish, gliding into a medieval landscape very like their own, using blades carved and smoothed from the shin bones of sheep strapped tightly to their boots. According to an early descrip-

tion, people skated just the same way in London as early as 1180, propelling themselves with spiked wooden staves. Even in the Bone Age they moved surprisingly fast: there are records of a 15-mile race from Wisbech to Whittlesey in 1763, with a winning time of 46 minutes.

During the early 19th century, fen skaters began changing over to the apparently clumsy steel fen runners or patterns, also introduced by the Dutch. On the long straights of the fen drains, these 15-inch Sheffield steel blades with curled-up toes wee actually capable of tremendous speeds, and the Fenland Championships seem to have begun on a formal footing with the founding of the National Skating Association in 1827.

They raced in straight lines between barrels set on the ice, turning sharply around them to double back, watched by huge crowds of men and women who would appear from nowhere, skating in from the apparently deserted winter landscape. From 1850 until the turn of the century, the fen skaters were practically unbeaten, even by the Dutch and Norwegians in the international races they entered. They kept on winning many of the big races until the early 1930s and nearly all the champions came from the same remote fenland village: Welney, on the Ouse Washes, the long flood-plain that runs between the New and Old Bedford rivers. None of these Welney men are ever mentioned in the fens without the prefix 'the legendary', and many of them also bore cryptic nicknames: William 'Turkey' Smart, his nephew George 'Flying Fish' Smart, and William 'Gutta Percha' See.

Gutta Percha's son George and Fish's brother James were the only two champions without nicknames, but it doesn't seem to have slowed them down. They all schooled themselves on the wide horizons of the Ouse Washes, skating in a headlong, forward-leaning style, arms flailing, with the giant raking strokes pioneered by 'Turkey' Smart, gliding 12 to 18 yards on each skate. (A modern speed-skating stroke is more like 6 or 7 yards).

Turkey Smart first skated to fame in 1854 when he beat the champion of the day, Larman Register of Southery, the skater who later raced and beat the King's Lynn to London

train between Littleport and Ely in 1870. Turkey remained unbeaten for over a decade: it wasn't until 1867, when he was 40, that Gutta Percha succeeded in beating him.

Championship races have always been arranged at short notice, when the conditions are right, and on December 18, 1878 a famous race was held at Mepal for a prize of £10, in which Turkey's nephew Fish Smart caused a sensation by beating the 16 fastest skaters in the country. Gutta Percha was drawn against Turkey in the heats and just beat him, only to be defeated by young Fish in the next round, who went on to beat Gutta Percha's son George See in the final. Fish Smart kept on winning until 1889, when his 20-year-old brother James beat him at Lingay Fen over one-and-a-half miles in 4 minutes 47 seconds. Later that year at Cowbit Walsh, James Smart covered ten miles in 36 minutes 39 seconds and went on to triumph in the 1891 Dutch professional championship at Heerenveen before a crowd of 50,000.

Speeds would naturally vary according to ice and wind conditions. With a following wind, John Gittam of Nordelph had once covered the mile in 2 minutes 29 seconds. But it was endurance that counted just as much as speed for the fens. It was quite normal for people to skate for ten or 15 miles to watch or take part in a race, and I know of a farmer's wife living in Wicken in the 1880s who would think nothing of skating along the Wicken Lode to Upware and thence by the flooded washes of the Cam to Cambridge and back in a day: at least 35 miles.

Every pub in the fens has its own versions of distance skating records, but most agree that, one January day in 1903, two King's Lynn men, S S Burlingham and his friend Ronald

Errington, skated 96 ¼ miles on a round trip from Salter's Lode near Downham along the Old Bedford River via Welney, Welches Dam, the Forty Foot Drain, the Old River Nene, Whittlesea Dyke, March, the Sixteen Foot Drain and Popham's Eau, returning home well after midnight on the mail train.

More recently Alan Bloom, the plantsman of Bressingham, skated the 66 miles from Denver Sluice to Cambridge and back in a day, retracing the route first skated in the long winter of 1895 by Dr W R Smith of Sheringham. In the Three Tuns at Welney, they also tell the story of Fred Page, the grandson of Larman Register, who skated 18 miles from Denver Sluice to Ely in just over an hour in 1897, then sped back again and across to Southery in time for a skating match, a total of over 50 miles in a few hours.

Beards and moustaches used to be fashionable in the fens, and the wind-chill factor would often cause the breath of skaters to condense and freeze, forming a crop of icicles that would have to be removed carefully by the application of hands at a chestnut-brazier.

Ice hockey began on the fens as a game they called Bandy, and, 100 years ago, many villages had their own teams, competing like a football league. It grew out of the same spirit of home-spun improvisation that inspired some claustrophobic fenmen amongst the RAF prisoners of war confined in the German camp at Barth on the Baltic coast of Pomerania during the 1939-45 war. Perhaps remembering that illuminated meadow on the way to Grantchester, they had the bright idea of flooding their parade ground to make a rink and improvising homemade skates from angle-irons unscrewed from the chapel benches, rounded off at the leading edge by illicit files, and screwed in nine-inch lengths to their army boots. The fashion spread to another camp at Heyderkrug in Lithuania, and hundreds of prisoners of war learnt to skate and play ice hockey well enough to compete against the Canadians in the same camps.

As the least visible of our great amateur sports, fenland skating has been quite used to an intermittent flowering, taking its chance with the weather, but the new warming of our world may pose a more serious threat to its survival than the odd mild winter from now on. Under the magical presidency of Jack Frost, skating in the wild fens remains far more vulnerable to our weather than cricket, and perhaps the only sport in which a commentator could write (in the *Cambridge Evening News*, Jan 1987) without a trace of irony: "It is to be hoped that the present bad weather will hold long enough to complete the championships over the weekend."

Originally taken from 'The Countryman'. Roger Deakin is the author of Waterlog, Wildwood *and* Notes from Walnut Tree Farm.

THE
BLACK
RIVER

BY
IRVINE WELSH

My father was always adamant that he didn't hail from the port of Leith, but immediately to its west, at "the quaint fishing village of Newhaven", as he was wont to call it. It's been a long time since that district of Edinburgh could rightfully be described in that way, the only remnant of its past being the old harbour and the lighthouse. This stands at the end of the breakwater at the harbour mouth, looking out over the cold, black tidal waters of the Forth estuary. Local youths would, usually after a few drinks, dare each other to walk around the ledge that tapered down to a few inches as it circled the tower, its beacon now long-defunct. Many fell into the river, with the occasional calamitous outcome.

My dad once told me a story about his courtship of my mother. One night, on about their third date, he got it into his head that if she could negotiate the lighthouse ledge, then she would be the one for him. When I asked her about this story, my mum, who can't swim and who has a pronounced fear of heights, ruefully confirmed it, adding that she was wearing stiletto heels at the time. "Somehow, mug that I am, I trusted him that I'd be okay, and that he'd be able to save me if anything went wrong." Fortified with gin, she didn't look down and successfully completed the walk. They tied the knot a year later.

My old man was pretty fond of 'tests' that involved heights and the river. When I was a small boy, he took me up to the top of Chancelot Mill, on an industrial estate overlooking the Forth, where he and his buddy, Benny Morton, made me go to the ballustrade-free edge of this towering building's roof. They then proceeded to hold me over by my ankles, and I recall being suspended upside down, watching the river and Fife from my perilous vantage point.

I recollect being excited, but not scared; I knew that my dad would never drop me. At that time, however, I was too young to be acquainted with the tendency men on his side of the family had towards extreme recklessness. Few of them have enjoyed long lives; his own grandfather died in relative youth close to the Forth at Leith docks, walking through a tunnel in front of an oncoming goods train whilst drunk.

Perhaps it was the river that inspired such madness and tradgedy. The Gaelic translation of River Forth is Abhainn Dhubh, which means 'black river'. Stretching for some thirty miles, the Forth is the uncelebrated pantomime villain of the major British rivers. You'd be hard-pushed to find much evidence of the romance that's occasionally lavished on the Thames, Tyne or Mersey, and even the Tay can boast William McGonagall's wonderfully awful poem about the disaster on its bridge.

"They then proceeded to hold me over by my ankles, and I recall being suspended upside down, watching the river and Fife from my perilous vantage point"

The Forth certainly doesn't command the affectionate relationship with my home city of Edinburgh that its counterpart, the Clyde, enjoys with nearby Glasgow. This is primarily because the Forth doesn't bisect the city, it merely defines its

northern border. For most people in Edinburgh, the river is
something tucked away behind housing schemes, industrial
estates and marginal communites that they'll never have the
occasion to visit. It's largely seen as this mysterious entity that
separates us from Fife, and many citizens, particulary those
who hail from south of Princes Street, probably wouldn't be
able to find it without the aid of a good map.

Being brutally honest, as it reaches the city limits, this
dull, manky stagnant-looking stretch of water lives up to its
gaelic name. Long turned tidal, and widened into an estuary,
even on a good day the Forth can still give off a positively sinister vibe. Rendered filthy by the petrochemical refinery up at
Grangemouth, it seems so still, yet somehow treacherous by
the time it hooks up with Edinburgh. It's a bit like the jakey
uncle who suddenly shows up at a family wedding, fresh out

of prison following a long stretch for a nefarious crime nobody can quite bring themselves to talk about. We know that it's connected with us in some way, but we can't quite muster up the enthusiasm to celebrate this fact.

I'll admit, however, that I'm basically seeing the river from a 'schemie' point of view. In the north Edinburgh council housing developments, few things were at their best by the time they made it out our way and the Black River was no exception. One of my first memories as a kid was the 'THESE MUSSELS ARE UNFIT FOR HUMAN CONSUMPTION' signs that adorned my local rock beach at Silverknowes on the banks of the estuary. The scarcely less-hazardous alternatives were the 'treats' proffered by the Seashell café, a building seemingly modelled on the World War II pillboxes which litter the islands of the Firth of Forth. These I can still list, as my school took them as house names; Inchkeith, Inchcolm, Inchgarvie, Inchmickerie. There were not enough islands for the purposes of our would-be educators, so the river gave the last house its title: Inchforth. Hitler's U-boats, in the event, never made it as far as the Black River. Whether the deterrent was provided by those military defences or the aesthetic qualities of the river and its environs, is a secret that has died with the Third Reich naval strategists.

The Romans got as far as the Forth, staying long enough to construct –then suddenly abandon- their most northernly British settlement on the banks of the Almond, a nearby tributary that flows into the estuary at Cramond. It's possible to catch flounders here, that strange, flat fish whose eyes move across to the side of their heads. Perhaps the Romans took a few sideways glances and decided that there were other things in life besides imperial expansion.

But it was the Scots' decision to jump on the colonial bandwagon that possibly constitutes the saddest chapter in the history of the river. Before the union with England, the independent kingdom of Scotland opted to invest in the concept of empire, and two boats set out from the Forth at Leith to establish a Scottish colony in Panama. When I inform English friends about this not-so-well-known historical detail, it often illicits gasps of stunned anticipation from them. It's like they sense what's coming next. Yes, the would-be settlers prepared in true Scottish fashion, carrying supplies of whisky, wigs, bibles and woollen blankets; ideal essentials for survival in the tropics. They were wiped out by disease within a few months, and the tartan imperial adventure died, losing half the nation's wealth in the process, thus precipitating the unloved and unwanted Union of the Crowns. So even history seems to exacerbate the Forth's sense of shame and failure.

To be fair, in its pre-tidal and pre-city youth, the Forth is an impressively picturesque river. My favourite view of it is from the top of the Wallace Monument on a clear day, as it meanders like a silver snake down from the Trossachs, through Stirling and the surrounding countryside. But I just can't equate this River Forth in any way with that dark and dirty firth that I grew up alongside. The Black River can be crossed for the last time before Edinburgh city limits at the town of Kincardine, where it turns tidal from North Sea flow-back. By the time it passes Grangemouth it's been corrupted by industry.

Industrial and post-industrial blight seem to define the river from then on in; the defunct shipyards of Rosyth and Leith, the former trawler port of Granton, the old fishing village of Newhaven, the oil refinery at Methil. Portobello beach, Edinburgh's Bondi or Copacabana, is and remains, the Forth's one concession to leisure. To this day it still attracts weedgie (Glaswegian) day trippers, even if the journey all too often ends up in the district's adjoining bars in order to escape the omnipresent drizzling rain and biting winds that tear down the estuary from the North Sea.

----•◦•----

While it's true that the river does facilitate a certain magnificence as it reaches the city, this is solely due to the impressive bridges that span its length. The Forth (rail) Bridge is one of the genuine wonders of the world. A magnificent piece of Victorian engineering, it looks like two rust-coloured armadillos sniffing at each other before they start shagging or fighting, and it makes the adjacent road bridge come over as a pretty scabby affair. Actually, this suspension bridge should be as magnificent as the Golden Gate in San Francisco. When I lived in that city, it was the comparison between those bridges that illustrated for me the essential difference between California and Caledonia. One constructs a large suspension bridge, does it in vibrant colour, calls it the Golden Gate and declares it a major tourist attraction. The other builds a large suspension bridge, paints it grey, saddles it with the humdrum moniker 'The Forth Road Bridge', and stoically informs us that it should make getting from Edinburgh to Fife easier. Some blame Calvinism for this crippling conservatism, others cite over three hundred years of London rule. Personally, I think the weather has a lot to answer for.

————•◦•————

Returning to my own first close encounters with that mundane stretch of the river, which I got to know at Silverknowes, my scheme of Muirhouse's local beach, the best part was the adjacent forested area. Here we would go to swing on 'Tarzans' or collect wood for bonefire nights. Unfortunately, we lived at the top end of the scheme and had to navigate back home through most of those unforgiving streets, encountering the inevitable 'raiders' who would batter you with cudgels and take the wood off you. We were usually lucky to make it back with a few twigs.

This relatively-concealed forest usually held imaginative dominion over the open, desolate, boulder and pebble beach, where our childhood cruelties resulted in the smashing of poor crabs trapped in rock pools, or unfortunate jellyfish ran aground. In those woods above the River Forth I had my first clumsy gropes, and while I didn't lose my virginity there, those maraudings paved the way for that imminently forgettable yet too-easily-recalled event. When you eventually found your feet in the romance stakes, there was Cramond Island, the one closest to the Forth's Silverknowes shore. You could walk out there with the object of your desire, then get 'accidentally' cut off by the incoming tides, and thus be compelled to spend the night on the island. The serious shaggers studied the tidal charts in the Evening News like the most dedicated Old Salts, and never left home without a sports bag containing a jumper and blankets. What was a liability in Panama in the seventeeth century remains a decided asset at home.

As with so many other things, it was Acid House that opened up the river to the people. An old passenger ferry called The Maid Of the Forth, which used to cross from Granton to Kirkcaldy, decided to install a sound system and throw parties. These were great fun, though even in the high summer it could

get bollock-freezing cold down on that estuary, again reminding you that the river being cut off from the people might not be such an intrinsically bad thing. One abiding memory was of the boat being moored on the Fife bank, near some field outside Kinghorn. Half the ravers were loved-up on those really good ecstasy pills, the other half were on some pretty strong acid. In the field a farmer was firing a crossbow at a target mounted onto a tree. The e-heads were going: 'Wow, that's so cool, I'd love a shot at that', while the acid heads were running off the deck, heading below, screaming: 'Some psycho cunt's got a fuckin crossbow!'

The rave boat seemed to herald in the winds of change. I recall, as a boy, having to cycle through a load of industrial estates on a Sunday, in order to pick up a parcel of fresh meat from a big warehouse by an abattoir in Granton. It wasn't far as the crow flies, but it took ages through an inhospitable warren of dead-end roads and diversions, with barred wire fences and Securicor guard dog signs proliferating. I remember thinking more than once: why did the shoreline on the Forth estuary have to be so cut off from everybody?

Other people evidently thought along the same lines. Now on this north side of the city, the Black River, once inaccessible and hidden from sight, has been opened up by developers. This area is now pompously refererred to (by them at least) as Edinburgh's Waterfront. It reeks of a total scam. The first wave of gentrification was one thing, with the sympathetic conversion of the old warehouses and whisky bonds at Leith. These renovated homes at least had a bit of style and substance. The new-build apartments that have proliferated in the last ten years, however, are poorly designed and badly constructed, with scant social amenities in the locality. There's a strong suspicion that they will be slums in ten years' time, and only about one in five of them actually faces onto the glum, oily prairie they call the River Forth. What is it with yuppies and water?

So I have mixed feelings about the continuing redevelopment of this part of my city. But I have to say that I had an uplifting experience at the Terence Conran patio bar at Ocean Terminal, a Forthside shopping centre in Leith, and resting home of the Royal Yacht Britannia. It was at this bar that I proposed to my wife, who thought (as did I) that I was going to pop the question in Paris, where we were heading that weekend. As I looked across the water, and loads of memories flooded back, I had a

> "Half the ravers were loved-up on those really good ecstasy pills, the other half were on some pretty strong acid."

sudden surge of inspiration. Waiting till she'd gone to the ladies, I ran into the nearby Samuels jewelers, purchased the ring, and had it in my pocket by the time she'd emerged to rejoin me in the bar. Switching my gaze from those still grey waters to her pale blue eyes, I slid down onto my knees and did the deed. The bar was empty, except for two tattoo-covered wideos who'd obviously been out on a sesh all day. I heard one guy pronounce in mocking sneer, 'Fuckin wanker', but lost in the moment, I wasn't at all bothered.

The next thing I recall, after we broke off from the engagement snog, was that one of the boys had sent over a bottle of champagne. They gave us the thumbs up as they exited, one guy shaking his head sternly, pointing at our drinks and saying, 'Fuckin lager? You're a comedian! Get him telt', he urged my bethrothed. It was true Leith class; he wasn't upset at me for making a romantic guesture, as I had thought, but sitting with a pint of lager. I'd broken protocol by going cheap on my bird and not doing things the right way. This perfect moment made me glad that I'd picked Leith over Paris, and yes, that the minging old Forth was there to share it. Stifling a tear, I looked over at those waters and I swear, that just for a moment, they were was as blue as my beloved's eyes. It struck me then, that perhaps that 'filthy old oil slick', as my dad used to call it, really could inspire romance. And I hadn't even asked her to walk around Newhaven's lighthouse.

Irvine Welsh is from Edinburgh. He is the author of eleven books, including Trainspotting, Marabou Stork Nightmares, Filth *and* Crime.

PALM-
READING
THE
HELFORD

BY
PETER KIRBY

Now I'm no mystic but my ghost disagrees. Water brings out the intangible in me. Maybe it's because we're two-thirds liquid that we all go giddy at the purr of a brook. Or maybe it's because one day far away from now, I'd simply love to die drowning. As Brian Wilson sang, "God only knows". And fish.

Wild water conjures up fate by the fathom-full and gees us on to go with the flow, even when it flows both ways, as it does here in the Helford. This is a river you cannot pin down. See, I've failed already. Geographically speaking, it's a ria, an estuary, a delta, a valley submerged 10,000 summers ago. Yet if you listen to an eddy, the Helford is an udder of the sea with teat-like creeks fed by the land and its century plus of springs. Time to trace one such source and chart its future.

WORVAL TO PONSONTUEL

Not the sweetest of starts. On all fours, I crawl through the slime of an industrial pipe beneath Skyburriowe Lane Bridge, deep in the conscience of the Lizard peninsula. Thirty-three knee strides later, I emerge with claustrophobia, wristbands of algae and my dislodged pooh stick.

I

am

taking

this twig

for

a

swim,

the

length

of the

Helford

River

The stream is my flock, the stick is my hound and Phil Drabble marks our card from his stile in the sky.

Nature is some boat-builder. She tickles the underbelly of the twig until it frees itself, sails a fair lick, before another snag at the bottom rung of my mother-in-law's garden, (aka Worval) where still waters run shallow. Rays of rusted sunshine rebound off the serpentine bed. Tiny trout spitfire upstream and nutmeg my rubber clogs. Distracted, I plunge thigh-deep into a pool, the very pool where my wife once sponged her Grampa Wally's back. God rest his trowel.

This is tropical Britain. Plants boast equatorial roots with leaves to match. I duck under some Gunera, the span of Michael Phelps. Wildlife gets wilder. Puff the Neon Dragonfly leads the way, drumming his wings impatiently. He waits…then…mush! We're off again. An afro of foam swirls round the stump of a sad elm; each bubble dredges up the past when the stream was a sewer to the local laundry and their killer chemicals.

The swamp thickens and I hurdle a barbed-wire boundary, drawing blood as I go. Curse those kisses of hate sat just below the surface. Brambles grow nearby to goad their man-made cousin. This is S & M passport control. I storm the gates and despite the punk appearance, the spikes don't hurt so much as violently rub.

My walk becomes a wade. I am up to my waist in *Apocalypse Now* bog with eau de Agent Orange. Ahead, the stream raises its voice to a river. Behold, the world's only ugly waterfall, made from catering vats of cooking oil. I name this dam 'Ni-Ogre Falls'.

The eyesore snowballs as tyres appear in one shape and many circumferences, followed by the tears of a torched car, the corpse of a caravan and the sunken soul of a speedboat burping lilies in a lay-by lagoon. Cue banjo, cue *Deliverance* and spare a thought for Ned Beatty.

Beauty regains its composure. A treble clef foxglove salutes a field. The fish are back, braver than ever and stand their water. The river writhes, a rabbit ga-boings, a dog yaps and a man stares as I pass his lawn, exchange 'awreets' and stoop off under a bridge.

The stick stops to sniff roots, marked perhaps, by the guard dog. A vine lassoes the bow of my baby boat up out of the water. Newton nods to gravity and bobs the stick back into its sea-bound path.

A grown-up forest has fallen into a teenage river, trunk upon prostrate trunk. This is an assault course for acrobat otters. I sail the stick under and steeplechase over. For one small second, it's Kirk Douglas dancing on oars in *The Vikings*, until the moss upends me. Like one-eyed-Kirk, I am not the man I was. Winded, I limbo beneath a clapper bridge and confront a landscape I call 'Heavenford' (as opposed to Helford). A celestial tryst of road, water and tree. These are the woods where alchemy lives. The epileptic light takes my logic hostage. Maybe I'm just tired, or thirsty? I drink the trail I'm on and realise all bottled water tastes of bin liners.

Salt smacks me round the face. Smell the weed of the sea. Bathe the blood away that is etched in 95 cuts below my knees, while the fish bite back at my sea-sponge toes. Time to change transport. And socks.

GWEEK TO GILLAN

Leg two = all arms. Take the kayak and paddle like a bastard. Kayaking is walking with your hands. Allegedly, it's also the chosen sport of palmists, or 'chiromancers' as their business card states. So, true to the laws of destiny, I'll make this up as I go along.

Take the plunge at Gweek glorious Gweek, gem of a village, bohemia of a boatyard. Here lie the bowels of the river Helford, where burst vessels seep into quays with sunken hips. Pampas grass graces the upper deck. Buddleia thrives in leftover lime from the kilns that once bore the brunt of man's industrial toil. Down the central spit grow a dozen conifers, feeding on dregs of yesteryear's guano (booby-shit baby-bio), which came from the South Seas to fertilise the fields. Above a slagheap of tarpaulin sits a lifebelt, all but an anchor, all but dead, nailed to a post where gallows strung up oyster terrorists many lives ago.

This given day, industry is rife. The 200 strong crew of Seacore set out to bore the ocean floor as they have done for 30 years. On land, the craftsmen of Working Sail recreate 19th-century pilot cutters with a deep love of wood and techniques that would make a shark weep. Across the yard, waterproof paint cloys the air, a toxic trip for all within nose-shot. Swan, duck and gull, the avian masons, meet up to talk eco-justice. At the gates, a silver-foiled beast squats its eight black legs over an unloved BBQ.

Amidst all this exquisite debris are boats. Boats to live in, sail in, fish in, potter in. Boats whose names are born on hope: *Halcyon*, *Clairvoyant* and, I dare you not to smile, *Puffit*.

I baptise mine 'HMS Worval' after her birthplace and launch her with the outgoing tide. From here, I shall guide her as the dragonfly did me. For now we are two boats. Time to stop pushing and start pulling. I tie the stick to the tail of the kayak-come-tug, climb in and let the hands meander to the tune of the river. We shall crisscross the waters, from creek-tip to creek-tip, to hear stories of folk who flank the foreshore and eavesdrop on songs sung by fish.

The weather is spiteful. 25mph of mizzle (drizzle + mist) pummels my enthusiasm.

However, the joy of a kayak is you can resist a rapid and the rip of the tide. Or else, freewheel the way of the wind. Choose the latter. Heave ho Geronimo.

Too many strokes later, I moor up at Tremayne Quay built for the arrival of Queen Victoria, but she never made it. Bitch blamed the weather. I'm not so sure. Camp here tonight, guilt-free, knowing the Vyvyan family of Trelowarren gifted the land to the public via the National Trust in the early 1970s, bless them. Erect the tent in daylight on a lawn so thin it does for my pegs what Uri Geller did for spoons. Store wood for a fire after the reward of the pub, then on with the voyage.

To escape the wind, I swing into Frenchman's Creek. At its mouth, I probe for bodies in a pleasure-boat wreck hoping to relive a scene from *Jaws*. It all goes eerily still.

Glide super slowly up the creek. Dust gathers on the surface, a film of phlegm that forms a landing bay for insects or possibly, very light aircraft. Pollock gulp flies. Eels bark. Bass gawp cockily; the Helford is a designated nursery, so although I can't hook them, I can nigh on pat them. At low tide, trees perform handstands and locals talk of a secret fish-well from pre-refrigeration days. But now, sitting here, motionless, I listen to dank silence and the river confesses that it dictated 'that novel' to Madame Du Maurier.

As I paddle, questions surface. It's as though the blade of the oar combs up ideas from the most fertile force alive, the sea. I stop to write these thoughts afloat. And just drift. Drifting, both mentally and physically, is a drug worth trying. Your mind becomes a cove and gathers all manner of flotsam, some absurd, some more so.

It's dark-o-clock. Stars hide. The moon is bound and gagged by a cloud cartel.

> Form a char...
> > an island
> > > made of river silt   ...live there a while

>   Line   nest
> >   every bird's
> > > > > > with pages of a novel
> > > > > to read their young to sleep

> > > > > > > Assign
> > > > > > Water postcodes
> > > > > > With no fixed abode

> > > bridge
> > a   to
> Build   unite
> > > the south & north banks

> concoct a   year
> >   monster   a
> > >   that   once
> > >   emerges

This is one bleak sky. With pie, pudding and pints as fuel from the Ferry Boat Inn, I kayak back to the tent at Tremayne Quay. My arms throb as I grind into waves the way a bradawl bores into wood. The wind has slowed a little after its all-day-huff but still spits spray at my cheap specs. It's all deliciously primeval. Leviathan meets Roger Dean-scapes on Temazepan. Conrad would love this world. The air is solid and mute but for the symbol brush of each stroke. The less I concentrate, the smoother the ride. The water turns to treacle. I see the quay. It is but mud. I am but blind. A hundred yards on, I reach the quay, almost. The tide is late and a good eight foot shy. Between dry land and me lies the bile of the landscape, sludge. I punt the kayak sideways. Lugworms laugh at my gondola-gone-wrong technique.

The island char I ordered earlier has built itself

Spark a fire with still-wet wood. Sap hisses, and coughs smoke back at me like a leper without a hand. In this blackness all that shines is an ember of life over Falmouth to the east. By head-torch, I read Tom Sawyer out loud to the gnats that gather round the citronella tea-lights, the fools. Each candle fades away as if to say hey, we're tired too. The yawn catches on.

I take the drifting thoughts to sleep. And dream that the fire sets the tent alight. I am burnt alive as fire-fish (yes, fire-fish) in flame-retardant sou'westers (yes, really) pelt seawater at the flames with their double-jointed tails. What exactly was in that pie?

Wake up, to my surprise, singe-free. Go about my morning pledge to leave a sculpture for the pleasure of the craft that sail, chug, row, tow and paddle past. Gather sticks of differing thicknesses and similar lengths. Jam each one into the top set of stones that line the quay, a foot or so apart. 159 toothpicks west of the steps, 59 east of the steps. As homage to the pincer-like arms of the harbour, I name the piece 'The Dentist'.

Blow a wish to the tooth fairy that sleeps beneath the quay

Time has galloped on. Havens to go, people to see, tales to hear, shudders to feel.

Among them, Merthen Woods, as dense and rare a copse of trees as Britain can boast. Tucked in under the canopy, my stick stares in awe at its ancestry. These medieval coppice oaks were planted, cut and charcoaled for the sake of tin, an industry that made our miners world pioneers of subterranean fame. The scent of bark stripped to tan leather still daubs the air, along with the faint whiff of sun-dried mammal. Why? In 1506, at the apex of these woods, Groyne Point was home to a 'dolphin abattoir'. Half a millennium on, the innocent ears of children at Gweek Seal Sanctuary can still just about hear the squeals on an easterly breeze.

Tucked behind this former bloodbath, at the nape of Polwheveral Creek, I find the river's resident carbuncle (as its landlord might say). Locals call it the 'ghost ship'. I call it art. I shout hello but no-one's home. Later, I discover the owner is hard of hearing and sadly, hard to track down. Like many a hermit, he gathers detritus and finds a use for it. His 'wonder-some' vessel is an experiment in seaworthiness and out-freaks the Huck Finn raft I made last night from ten pole buoys lashed around a tongue 'n' groove door. His keel wears a pair of giant polystyrene stabilizers, while the engine house is a Renault 5. Charlie Pugh, king of this 'scruffily beautiful' creek, recounts the ghost ship's one and only voyage, a 100yard venture upstream, where he ran aground until the next spring tide U-turned him back him to his Calamansack roost. As I go, Charlie leaves me with words ending in age...anhorage, keelage, bushellage, killage, pannage...and I ponder the futurage of Helfordage.

Ghost steals my notebook to line nests with fake Twain words

The river has always lured hobos and travelling wilburys. As a boy in the late '60s, Sir Ferrers Vyvyan (High Sheriff of Cornwall) befriended a tramp that hunkered down in the hidden room at the back of Tremayne boathouse and bought hand-made holly pegs from the gypsies encamped in the woods. Inspired by these outsiders of society, he and Richard Winfrey would wade the channels at ebb tide to harpoon flatfish on sharpened poles, and head home with 4ft high kebabs.

I want to trespass, but I'm not sure how. KEEP OUT! signs only beckon people in. What's private is, in a way, public, as long as you ask. On the waters, there is no 'right of sway' to row against. Only if you moor up to a withy and dive for scallops, will they trawl you in. We trespass by what we do, not by where we are. WWII proves as much. On the steep banks, petrol tanks fed pipes to the beach and out across the river so a flame barrage would fry the enemy alive.

One Nov 5th, build a tightrope of twigs across the river and set it on fire

Anarchy once ruled these bayous. Cash-in-hand smuggling fed families, who got shot if they weren't on their toes. To this day, drugs swan in under the radar of HM Customs who, to the joy of barons everywhere, moved from Gweek to Bristol.

Like the National Trust and The Duchy, you sense the authorities are out of touch with the day-to-day doings of the people who live (and dock) here.

Take Phil Badger, doyen of the lower reaches. His family of Badgers once occupied two-thirds of the beds in the hamlet of Durgan, until the National Trust muscled in and cranked up the rent. Tourism may bring in the bucks but it also triggers social schizophrenia. Holiday homes have sapped the soul from the east of the river mouth, where locals just can't afford to live. Those who can are here, at a push, a month a year.

Communities are built on diversity, as the water knows only too well. Over 80 fish share the river and must wonder why we make such hard work of things. One day in the late 1960s, the river swarmed with pilot whales and half a dozen different species of sharks. Creatures get odder still at the Animal Chapel above Penarvon Cove. Built for a congregation of one, you kneel before a carving of a dog on hind legs baying at St Francis, with a rabbit on his lap, 2 frogs arm-wrestling his feet, a lugworm at his toes and a chough whose beak rests against his temple. Built in 1933 in honour of Leo O Neill by his sister, it is the tiniest and warmest house of peace I've ever set paws in.

Hostility, like ugliness, is hard to find. Still, I fancy a stir as I grew up in St Ives and went to school in Penzance. In their bitter hearts, I was a scaly-back (after the fish wars when 'we' sailed round and stole their catch). Is there a North v South? Not to Phil Badger, whose mates were all southerners. He'd row across to the Shipwrights Arms, down a boatful of beer, sing a sea-shanty or ten then (try to) row back.

So, I ask Mother Ocean. She draws me a diagram, true to the compass.

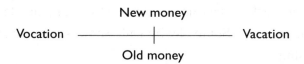

Every time I set foot back on land, I realise the kudos of the Helford. It carries gastronomic weight. There's a food micro-movement gaining momentum here. Helford Creek Apple Juice, Roskilly's Ice Cream at nearby Coverack, and Cornish Sea Salt of Porthkerris, are all on the up. Along the coast a little at Roseland, Britain's first plantation house grows its own leaf of tea. Near the border, Camel Valley fizz is champagne in all but a beret. Asparagus next, so hopes Gweek's Jo Cain. And kiwi fruit may even follow if the old vine at Bonallack has a say.

Best in show goes to the oyster. Not just any old mollusc. No. The Native Helford Oyster that Keith Floyd used to harp on about between bottles of claret and smokes. The oysterage dates back to 1580 and has passed into energetic new hands. Finally, I find a fight.

Before the blood, some background. People oppose change the further SW you go as my own father found when we arrived in the mid 1970s and our humble plans for a porch were turned down on account of his Midlands accent. Minds have moved on but still err on the conservative. Fair enough, protect and preserve a river that could out-pageant any other in this book, come sleet or shine. But milk the Helford too. It is blessed with oysters to drown for. They are nature's water filters. Ask Chesapeake Bay, America's biggest estuary that silted up into a coma when the oyster farms packed their bags. If the Helford bore 100,000 a week a generation back, it can do so again. How they are farmed is the sticking point. Some say by sail. Some say by cage. Some say nothing.

In the middle of the bun-fight sits neutral Nick Bailey, the latest in a long line of ferrymen. The crossing is medieval and until 1929, was a rowing boat that ran alongside the 'horse boat'. No lie. At Bar Beach, wagons and carts edged onto a craft while horses swam behind on a long rope, no doubt led on by sugar.

Nick tells me of the reciprocal circle, a back-scratch conga that makes things tick on both sides of the river. Like everyone I've met, his mood is in tune with the moon. A low-tide morning means a high-tide evening when everyone crams round the pub. Many admit they sense the pull of the water even when they wander inland. Full fat moons rub us all up the right way.

Water postcodes: NSHL Neap Spring High Low

The biodynamic forces start to get to me. I see early stars out to play and plot the astrological chart according to the opera above me. Down below, the eelgrass, our only underwater flower, shuts its blossom for the day.

THE END TO WHEREVER

"Seadogs and mermaids, we are now in the closing stages of our tour. To our portside, Rosemullion Head, to our starboard, Nare

Point, to our stern, 27 miles of foreshore, to our bow, the deep green abyss. Goodbye Duchy, hello Crown Estate."

As I cross this vague finish line and free HMS *Worval* into the ocean, deeper thoughts rise to the surface.

There's something about the shape of the river and the land that engulfs it. Staring at my map, worn bare through wear, a gaff hook strikes: The Helford is a miniature Amazon. The Lizard is a miniature South America. Geometry and orientation are one and the same. Even the vegetation marries up. Trees hang in a mangrove manner. Egrets are on the electoral role, while sunfish and barracuda stalk the bay. How long before piranhas hitch a ride up the Gulf Stream to lay their hat, and their eggs? Or malaria stows in with mutant mosquitoes, as it did in the 1700s. Climate change means we have the earth on the hob; the fridge door open and the ocean on simmer. I gaze at my stick-ship, its epic journey and wonder when we'll be logging the old woods to make ends meet.

Be the boy with his thumb in the dyke, my conscience tells me. Consume nothing, recycle everything, and generate my own energy...somehow. Paradoxically, the answer is staring me in the backside. Hydropower. Water, rivers, tides – use the most powerful thing on earth, rather than what's in the earth. Capture the elemental force of the sea as it overflows and we could enjoy the happiest accident of all time.

My time in this river is done. Cats-cradling the creeks, I've left a wake. As apt a word as any, as land surrenders to sea. If we admit defeat, this becomes the Last Will and Testament of the River Helford. If however, we attempt the absurd, we can achieve the impossible and save the planet's skin.

The river is in good hands. I stare at my palms, and beneath blisters, I see tributaries. Another collision of joy, the creases and curves of my hands seek out their soul mates in the arms of the river. To each palm line, I allocate a creek. To each creek, I entrust a guardian. To each guardian, I suggest a motto.

CREEK	LINE	GUARDIAN	MOTTO
Porthnavas	Head	Phil Badger	Make the old think young
Polwheveral	Life	Charlie Pugh	Propagate peace
Gweek	Heart	Jo Cain	Fly your own flag
Mawgan	Fate	Ben Kirby	Laugh when the fish do
Ponsonteul	Marriage	Maud Tregoning	Take a stick for a walk
Gillan	Luck	Anthony Jenkin	Sailing keeps the wind busy
Vallum	Fame	Sir Ferrers Vyvyan	Success is what you believe in
Bonallack	Money	James Lyall	Invest in trees
Helford	Travel	Marie King	Go by sea, it's free
Penarvon	Health	Virginia Richardson	Dogs are the heart's best friend
Frenchmans	Spirit	Mr Ghost Ship	Sod off

To the ebb tide, I entrust the Wright Brothers to sift the silt and flourish the shellfish. To the full tide, I entrust Nick Bailey to ensure everyone's glass is full, come sunset.

Hands up, astrology is science wearing a fictional dress, but if we bank on the moon to control the tides, then it may just control the future. Reading between the lines on my palms, that long term forecast ain't so bad.

Deep thanks to: Phil, Charlie, James, Jo, Ferrers, Ben, Rob, Virginia, Robin, Marie, Nick & Anthony. Without you, I'd be Virginia Woolf'd. Peter Kirby is a writer and artist who built the steps to his house from material he found on the banks of the Thames.

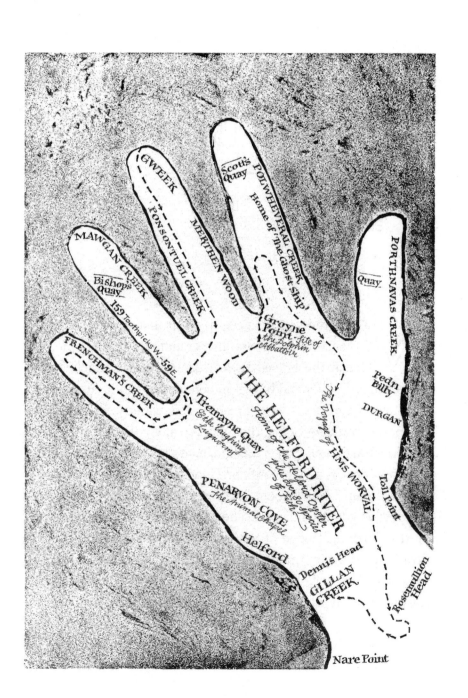

To Fish
The Burns

BY
EDWYN COLLINS & GRACE MAXWELL

My grandfather was a good fisherman. A good poacher. I suppose my grandfather taught me. To fish the burns. Brown trout. 10 or 12 inches say, wee things. Golden and brown in colour, red spots. First of all, the burns. They are slippery places. The water is fast moving. You better watch out. You kind of move along the water's edge. Quickly. You carefully drop the line in, feed it out and wait. Three minutes tops. You've got a fish? Good. If not, move on. Once I got a salmon! I was fifteen. That was at Langwell Water. I was pleased, as you can imagine. The places I fished. Ousdale Burn, on the north east edge of Sutherland, Kilpheddir Burn, in the Strath of Kildonan, the Craggie, up Glen Loth. All rough stuff. My bait? Worms. Not any more, since my stroke. I'll cast from a rowing boat, on the lochs. That's easy. Not like the burns.

Edwyn Collins

dwyn's grandfather taught me to fish too on my first visit to Helmsdale in 1985. Not on the Helmsdale of course, that's for the super toffs. Prince Charles comes up most years. Although his grandfather was an expert salmon fisher himself, he preferred the burns that come tumbling down the craggy hillsides and down in to the river. Rough stuff indeed. I spend more time on my arse in the burns than anything else. Edwyn's description is perfect. It's not proper fishing. It's a bit mental really. It's just rocks and really steep sides and getting your hook snagged in the gorse and the alders and getting eaten alive by the midges. The trout taste great though. I'm better at getting them than Edwyn because I have more patience and also obey the grandfather rules to the letter.

One day when he was little, Edwyn and his sister were walking up the Strath with their grandpa and an old tweedy toff was fishing the river with his ghillie. He's got a salmon on the line and grandpa's going: "Oh dear he's an old man. He's struggling, look. He's too old, you see. He's handing it over….." and on and on. They run into him later on and he says to grandpa, "I did so enjoy your running commentary. Would you care for a fish?" And proceeds to show off his enormous haul in the back of the car!

Grace Maxwell

Grace is the wife and manager of former Orange Juice singer Edwyn Collins. Their first book together is published by Ebury in 2009.

Not Caught By The River

BY

JOHN NIVEN

He seemed like a 'big boy' to us at the time although, of course, looking back now, he was just a kid. Thirteen or fourteen. Wearing one of those green army jumpers with patches at the shoulders and elbows. How he cried.

My little brother and I had come along the bank of the river Irvine, in Ayrshire, thirty miles south of Glasgow. We'd been spinning for sea trout up at the weir. The serious fisherman went for the salmon with flies further up river, in the shadows of the great Victorian railway bridge. I remember it being a cold spring morning, incredibly sunny, maybe the Easter holidays then. When we came around the bend towards the bridge, there was already a good crowd there, maybe a dozen or so fishermen, old boys and some kids our own age, just, or not quite, into their teens. They were all watching as this kid – his rod bowed into an upturned 'U' – did battle with something huge. There was an air of real excitement, and you got the feeling that this had been going on for a while.

The kid was flanked by a couple of the men, both giving him advice – when to play out some line and let the fish run, when to lock the reel – but neither touching the rod or interfering too much. They were going to let him catch it himself.

I remember his trainers slipping and skidding on the greasy boulders of the bank, the great anxiety and fierce determination on his face. The fight went on for a long time, an hour or so, and for a long time nothing seemed to happen, no one seemed to be winning, and then one of the old guys said 'Christ' and everyone was piling up behind the kid, straining to see down into the water. We got a glimpse of white belly as something turned fast a few feet from the surface. The kid saw it too and suddenly he looked scared, as though he knew for sure now that he had the fish of a lifetime on the hook. His legs were shaking, his hands trembling as they changed position on the rod.

Then, suddenly, with a rush of foam, it broke the surface, leaping clear of the black water. A great gasp went up. A big salmon, plump and perfect in the Scottish sunlight, the proud hook of its lower jaw.

More people gathered – other kids fishing nearby, people walking past, a crowd maybe thirty strong watching now as the battle went on. There were many moments where it seemed certain the line was simply going to break and it would all be over. But it didn't. The kid was good. Patient. The fish was tiring. Finally one of the old guys clambered down into the water with a green net. There was a terrible moment as he tried to get the net under the fish, one hand on the twanging line – taut as piano wire – where we were sure the line was going to snap. Another man scrambled down there and it took two of them to swing the fish up onto the concrete wall. Everyone jostled to look.

The salmon lay quite still. The enormous swell of its milk white belly, the iridescent perfection of its colour – blue and silver and flecks of rose and pink, the great head the size of a man's fist and almost black. The kid leant down over his prize, exhausted and triumphant. The salmon was almost as big as he was, over three feet long. Maybe thirty pounds. Worth fifteen or twenty quid easy at the fishmongers: an unthinkable sum for a teenage boy in a recession-hit, early '80s Scottish town. (I remember vicariously picturing the looks on my parent's faces if I had staggered in the door holding such a prize.) And there, in its jaw, was the boy's red and gold spinner.

In the outside of its jaw.

Everyone saw it. The kid looked up hopefully at one of the old guys who had helped him land the fish. 'Snagged it,' the old boy said sadly. The fish had not taken the bait. It had been hooked illegally. It had to go back. The kid looked at the salmon. He looked at the old guy. The old guy put his hand on the kid's shoulder as he leaned in with the pliers.

It took two of them to lift it back into the river. It didn't swim off right away. It turned slowly in a figure of eight in the shallow pool for a moment – as though showing the kid all that he had lost, all he would never have. Then, with a nonchalant flick of its great tail, it vanished into the depths. The kid – physically exhausted, emotionally destroyed – burst into tears. The old guy folded him into his arms and held him while he sobbed. 'C'mon son,' he said. 'There'll be other fish.'

We all stared at the river in silence. Finally someone said 'Whit a boot in the fucken baws,' and you were powerfully reminded that you were in Ayrshire, where bad is expected, where defeat is met with cheerful understatement, and where tragedy is routinely rebuffed with humour.

A fine part of the world.

John Niven is an author and journalist. He recently published his second novel, The Amateurs.

THE KENNET
& AVON CANAL

BY
JOHN MOORE

My favoured part of the river is the stretch between Tile Mill and Sheffield Lock which meanders with quiet purpose through meadows flanked by woodland of ash and oak, then closes to a narrow path lined with blackberry bushes, aspens, rosehip, and fluorescent red–for-danger berries whose name always escapes me, but which I know to be highly poisonous.

The first part of the walk can at times be anything but relaxing, and there have been occasions when I've been tempted to go elsewhere for spiritual sustenance. Reaching the plateau of tranquillity can involve the negotiation of a large herd of bullocks – enormous, supposedly docile beasts, each weighing as much as a large motor cycle, and possessing horns that could have your intestines out in a trice. When they are going about their business on the far side of the field, everything is fine, and I breeze by with my thoughts lightening and my troubles evaporating with each muddy step. However, I often seem to time my ruminative walks for the precise moment when the beasts become thirsty and playful, and swarm en masse down to the river's edge for a drink and a wallow. Whether some sort of hitherto unrecognized bovine ESP is in play and they sense the approach of philosophical turmoil in the shape of a man dressed inappropriately for country rambles, and decide – out of devilment or plain boredom, to get in his way, give him a scare, and try to get shit all over his city shoes I can not prove, but I wouldn't put it past them. I've heard stories of bullocks turning nasty and putting their bulk to fatal use – I suppose if I'd had my bollocks whipped off by a member of their species I might harbour a grudge as well. When faced with this picket line, bravery disguised as nonchalance is the only way, and I push through them like Marlon Brando in *On The Waterfront*, imagining my pitiful obituary should they decide to push back, and keenly aware of the fact that but for the ability to produce several buckets of semen at a sitting, they are, for all intents and purposes – Bulls. They know it and I know it, and they know that I know it, and all the way along, they give me the intimidation stare that says – some day you won't be so lucky, punk.

Once the threat of *Animal Farm* recedes, the beauty and majesty of nature truly sets in. On the horizon a train heads west, an aircraft flies overhead, and the hiss of the A4 is occasionally discernible, but rather than breaking the spell, it increases it. Here, in this magical reserve, the world spins slowly. Swans glide by with their signets – there's no question of bread being offered or requested – nothing so crass – we're all ghosts here.

A narrow boat ties up for the day, its occupants, weary from Reading's escape, contentedly sipping red wine and preparing supper, ready for tomorrow's push towards sinister Aldermaston. Wood smoke, plain sailing; nice types, whose children have flown the nest, satisfied that they have now fully mastered the locks.

Here, the cyclists are polite, exchanging friendly grunts with the dog walkers who step aside to let them pass; and never a Rottweiler in site. As the near-distant planes trains and automobiles burn carbon swathes through the rat race world, this quiet stretch of waterway is infused with the civility and courtesy of a bygone age – unless it's something they're working on at Aldermaston that has leaked into the river.

Of course, these walks aren't all solitary rambles to recalibrate a tormented psyche.

Quite often, I have a daughter and mother in tow. Three generations of Moores taking the air, the youngest gathering sticks, leaves and interesting stones which I must carry in my pockets, the oldest, a font of knowledge, identifying all flora and fauna (with the exception of the poisonous red berries – which she'll Google as soon as we get home – but always forgets to) and making incisive observations about the wildlife, such as "I suppose even sheep must have a routine".

We make for our spot, a bench on the opposite bank, across the Troll's bridge – a manual wooden swing bridge, that does make a fine 'trip trap' sound as the three billy-goats Moore gamble across it, and we sit there and ponder the universe, the passing of time and the ripples in the water, or perhaps how long we should give the bullocks before heading for home. Pictures are usually taken – images that show another month of our family history, which will one day be seen by great great grandchildren, and viewed with the same detached familiarity as the sepia portraits of my own dearly departed forebears. We smile and are happy, knowing that long after our physical presence has been reduced to nothing more than pixels on a screen, our spirits will still be here – walking by this beautiful river – even if it's become a housing estate by then.

John Moore was a member of the Jesus and Mary Chain. He is a member of the popular music group Black Box Recorder, and Sports Editor of The Idler *magazine.*

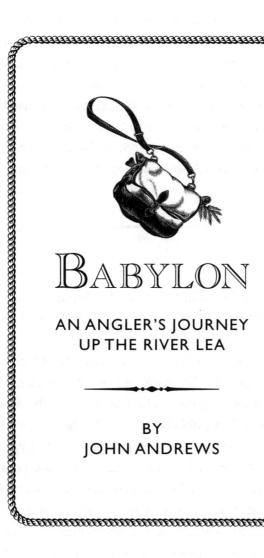

BABYLON

AN ANGLER'S JOURNEY
UP THE RIVER LEA

———————•◆•———————

BY
JOHN ANDREWS

*"It is an extraordinary sight to see the interior of
Liverpool Street Station on a Sunday morning when the
early trains are starting. Fishermen, fishermen, everywhere, and
what a variety! Here the little pale-faced weaver from
the looms of Bethnal Green, then come the chair workers,
shoemakers, stonemasons, literally hundreds of them.
All of them with 'labour' stamped on hands and clothes
as plainly as a calling could possibly be stamped."*

J.P Wheeldon, *Angling Resorts near London,* 1878

Then J.P. Wheeldon wrote those words, he was describing a solemn exodus of anglers which occurred weekly in Victorian times to a river situated to the north, north east of London which inspired arguably the most well-known but least popular, amongst anglers, of all angling books. *The Compleat Angler* written by Izaak Walton was first published in 1653. The Lea, known also over the years as the Lee, the Lyzan, the Luy, the Lyge and the Leye is London's forgotten river. It may play the poor cousin to the pearly king, the sickly vein to the lusty heart, but in a number of Londoner's minds, both old and young, it is more significant than the River Thames into which it flows at Bow Creek. Today those Londoners who fish the Lea are relatively small in number but in the early Victorian era, the River Lea was Babylon, a Mecca to a giant population that had seen off the plague, drunk themselves through the Hogarth years and were now building the world's greatest capital city with their bare hands. To the pale-faced weaver who shunned the church door, true redemption came in the form a cheap railway ticket that would take him out of the blackened grimy maze of London streets to any number of what Wheeldon described as resorts. The coalman would fire the engine until a head of steam would lead the packed carriages out along the iron over Lea Bridge past Tottenham Mills to Bleak Hall and Cooks Ferry. Onto Chinkford over Shurey's Water to Sewardstone and Enfield Wash. The country opening out at Waltham Abbey and Cheshunt into Nazeing Marsh where the world threatened to end due to stillness, on, on to Wormley and Broxbourn Bridge to Pages Water, Hoddesdon and Rye House. The train delivering men by their hundreds and thousands, discharging them at places along the way, as if they were disciples falling prostrate in prayer in front of the stations of the cross.

They stood out as surely as if they were carrying crosses to some holy place -blackened men with gin gums and swollen paws for hands. By the time Patrick Chalmers came to describe them in his book *At the Tail of the Weir* in 1932, long after the Lea had been poisoned along half its length by sewerage systems, their look had been honed to a strict uniform and they had become London angling's old soldiers: "He wears a black, blanket-lined 'oily' and a scarf of red tartan, his pole and folding net are packed compactly in a waterproof cover. These he carries over his shoulders, at, what a rifleman calls 'the slope'. But his gait is not soldierly, for, slung upon his packed pole, he bears over his shoulder the box without which there would be no roaching. The box is of wood and it is painted black. It has a strap of leather athwart it, side to side, for handle and support. It stands two foot and some inches high and its beam is one foot. It contains tackle of all kinds but its real use and excuse is to be the throne of the bank angler."

But exactly what was this place to which the chair weaver and his brothers went? A small arm of the River Thames which rose at Leagrave in Bedfordshire and whose path, a journey of fifty miles through Hertfordshire and Essex became epochryphal. The memory and meaning of its name alone burnt itself into the consciousness of every London angler. Long before gentlemen in West End private members' clubs invented dry fly fishing, or army officers chased mahseer in India's mountainous river, long before there was even a distinction between coarse or game fishing, the River Lea was legendary. Walton immortalized it in 1653, three centuries before Chalmers described his Lea angler. But the river that Walton described was already growing old, it was stately and grand, revered and worshipped. Above Tottenham Mills, it flowed up to a mile wide for much of its length. Perhaps if Eden did exist, it was not south of Tasmania, as advertised in the newspapers of the time, but north of Tottenham. An ocean contained in the last drop of gin in the bottle. Salter wrote of it in 1815, "For many years, this was a favourite and well-frequented place by the lovers of angling of the old school". What was the old school in 1815? Such as it was Salter claimed that it had become 'much neglected'. It was made up of men who had grown up sniggling eels using thumb reels, 'hickery' rods and bell wire, men whose boxes were filled with bank runners, cork and men o' war trimmers, cork floats, plug floats, winches of brass, their feet punched with holes in order to bind them to the rod butt, coffin leads, drag hooks and clearing rings. Experts in loop draw-knots, wise old heads who knew that live gudgeons could be purchased from Mr Isaac Jacobs at No 30 Duke Street in Houndsditch and that they could be fished on a gorge and snap tackle under a red painted float. Gudgeon baited up for fish like the one described in a London newspaper in 1765, "a fish which weighed upwards of twenty – eight pounds and was sold to a gentleman in the neighbourhood for a guinea. On the cook's opening it, she found a watch, with a black ribband and two seals, in the stomach of the fish, which proved to have been the property of a livery servant that was drowned near the place about six weeks before. The watch was kept for the inspection of the curious."

North of the River Lea's oily tail stretches at Stratford, Bromley and West Ham where flounders mixed up the catch, the tide made the banks dirty and slippery and the river split up into salty creeks where Magwitch look-alikes hid, the Lea became a river as much of remote public houses as it was of slow freshwater glides and wide luxuriating bends, deep holes and willow-laden undercuts. Public houses which served the every need of the anglers who fished the river. One of the most infamous of these establishments was the White House which stood on the banks of the river at Hackney Marsh. In the years immediately before one of its many forms was 'consumed by fire' in 1813, a man calling himself Robert Johnson was selling tickets to fish in its waters. An engraving of one such from 1810 shows anglers on both banks and on the bridge which crossed the marsh and led to the house. But the White House had been there long before the 19th century. There it is on John Rocque's Map of the Parish of Hackney, surveyed and drawn in 1745, a tiny black dot on the north bank of the "River Lee". According to the 'Victorian History of Middlesex', if you wanted to reach the White House you could travel by ferry from Tyler's directly upstream "to the isolated White House". There, in crystal clear waters, you could fish for barbel "as fat as pigs". Fish which were mounted by taxidermists working before the trade of beast stuffing had allegedly even been established in this country. It was Wheeldon who spoke of it as late as 1868: "There used to be in the large room at the White House the trysting place for the subscriptions to this water, a really grand collection of preserved fish, all of them taken from the water attached to the house." *The Anglers's Guide to the Horse & Groom Fishery, Lea Bridge and White House Fisheries*, published in 1841 by H Brown at Cripplegate in London, talked of the barbel in particular: "There are two at the house (White House) stuffed (among many others including chub, perch,

roach) one of which weighing eleven and the other fourteen pounds". Giant fish which were caught on tiny baits, maggots or gentles as they were then known, often reared over a summer by the anglers themselves. Salter took them when they were green from Mr Rastall's at No 8 Sleep's Alley in St John Street, Clerkenwell, and would feed them daily on a small piece of fresh flesh or liver until they grew to the right size. Marsh worms were as popular as gentles, as Salter describing the nightly movements of the workers who kept the anglers supplied proved, "The poor people who supply the London tackle shops with worms, get a great number of marsh worms on Kennington – common in the night, using a candle and lanthorn to see the worms." Shrimps were used, too, along with blood worms, tag-tail worms and the spawn of salmon which was fished either boiled or raw. At that time and in that era, the salmon was not a revered fish. It was viewed as an invader, a marauder from the sea, a crude and rather stupid fish, dumber than a chub. Salter loathed it, "There are several salmon in this part of the river (Hackney Marsh) which frequently disturb the quiet angler when fishing for roach." And fishing for roach was what more anglers did on the Lea than any other kind of fishing. If the Lea was Babylon, then the roach was holiest of the fish that swam in its waters. A relatively small, coarse fish but one of such mesmerizing beauty with its silver scales, blood-red fins and dark brown eyes that the labourers of London gave everything to fish for them. Wheeldon recognized it: "A curious point about the regular habitue of the Lea is, that nine out of ten one sees are roach men and never think of going for anything else." It was roach men that both he and Chalmers described and of whom Edward Ensom later wrote: "the roach pole may be fairly termed the Londoner's style as so many London anglers are experts in its use".

———•◆•———

Before the railway took the angler to places such as the White House, many would travel by foot as in the journey of Walton's piscator and some would go by 'Stages' drawn by horse and travelling frequently throughout the night and day from the Angel at Islington and Clapton. A few unfortunate occupants would not even reach the river, persuaded instead to take a drink when the horses themselves stopped for water. At the Halfway House in Stoke Newington, one of the last stops on the road north to the Lea, anglers were often drugged by bar-room con men and taken by force to Shacklewell Lane, where their throats were cut and their pockets emptied. Assuming their friends had left the premises to take pleasures elsewhere, the remaining anglers would travel and deposit their friends' tackle in lockers built specifically for rods and reels where it would stay, a memorial to days spent innocently amongst the marshes. The risks for anglers on the streets of London were great, the 'roughs' knowing that already their minds were elsewhere and their eyes intent on a float rather than on the road before them. The swims that these fateful anglers were dreaming of were often named after their characteristics ('High Banks', 'Pigs Stye', 'Bee-Tree', 'Chingford Ditch') but sometimes there were lasting memorials to anglers who never made it out of the city for one last cast on 'The Gordon', into 'Brocksopp's Hole' or at 'Watt's Swim'. Even on the marsh the danger had not passed completely. It may have been a place of "pleasant and enlivening scenery, the tranquility and quietness of which is disturbed only by the soft song of the birds" (Brown 1841), but, writing in *The Rod and Rail* in 1867, Greville Fennell warned anglers not to fish without companions or dogs, or even both on certain stretches where 'marsh men' waited to "'remove' anglers by robbing them and pitching their bodies into 'the Porridge Pot'".

To fish the stations of the Lea was not just risky, it was expensive. The river swallowed wages quicker than the ale house or the bookmaker's bag. A season ticket on the Horse and Groom cost ten shillings and sixpence per annum or one shilling per day in 1815, enough at that time for some men to be taken off to fight Napoleon and never to return. The proprietors of the waters guarded their fish and their livelihoods with a lot more prudence than they did the welfare of the unfortunate

"Anglers were often drugged by bar-room con men and taken by force to Shacklewell Lane where their throats were cut and their pockets emptied."

anglers who fished at their own risk. Before recognized water bailiffs even existed, freaks of nature would be hired to patrol the banks and threaten gangs of fish rustlers. On the Old Ferry Boat Inn (which still stands today and serves pies to the carp anglers on Walthamstow Reservoirs) stretch at Tottenham, the river was 'infested by gangs of the most determined netters'. Their nemesis came in the form of the keeper, one Jimmy Lifty who was described by the newspapers in mid-Victorian times as 'a bit of a character'. It was said that he regularly sparred with Da Costa 'Prince of the Lee Fishers' who "with a troop of dependants will be found tearing 'em out by the scruff of their necks". A reference not to the netting gangs, who would have fled upriver, but to Da Costa's favoured quarry, the common bream; a tasteless fish with flesh like glue, whom he murdered by the hundredweight using a 12 foot rod, a drilled bullet and a bait of bright red worms and brandlings.

———•·◆·•———

When Liverpool Street Station could take no more passengers on a Sunday morning, a number of paddle steamers were built and commissioned to carry anglers and sightseers up the Lea from Old Ferry Boat Inn. These gaudy ships were in truth early gin palaces and amid the noise of the barrel organ and the constant cacophony of drunken passengers, stoic anglers would step off the plank and take the bankside walk north to Bannisters Water or Bowerbanks trying hard not to fall down holes which had been created by too much eel sniggling. At Cook's Ferry, later the site of Bleak Hall described as "a house for the accommodation of anglers", eight miles out from London at Edmonton, the waters were "well stored with fine large carp, barbel, chub, jack, pike, roach, gudgeon, perch and eels". The water was controlled by the landlord James Cook whose father Matthew was consistently rude and kept two dozen cats which he used to pester anglers for their catch. Those fish which escaped the paw or the pot were preserved in glass cases which lined the walls for decades. Further upstream between Bleak Hall and Waltham Abbey stood the Swan and Pike Public House taken over by a landlord in the early 19th century who despised anglers and refused to issue tickets or let anyone fish in its waters. North at the Carthagena Water, there was good roach fishing to be found beneath the willows on the Cat and Fiddle swim where the most popular groundbait was clay balls dug and shaped by hand and filled with carrion fed gentles, and fat chub to be snared using the bait that Walton recommended: "a black snail, with his belly slit, to show his white", and during a shower of rain the final words from the Piscator's song to ponder,

> *"Or we sometimes pass an hour*
> *Under a green willow,*
> *That defends us from a shower,*
> *Making earth our pillow;*
> *Where we pray*
> *Think and pray*
> *Before death*
> *Stops our breath*
> *Other joys*
> *Are but toys,*
> *And to be lamented."*

A man called Nipper kept the waters at the Crown Public House in Broxbourne, whilst at the George Inn in Hoddesdon a number of large wooden tanks had been built in which were stored the prize water pigs – giant carp and barbel and pike, kept fresh for their final run to the Friday markets in London. At St Margeret's where the path from London was now 22 miles long, gentles were discouraged and the favoured bait was the black beetle fished always under a large reed or quill for here the river was deep, slow and quiet. Perfect water for the roach-men who fished their quills under rods that did not have brass winches and were not made from greenheart as others were. Roach men used long poles made up of sections of Carolina white cane averaging 18 to 22 feet in length and constructed by makers such as Bazin, Ebeneezer Creed and Sowerbutts in the city of London.

Poles became synonymous with roach men who in turn became synonymous with the Lea spawning the words that Ensom wrote a century later in 1953 about the roach pole being fairly termed the Londoner's style. The style of fishing evolved from fishing a fixed tethered line much as Piscator would have done in the seventeenth century whilst singing his lament under the willow at Carthagena. Roach men were purists, prizefighters – many of them were the men who filled Liverpool Street Station with their poles and their boxes and they clung to the idea of the Lea as Babylon longer than anyone. They clung to it long after the last of the lockers had been shut at the Horse and Groom, long after the doors of the London Orphan Asylum which overlooked the Lea at Lea Bridge were closed and the last of its children looked wistfully to the distance and watched the lonely angler make his solemn way up the bank to his few hours of freedom. The roach men clung to it beyond the days when builders knocking up cheap streets in Leytonstone in 1875 put the last brick into the sewer pipe which took the

new suburb's waste directly into the river and killed every fish below it within days. A slaughter which in turn closed the doors to the White House as a subscription fishery and made it a gambling den in 1911 when the last photograph of it was ever taken. The only one where outside there is not standing an angler and two or three attendants and a loveable mongrel of a dog. A photograph which Alfred Wire, working for a Leyton paper, exchanged for a pint of Benskins stout – brought down by barge from Hertford to fill the pub's cellar. A pint which became one of too many as the White House grew into one of the most notorious and riotous late-night gambling dens in the capital until the LCC refused it a licence and the pub was demolished on the eve of the Great War in 1913. Even then, roach men walked up the river or stared out of the window as the train took them north whilst sitting opposite in carriages, twitchy clerks read penny dreadfuls and coughed with the first ailment of the winter at their throats.

After the Great War ended in 1918, the Lea's status as the forgotten river was sealed. With the passing of every decade fewer and fewer anglers lined its banks. The London Anglers Association and its many clubs held sway over its most celebrated stretches but, after two wars and a depression in-between, some of the clubs were down to a handful of members. The birth of the electric train swelled numbers again in the 1960s when in comfort a sixth generation of roach men could reach every fishery from Liverpool Street to Hertford but the social changes that London itself was undergoing meant that many of these anglers boarded trains on a one-way ticket and once there was little of London to take out to the Lea, it lost even more of its identity. At some point in the 1990s, the River Lea became a vision of the future rather than the past. Once a waterway fed by the crystal clear chalk streams of the Mimram, Beane, Rib and Ash in Hertfordshire and written about for centuries, it had become abstracted, polluted, neglected, ignored: the broken needle in London's arm until in time it was forgotten. If you walk it today, you will still find anglers fishing on, and many of them still catch giant chub, barbel and carp, but equally there are many stretches of bank which never see an angler from one week to the next and many parts of the river bed which are barren.

There is talk of regeneration, the promise of the Olympic clean-up which may turn out to be nothing more than a cosmetic act and one which is already ridding the river and its plain of any last vestiges of a 20th century life past on the stretches close to the Olympic park. Portakabin caffs, allotments, scrap-metal merchants, caravan sites, container yards, tyre and brake centres, amateur football pitches, pylon parks, abandoned railway lines, derelict factory units, thunderstruck oaks, graffiti-tagged bridges, stolen car and shopping trolley graves, a thousand single shoes and half-a-dozen Georgian pocket watches once swallowed by pike and lying under a foot of black silt, all will be cleared, erased, or purchased compulsorily and built upon.

———•◦•———

But all hope is not gone. Under the bridge at Coppermill Stream, up river from the garden where Mr Day used to keep carp in a moat and feed them on apples from the next door orchard, something moves. It is a golden flank, a descendant of a White House barbel, whose spirit escaped through a broken pane in the side of the case and can be traced in the fish which lies up in less than three feet of water. You can barely see it as you hurry along the tow path conscious only of the imminent bell for last orders in the Old Ferry Boat Inn, a passing bus rattling the bridge overhead as drops of water fall from the ironwork with a lonely echo, but it can see you, a shadowy figure, a blur, and it slips under a tiny mat of weed as the vibrations of your footsteps pass through it and you move under the bridge and walk away across the meadow. Sirens carry on the wind and night falls as it has done on a million Lea nights and the fish noses its way upstream creating a small bow wave that can just be made out in the sodium-lit gloom. Onwards this barbel goes, through a thousand swims: over Forty Guinea Water, through Black Pool and October Hole past Black Beetle and Half Moon to Cordless Point and the Punch Bowl. Tracing the steps of Walton and his Piscator, of the legions of chair workers, shoemakers, stonemasons and weavers who followed in their wake, of John Rocque the mapmaker and Salter the guide, and Cripplegate Brown, of Wheeldon, roach men and roughs. Passing the ancient places that were guarded by Lifty, Da Costa and Nipper, black ink spots on a hand-coloured linen bound map of Babylon, folded up and locked away in a drawer in a crumbling Georgian house somewhere unknown, deep in the heart of the city.

John Andrews is a contributor to the magazine Waterlog *and dealer in vintage fishing tackle, www.andrewsofarcadia.com.*

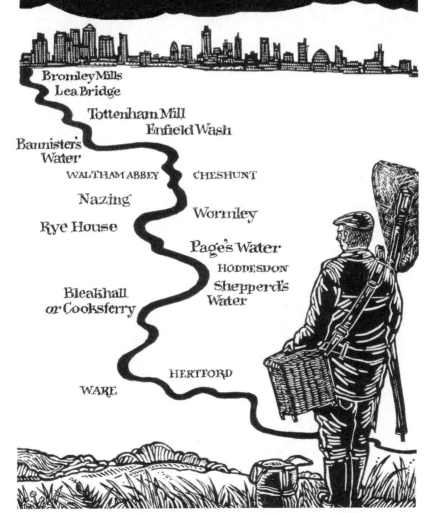

The Lea, a clear stream in its shallows, pools and flowery banks; the shady trees, the odourous honeysuckle, the green pastures, the disporting of the lambs, the hum of the bee, the clouds and the sky, and the song of the linnet and the lark, the blackbird and the thrush.   *The River Lea or Lee.*

Bromley Mills
Lea Bridge

Tottenham Mill
Enfield Wash

Bannister's
Water

WALTHAM ABBEY   CHESHUNT

Nazing   Wormley

Rye House
                      Page's Water
                      HODDESDON
Bleakhall   Shepperd's
or Cooksferry   Water

                      HERTFORD
WARE

Valley Of The Dead Cars

THE LOWER LEA

BY
BOB STANLEY

I went to school in Croydon but even there, in a home counties joke of a town, the field trip to Ironbridge gorge was a given. You study history? Economics? Geography? Well, it's the birthplace of the modern world, don'tcha know. No matter that even back in the early eighties there were folks laid off from British Leyland dressed as authentic milliners, furnace stokers, and candlestick makers, with all the joie de vivre that goes hand in hand with a low paid Black Country job. Toytown or no, this is where it all sprung from. Plus the bridge was very pretty.

That's not a word you would use to describe the lower Lea Valley. So it came as something of a shock to find out that an area of unspeakable pollution, poverty and decay – Bow, Bromley and Homerton on its west bank, Canning Town, Stratford and Leyton on its east – is at least as historically important.

I don't know anyone who has ever been on a field trip to the lower Lea Valley. It's the kind of place you would never visit, and only intrepid cyclists seem to know it exists. So what's the lower Lea Valley ever done for us? Petrol was invented there. Plastic was invented a hundred yards up the road. The Labour Party was born there. How's that, Ironbridge?

All I knew about the River Lea until a few years ago was that it was the only tributary of the Thames that was still clearly visible in London – RIP the Fleet, the Tyburn, the Westbourne, all buried under Victorian London, just occasionally rising up in anger after heavy rainfall to flood an area of Kentish Town or Farringdon. But the Lea meanders down from Hertfordshire to create a physical barrier in our mental maps of London – East of the Lea is most definitely East London. A friend of mine who went for a bike ride down the Lea and thought – with my love of derelict Victoriana and all things mossy – I would love the area south of Hackney Marshes. Besides, they were planning to build the Olympic village on it if (as if!) London won the Olympic bid.

He was right, I was hooked. Right now, much of the area is rapidly disappearing. It is too late to catch a couple of the area's landmarks: Hackney dog track, which had been fully restored in the nineties only to go bust in a matter of months; and the fridge mountain, a heap of thousands of CFC gas filled death traps off Carpenders Road. It had been Europe's largest – another continent conquering, ignominious record is that the area currently has Europe's highest incidence of TB.

Further north, bird life is abundant on the Lea: Canada and Greylag geese, swans, coots, moorhens, mallards, herons, great-crested grebes, little grebes, kingfishers even. At dusk, pipistrelles and noctules feed over the river near Stamford Hill. The water quality of the Lea deteriorates suddenly below Tottenham Lock, where discharges from sewage works, run-off from roads, oil and gunk from factories and boats cause eco-chaos. The result is, waterfowl aside, nature is put firmly in its place by a man-made mess. Below Hackney Marshes, a delta of channels and canals, the water is worst of all.

The best way to get an idea of how the Lower Lea looks is driving east on the A118, between Bow and Stratford. Get past the Bow interchange and to your left and right, as far as you can see, are armies of electricity pylons, towering over grubby waterways and barely breathing industrial estates. It's a hellhole.

The first pitstop on my Lower Lea field trip was the now defunct Cosy Cafe on Waterden Road, just a little way down from where the dog track used to be. Everybody in there wore an orange jacket except for the two women who ran it. There was a sun-faded picture of the young Blur on the wall. Outside were plastic tables and chairs and strange giant-size wooden flowers. The caff itself was made out of an old metal container and the food was unbelievably cheap. On the counter, unapologetically, were pirated dvds in clear plastic slip cases, the titles written on the discs in marker pen.

Be brave. Explore. Take out your *A to Z* and find White Post Lane. Still intact, the stretch that crosses the Lee Navigation and slides down to the Lea Tavern (with its David Lynch-like sign reading 'hotel') looks like something out of *Saturday Night And Sunday Morning*: Victorian mills and warehouses, mostly now artists' studios and small workshops, soon to be waterside luxury pads with tacked-on black metal balconies you can't actually walk on.

Turning right into Hepscott Road there's what remains of one of these buildings. Now only the ground floor exterior wall exists and inside are a bunch of demolition lorries and equipment. This was the place where petroleum was first refined – the inventors tried to copyright the name 'petrol' but were turned down. Turn a corner into Wallis Road and there's a desperately unremarkable brick shed with an apologetic plaque on the wall announcing it was the birthplace of plastic – or 'Parkesine' as its inventor Alexander Parkes called it in 1855. Right here in Hackney Wick, they invented the future. It should have flooded the place with money, mansions for the owners and model dwellings for the workers, but both ideas were adapted and improved by the Americans leaving nothing in the lower Lea Valley except a bunch of low-level factories. Chemical processing, paint manufacturing, God knows what with animal products (one factory was called Retriever Meats, which sounds awful whichever way you read it). It smells bad enough now; imagine it in the nineteenth century.

———•◦•———

Go back to your *A to Z* and have a snigger: Autumn Street, Pudding Mill Lane, Sugarhouse Lane, it all sounds so romantic! Sugarhouse Lane is definitely worth a peek, a long meandering dead end lined with empty factories, post-war Park Royal stuff that you rarely see anymore. They all back on to the Three Mills Wall River (another quirk of the Lea is that if you try and follow it upriver from Leamouth you'll end up in one of its strange tributaries with names like City Mill River, Channelsea River, Waterworks River... some of them stop dead in a murk of green slime, shopping trolleys and car skeletons. So confusing that, depending who you're talking to, and which stretch you're on, the name is spelt Lee or Lea). Right at the top is a now empty dye factory – yes, synthetic dyes were invented here too – which is on the site of the Bow porcelain factory where bone china was first dreamt up in 1749.

Back up the Lee River Navigation at Old Ford locks, next to where the Big Breakfast used to be filmed, there are the only remaining multi-storey stables in the country (well, think how many horses used to work in the area). They're on Dace

Road, just opposite the Percy Dalton peanut warehouse. Go up to the top of the road and there's the beginning of what looks like a disused railway line up an embankment. It isn't – it's the Northern Outfall Sewer, a gigantic sewage pipe that you can walk on, past a zillion abandoned tellys and bits of twentieth century junk, all the way to Beckton, 14 miles east of London Bridge. The sewer was fed by the highly ornate Abbey Mills pumping station east of the Lea, a cathedral of sewage that makes St Pancras station look minimalist. As I write, Philip Glenister is in there with a film crew shooting *Demons*, a "contemporary spin" on the legacy of Bram Stoker's *Dracula*. Yes, it's that gloriously creepy.

Down near Leamouth, near the beautiful but abandoned Bromley-by-Bow gas works, is the Gas Museum. Like almost everything else, it has closed down, but I love the idea that a Gas Museum existed, full of invisible exhibits. And opposite is the disused Bromley dock, the final resting place of the Euston arch.

As it meanders, widely and severely, into the Thames, the Lea becomes covered by a network of dual carriageways. The name of the river changes to Bow Creek. It is impossible to walk this stretch but a side road called Orchard Place leads you past low-level warehouses, mostly dead, to the urban hamlet of Leamouth, where the Lea meets the Thames. It's as odd a place as Dungeness, and the oddest community in all London. On the east side is a salvage company, piles of rusting metal just a few hundred yards from the late twentieth century towers of the financial centre. On the west is Leamouth. It consists of the Trinity Wharf lighthouse (the only one in London, now an art gallery), Container City (futuristic homes made from converted metal containers), and Fatboy's Diner, a genuine thirties US train carriage transported to East London. And that's it. Get yourself a stack of pancakes, then descend the steps of the 1822 river wall. The Lea lapping at your feet seems a friendlier fellow than it does anywhere else, relieved to have clocked off, mixing it with old father Thames. Opposite is the Millennium Dome. It is a very hushed place. You may want to take a book.

What the Olympic village doesn't erase will be lost in time to property development. The recession has come just in time to preserve chunks of this greasy backwater a little longer. Iain Sinclair will be chuffed, but frankly something had to change. The only housing estate in the lower Lea Valley was the dreadful seventies clammy-red brick Clays Lane estate, completely isolated from the rest of humanity. The poor residents have now been rehoused somewhere within walking distance of a shop and not directly underneath a 110kV pylon. The pylons will – budget allowing – all be buried underground, the Northern Outfall Sewer will become a majestic grassy thoroughfare, the Eastway cycle track will be replaced by a new Velodrome, the waterways will all be cleaned up. But lovers of urban decay and fabulous dereliction are urged to go there before we get too close to 2012. It's your last chance to take a field trip the birthplace of the twentieth century in all its beautiful, chaotic squalor.

Bob Stanley is a founder member of Saint Etienne. His writing has appeared in NME, Melody Maker, Mojo, The Times *and* The Guardian.

A Rainbow
In Flight

---◆•◆•◆---

BY
JUDE ROGERS

L ast summer, the sun low in the clouds over the Reverend
James, we went down to the river for the very last time.
I could walk there in my sleep, I said to him, narrowing
my eyes, trying to ease a smile from his cold, weary mouth.

It's like this.

My front door, turn right. Past the boys that I used to
babysit, smoking fags in the bus shelter, and the house where
the dog, now long gone, had me screaming blue murder in my
little red coat. Then turn left. Past the path, now grown over,
where Grandpa would fill bowls with blackberries, and his
house, only Grandma now, peering at us through its pebble-
dashed eyelids. Down the hill where I'd toddle, past the pub
where I'd land, over the road, nearly there.

The path behind the houses, the mud and the leaves, and
then, there she is: the long, wide, sandy ribbon stretching
north to the mountains, its mouth opening here to the curve of
the Gower.

In Welsh, I told him the first time, this is not the River Loughor. It is the River Llwchwr. You blow those double ells with your tongue behind those sweet little teeth. You say the double-yous like the hoots of an owl. You purr that last arr like Eartha Kitt after a night on the Buckleys. He would try to, then laugh, burying my head in his shoulder.

Then, we would walk. We would look across the estuary to the cockles of Crofty and the chimneys of Bynea, and then return to our shore. To the boating club where I would wait, as a young girl, for the arched arms of boys to fall over my head. To the bench where my first boyfriend kissed me as the wind hit the water. To the ruins of the castle where, over the years, I'd look out like a look-out, thinking of the Romans and the Normans who had treasured this land.

We had stood there together once, I remembered, braving the rain. Today, it is clear, but we can't see what is coming.

We let the light take us. It takes us upstream. I think about what would happen if we carried on. We'd see the river reaching the eleven arches at Bont, and the land that had once held the church of St Teilo's. If we made it further, we'd find the underground lake where the Llygad Y Llwchwr would blink us its welcome. The Eye of The Loughor, drawing us beautifully into the blue.

But this is old news to us, as we are to each other. The river sits flat and heavy, and our hands set in our pockets. Maybe this is just another rivermouth, I think, as I look out at the water. Maybe this is just another way that it ends.

And then the kingfisher comes.

He sees it first, a tiny flash of blue on the edge of the marshes. He gives me his hand, and slowly I come.

We stand there, still as statues.

The flash comes again.

It's lovely, he says, like a rainbow in flight. I watch it move, phosphorescently, and our fingers clasp tightly. One last shimmer he gives us, one last beautiful dance in the afternoon sun.

And then, as soon as he appeared, he flies away.

I remember us looking at the space, our hands slowly unfurling, the eye filling with water, the mouth full of tears.

The place where he once flew lies empty now, like a memory rubbed clean. I walk here in my sleep. Sometimes, you are with me, sometimes I am alone. I turn back to the river, this time, by myself. No kingfisher has come yet, but the river is always here, its eye, its mouth, and its heart still opening and living. They promise me everything.

Jude Rogers is founder editor of Smoke: A London Peculiar, *a quarterly magazine-shaped love-letter to London. She is also a music columnist and feature writer for* The Guardian, *a writer and reviewer for* The Observer *and* The Word, *and an arts critic for the* New Statesman.

MERSEY

LIVERPOOL

—————•———•———•—————

BY
MATTHEW DE ABAITUA

Terry showed me his packed lunch: corned beef and ketchup sandwiches swaddled in a foil blanket, a packet of salt 'n' vinegar crisps and a can of Coke.

"This is my one luxury," Terry said. He opened the can of Coke and fingered the cutting tongue loosed by the ring pull. At his right hand, he kept a packet of twenty Embassy filters – short, strong cigarettes designed for a working man to suck down between tasks, as opposed to the extra-long Superkings that were fit only for idlers, a baton of a fag to be savoured while watching telly.

"Six pounds an hour. Twelve hours a shift. Six shifts a week," Terry divvied up the numbers. "Taxman takes his lump. National Insurance. Then the missus and her kid take their lump. End of that, I only have enough money left to buy me packed lunch. I don't need the can of Coke. I could do without the Coke."

"It's not essential."

"Right. But it keeps me awake on the night shifts. And I like it."

The security guard uniform consisted of a nylon blue shirt tucked into black polyester trousers, an open brass-button blue jacket with Neptune Security insignia on the arm and a clip-on blue tie. Two peaked caps set aside on a melamine table. It was long after midnight and long before dawn: Two men adrift in a windless night.

Either Terry was unconvinced that I appreciated the tragedy of his situation, or he felt that that we had plenty of time to go over it again.

"Her kid needs stuff. There are bills to pay. All that is left over for me is this."

The can of Coke, which I watched him drain sip-by-sip. The cigarettes, which he did not share. The two-ring baby belling stove on which we cooked bacon and eggs at sunrise.

The portakabin was in Huskisson Dock, one of the North docks on the east side of the River Mersey. The history of the docks is rich, an epic tale of labour and its opposite that built and then dismantled the city of Liverpool. But I was only eighteen years old and knew nothing of such history. I was in sore need of an education. When Terry described the economic realities of his situation, it was delivered as a cautionary tale, a lesson he felt my books did not contain.

Every hour, I took the long-handled maglite torch out for a patrol of the decrepit warehouses. The beam picked out stacks of timber and empty pallets. My footsteps echoed in the rafters up where the pigeons roosted. The berths were empty enclosures of black water.

"When Terry described the economic realities of his situation, it was delivered as a cautionary tale, a lesson he felt my books did not contain"

Downriver, the container cranes of Seaforth Docks worked all night to unload and repack a freighter. Under floodlights, the four-legged straddle carriers zipped along the container bays, selecting the required crate, then hauling it up into their belly and zooming off to the quayside. The straddle carriers were three or four storeys tall and set about their duties at forty miles an hour. Before they were launched, a siren sounded to warn the security guards like myself who were out in the bays to abandon our work checking the seals on the containers and take cover. The drivers had very limited visibility high up in their cabins. From their perspective, a security guard was a mouse on a motorway.

I worked shifts all along the docks and sometimes away from them too.

Nights spent in the caged office of an all-night garage in Fazakerley, where the attendant called Spider played me Prince bootlegs. He kept a stick next to the till, a chair-leg reinforced with steel bearings and the legend Nukklebraker stencilled along its length. The junkies tried to cadge change when they came around for their nightly fix of Kit-Kats. In the morning, the forecourt was littered with abandoned chocolate wafers, the precious silver foil spirited away. That was what I thought about when Terry showed me his packed lunch: its generous wrapping of silver foil.

Some shifts would be spent riding around in a van checking on alarm calls. I was tall and strong and green, and so was sent in ahead. Feeling my way around the dark passages of a clubhouse, I eased a door open with the head of the torch and saw a silvery shadow opposite. The boss flicked the lights on and I came face to face with a terrifying full-length reflection of myself. Long periods of boredom were enlivened by brief outbreaks of terror, like one of Stalin's dinner parties.

These were diversions from the main task: guarding the industry of the river. Before I started work on the docks, the Mersey meant nothing to me. Its heyday was long gone. The family told stories of crowds coming in from the ships, of

lunchtime at the Cavern and then back to work again at the BAT office. Those crowds had moved on, the offices closed, John Lennon dead. The ferry still ran but I never bothered to take it.

I walked down to where large hewn boulders were stacked upon the riverbank. Rats moved in the angular shadows in between. The Mersey was a black twisting void. I had wandered so far that there was not another living soul for a mile. Alone and adrenalized by the fear of the unknown, my thoughts took on a baroque apocalyptic form. The bombed out churches and abandoned pubs and collapsed warehouses of the Dock Road were infested with imaginary figures from an industrial gothic: vampire welders, birdmen in diesel-smeared dungarees roosting on the sugar conveyor belt that ran over Regent Street.

An ark was moored at Pier Head and they were taking on the last evacuees, two by two.

The Mersey is an industrious river. Too wide and cold for pleasure boating, its toil is visible in the treacherous contrary current. At the Runcorn gap, its course is bounded by Runcorn Railway Bridge, a bracing engineering marvel of wrought iron lattice girders. The arch sweeps overhead like rollercoaster track. The engineering of man and nature compliment one another. Under dour daylight, the Mersey runs muddy and rusty. At dusk, it turns belly-up, showing a pallid steel hide. Neither nature nor industry is built to the scale of a man. To stand under a giant bridge that passes over a great river is to be doubly dwarfed.

———————

At night, the Mersey was as immense, cold and untouchable as the iron hulls of the ships I was employed to protect. Dawn was a blessing: a parabola of silhouetted gulls arcing from one sandbank to another against the ebb of new light. I returned to the portakabin to make my breakfast. Terry was outside blowing clouds of cold smoke and stamping his boots to get the blood flowing. Other guards stopped by on their way home. Some told bawdy stories about prostitutes who offered them the choice of a beer or a blowjob to let them on board ships. The guards warned me that the whores would catch a whiff of my fry-up and stop by for a piece. "She'll pick up that sausage, lick it, and then throw it back in the pan: then she'll say 'I've just been sucking off Turkish sailors for twelve hours – do you really want to eat that?'" For all these stories, I never saw any prostitutes. There were enormous piles of pornography lying around. Each post had its own well-worn collection of magazines. Some of the guards' tales sounded like they had come straight from the letters pages of porn rags, fantasies cooked up over long and tedious shifts and passed down from one guard to the next.

A week after I started, a docker was killed when the straddle carrier he was driving overturned. On the morning of his funeral, the place was deserted, but by the afternoon the men returned in a rueful generous mood that meant – for once – the divide between guard and docker was breached. Sometimes the dockers would make me breakfast then shove a copy of the *Morning Star* into my hands. When I told my father about this generosity, he laughed cynically. He had worked the Dock Road as a young bobby, patrolling the

> "The guards told bawdy stories about prostitutes who offered them the choice of a beer or a blowjob to let them on board ships"

foggy, dirty-bricked streets, arresting thieves and drunks. This was before the days of walkie-talkies, so if he collared a thief or a round-eyed sailor, he had to drag them a few miles to the nearest police box. He did not share my idealistic view of the dockers. As I told him about the enormous fry-up they made for me, he stood up and mimed the dockers creeping away behind me carrying great crates of this or that. Like Terry, my father knew the river could teach me something about human nature, its tragedies and its schemes and that was why he had pulled strings to get me the job, as I was underage for security work.

———◆•◆•◆———

The morning is box-fresh. The sky is minty. The tide is out and the sand forms hard, wet furrows, some in close creases, others sinuous and relaxed.

A hundred iron casts of the naked body of artist Anthony Gormley are evenly spaced along Crosby shore, some immersed in the tide, others standing inland. Each gazes eyelessly out into Liverpool Bay toward the entrance of the River Mersey. The salt air is eroding the iron men. Rust blooms spread from ear to chest in fleshy scabs. The arms of each figure are set passively at their sides and their feet are close together: a stoic pose, accepting the long torture committed by the elements and time. Gormley's iron alludes to the city's lost age of heavy industry.

A few kilometres beyond the coastline, the mysterious sentinels of wind turbines stand on Burbo Flats, where the fishermen used to clean the keels of their boats. White blades turn over blue water – the promise of new technology. The Mersey is cleaner now and salmon swim its waters. The river has a new job in the service industry as a backdrop to pent-houses. Time flows ceaselessly out to sea. Endings merge into new beginnings. Even iron men rot.

I don't know if Gormley's figures are gazing into the future or mired in the past. The city is equally ambivalent. So am I.

It is twenty years since I discovered work on the banks of the Mersey. Now I am unemployed again and walk the sands with my wife and three young children. Looking along the coastline I try to calculate how far we have come and how far there is still to go. I think of the Yoruban proverb: "our culture is a river that is never at rest."

Matthew De Abaitua is the author of The Red Men *(Snowbooks), which was nominated for the 2008 Arthur C Clarke Award. He is also one of the ne'er-do-wells behind* The Idler.

Mersey

MANCHESTER

———◆———

BY
JEMMA KENNEDY

I have always felt nostalgia for the north of England. Which is odd, as I grew up almost exclusively on the south coast. I was, to all intents and purposes, a northern novice when I found myself living in Manchester in my early thirties. I'd gone there for a change of scenery and a vague desire to put down roots somewhere far from my previous homes. I was also a novice to rivers, having been raised by the sea, and, during the long summer holidays, largely in it. The only rivers I was acquainted with were fictional, beginning on the overpopulated banks of Kenneth Grahame's Edwardian river society (based on the Pang in Berkshire), following a tributary to Mark Twain's quaint Mississippi and progressing on towards the darker adult territory of Conrad's treacherous Congo.

My relationship with the north was similarly imaginary, although I didn't know it yet. That peculiar second-hand longing of mine for all things northern had begun in childhood and been consolidated as a teenager by the now iconic records of 1980s Mancunia, paintings by Lowry, the novels and plays that captured the iron grip of industrialisation among the mills and the slums of Salford. I was sick of the robust, wealthy south; the insistent jolly glare of golden sands and sparkling water, the smugness of London, the propagandistic sale of pleasure as the south's inherent natural resource. I wanted a physical landscape that matched my interior one (soulful, grumpy and damp). In my head this involved soot, Guinness, melancholy, canals, electric guitars and the spectral blare of the factory horn. But the Manchester of the early 21st century had changed beyond recognition. I found a city held firmly in the suede-gloved hand of the regenerationists (developers, retailers, and so-called culture industries), and apparently having the time of its life.

This force of progress was also reputed to have reached Manchester's great waterway, the River Mersey, which had become a triumph of conservation over the last twenty years. Local friends of mine enthused about the nature reserve at Chorlton Ees, the freshwater wildlife – a rural riverbank paradise. I was dubious. Two hundred years of industrialisation would take its toll on any stretch of water – it took until 2002 for levels of oxygen in the river to reach life-sustaining levels for fish again. But this was all fine with me. I would have been happy if the current had bobbed with the corpses of mill workers and empty ale bottles. It was what I had come for, wasn't it?

"Our neighbours included junkies and falling-downstairs drunks and restless, school-dodging children whose hobbies included throwing water bombs"

It wasn't until my second year in Manchester that I became properly acquainted with the river, when I moved into a friend's tiny ex-council house in the southern outskirts of the city. This part of the Merseybank Estate had so far escaped gentrification; our neighbours included junkies and falling-downstairs drunks and restless, school-dodging children whose hobbies included throwing water bombs through our front windows when they were feeling friendly. Across the cul-de-sac was a path leading down a grassy slope littered with rubbish to a riverbank. There it was – the River Mersey, rushing past on its way to the Irish Sea.

It wasn't much to look at. The Mersey is a river of noble pedigree, created from the tributaries of the Rivers Etherow, Goyt and Tame, which traverse Lancashire, Derbyshire, Cheshire and West Yorkshire before they conjoin at Stockport. I've seen photographs of these three rivers closer to their source; land-scapes featuring peat moorland, mossy Roman bridges, a bleak Pennine beauty. In Stockport everything changes. The Mersey officially begins beneath a concrete shopping centre.

———•◆•———

So far so good, concerning my mythic northern blueprint. Half a mile down the river path was the entrance to the Chorlton Water Park; once a gravel pit, now a small lake fringed with local fisherman in army surplus who sat stolidly on camping stools holding their lines like a silent militia. There were trees, swans, pre-teen kids pestering you for cigarettes. Urban nature. The Mersey itself felt similarly manmade, fortified with steep flood banks, concrete bridges and the roar of traffic from the nearby M60. No water rats eating Gentleman's Relish sandwiches and quoting Keats. Just solitary dog walkers, cyclists and the occa-sional scrambler bike ploughing up the path. I joined the traffic and began walking.

Every other day for the best part of six months I took the same route along the river to the Northenden Bridge and back again. Past the football pitch, under the spray-painted footbridge then on for a half-mile around the bend that hugged

the golf course until I reached my turning point. The brown
water slopped and swirled and occasionally raced with a raging
current, on top of which ducks whirled around like waltzers
at a fairground. Slowly I discovered the river's secrets and
eccentricities. The adjoining field of silent, anorak-backed men
who flew radio-controlled aeroplanes in all weathers. The giant
lime tree that hummed with invisible bees in the summer. The
angry geese who colonised the river path and whose hissing
sometimes made me run for safety. The infamous Jackson's
Boat pub, a short stagger across the Jackson's Boat Footbridge
just before the sluice gates, which was reputedly a hangout
for Jacobean sympathisers back in the days of Bonnie Prince
Charlie. It retained something of its suspicious nature; I had to
steel myself to enter it alone. This was not destined to become

a gastro pub. The Mersey had outwitted the regenerationists and kept to its own natural laws of dawn and dusk, flood levels and seasonal change, laws upheld by its own riverbank society of anglers, cyclists, teenage lovers, family Sundayers, graffiti-sprayers and dogs. Somewhere between my front garden and the Northenden Bridge it dawned on me that I had wanted to try on the north like a new hat and see how it fitted. The truth was, of course, it didn't fit at all; moreover the hat I had chosen was entirely outdated. But by then I didn't care – I had the river, and the river had me, and I found more of myself (and of 'real' Manchester, perhaps), in that mile and a half of wet grass and rushing water than I had in years of dreaming about who I might be a few hundred miles north of my upbringing.

To me, Manchester, like Liverpool, feels like a tribal city, with its warring football teams and its out-of-bounds neighbourhoods and its fierce civic pride. Its major river reflects this. The Mersey doesn't have a tranquil beauty (at times it feels more Congo than Pang) but it remains stubbornly resistant to the new industrialists, the ones who install the cranes in the city centre and divide up the luxury apartments into 'units'. Somebody told me the name 'Mersey' means 'division.' They were close – apparently it stems from the Anglo-Saxon world for boundary. The River Mersey represents many boundaries both literal and symbolic; between Cheshire and Lancashire, between the two great British northwest cities, between Manchester's historical past and present, and in my case, between my romantic imagination and the reality of life in the north. Walking along the Mersey regularly for two years burst my bubble and wet my hems, but I fell in love with it anyway.

I moved back to the south eventually, of course. Recently I heard that the Jackson's Boat pub has been refurbished under new management. I don't miss my northern fantasy. I still miss the river.

Jemma Kennedy is the author of the novel Skywalking.

FISHING WITH JAKUB

BY
JEFF BARRETT

I t seems the only way I get to see a fish on the bank these days is by going out with Jak. Last week we grabbed a day and headed over to Oxfordshire to fish a big old estate lake. Not at a bite for me but Jak took a 9lb Pike on a spinner in the morning and a 10lb Mirror Carp to a boilie at dusk.

Then, on Sunday, when the weather was really weird – sunblock on Feb 10th – Jak took me over to Cobham to fish the Mole. It was beautiful. I hadn't seen it before. We parked up by the mill with plans to fish the weirpool but we were too late. All three swims were taken. Looked really good too. So, off we walked across a frosty meadow, following the river along the wrong side of a barbed-wire fence until we came to a place where we could get over it and into a wood. It was magical. The garlic was already up and as we broke the leaves underfoot the smell was amazing. We had walked into spring.

Over snowdrops and quietly to the bank. There were two dream swims and within minutes I had a John Richardson goose quill trotting downstream. I was going to get a bite. I was going to catch a Chub. I was convinced that the float was going to bury just as it reached the bend and held back below the willow... but, nope, not a thing. So, we walked and walked and then we had to sit a while and just take it in. A million miles from the Uxbridge Road, no traffic, no people, no sound but birdsong. No fish either. Didn't care. Getting used to it anyway.

We made it back to the weirpool just before dusk and the swims were free. Jak spotted a fish roll about twenty feet out, right beside a really horrible snag. A Barbel he said, a big one. Four red maggots on the hook, dropped right on the spot. Feed a few more and wait. It will come. And it did. A great big beautiful Barbel weighing in at 13lb. Jak's the man with the mojo right now.

Me, I'm still searching for the spirit of Brendan Behan. One day...

Jeff Barrett is part of the team behind the angling and culture website Caughtbytheriver.net. He is the co-founder of Heavenly Recordings. The seeds were sown for Jeff in the 1970s on the banks of the river Trent; fishing at Beeston & Attenborough, football at the City Ground, and rock 'n' roll and northern soul at The Boat Club.

RIVER MAN

BY
HANNAH HAMILTON

Gonna see the river man
Gonna tell him all I can
'bout the ban
On feeling free.

Nick Drake, 'River Man'

—————————◆•◆•◆—————————

Rivers can be metaphors for many things. Metaphors for life, for its twists and turns, for the suredness of its path, for our uncertainty of what lies ahead. For times of peace in deep, calm waters, for times of struggle in the turbulence of the rapids, for times of submergence when hard bedrock yields to soft sand, creating hidden whirlpools and turnholes that threaten to suck us under their untroubled surface. Metaphors for the flow of time that's constant in its pace but relative in our experience of it: going fast when we're paddling frantic upstream, and slow, when we're floating down, on our backs, gazing up at the clouds, letting the current do with us what it will. And metaphors for memories. That ethereal lifeblood that courses through our lives just like a river, connecting the babbling brook to the broad estuary, giving us a place, a direction, a stage, a reflection.

Rivers flow in all of us, and us in them, and in the sublimeness of their presence we find ours.

In his own way, my father taught me this. Not in words, they were not his strong point: as a peasant child in 1930s rural Ireland, he emerged illiterate and innumerate from two years of schooling, greatest impact of that experience was felt on the temples of his head, the lobes of his ears and the palms of his hands. He recalls being beaten by the teacher for 'being thick', so he wouldn't go to school, and instead opted to be beaten at home by his father for truancy. School registers from the time record one of two excuses: 'Wet day no clothes' or, more frequently, 'Gone fishing'.

What I learned from him came in more subtle ways than that of lecture, both in retrospect and in riddle, that required a certain amount of water to pass between the arches of my bridge to be understood. But now, I understand.

Because that scrawny malnourished child with no shoes and no electricity, that picked stones out of pratie (potato) fields for pennies and knew the fear of God like the back of his hand instilled in his child, a child of 1980's relative affluence with a full belly and nothing to want for, a sense of what it is to know oneself through nature, to find your place in this world, and in that place be free. His lesson was his life, and his classroom his river.

———•◦•———

Aside from the mechanics of classic cars to which he devoted 40 years of his professional life, my father's greatest passion was fishing, and I remember my first proper outing with him like it was yesterday.

I was five, and visiting my Granny Ireland for a fortnight on holiday – an annual pilgrimage to the paternal homestead. Holidays to me smelled like burning turf and tasted like red lemonade, Galtee cheese and soft-whip 99 ice creams. My daddy was my hero. He was taking me fishing For The First Time and I knew it. Green wellies with frogs on the toes, dungarees and a lick of white blond hair, bounding eagerly over rickety fences and through meadows, leaping into mansize footprints in grass, desperate to share, to the banks of the chattering Nore.

I remember watching enrapt and bewildered at his rituals: threading the cast through the eyes of my little rod (black, with red threading and a cork handle) and knotting the end deftly around the eye of a huge (to me, at least) hook and moulding a blob of "Ssssh Hannah Don't Tell Anyone" orange Playdough (salmon spawn, highly illegal, even in 1988) around its barbaric-looking barb. He sat me down on the bank at the top of the rapids and cast my hook under a large overhanging Sally tree and into a sandy hole he knew well. He handed me the rod, and rifled through the flaggers (long riverside grass) for a gabhlóg – a Y-shaped stick – to act as my rod rest. He found one, dug its tail into the earth, rested the neck of my rod in the V and hunkered down to look me square in the eye.

"Now, Han, this Is Very Important. When the tip of the rod goes like this (cue his forearm in electric shock), you call me. Ok?"

"Ok."

Thoroughly determined, I remember focusing on the top of the rod and willing it to move. I was sure it would if I just tried hard enough. And it did. Having made it no more than 30 yards upstream, he heard my urgent squealing: "Daddy! Daaaaaa-deeeeeee! The rod's shakin'!"

He strode over in no great hurry, and I remember feeling frustrated that he wasn't sprinting. "Are you sure?

Maybe it's just settling down in the current," he offered, in his wisdom.

But no. Out from the water emerged a slippery, silver prize, more precious than gold, struggling to escape the confines of my net. He caught it in his big fist, stuck his fore and middle fingers down its neck, snapped its head back and, in my triumphant hands, he placed a half a pound of glory. I shone, nay, beamed with pride.

He took a clutch of grass, put it in our old battered fishing bag and gently lay the trout to rest on top, before casting out another blob of Playdough (this time with two little hands helping). Again, I sat and waited, and again – in a matter of minutes – the tip of my rod went into a violent spasm. Again came the squeals, the splash, the crack, the glow of father/daughter pride. Five times in total, if I must boast. Beheaded, gutted, floured, peppered, fried. That first time remains etched in my mind's ore not just as the first time I went fishing, but also as the only time I was ever to catch more fish than my father. He only got three.

But he played a clever game, knowing that if there was any chance of me becoming a fisherwoman, I had to catch a fish on my first go. (Later, I found out, that that was the one and only time he had ever used salmon spawn – or trout's heroin, as it can be known – to lure a fish, and that I was the intended prey.)

I have tried to repeat that first success many times, albeit with less advantageous bait. Pails of warm soapy water brought forth maggots from Granny's back garden, though all I seemed to catch with them were hideous eels that squirmed and twitched, even after their heads had been chopped off. (My cormorant uncle always gave them a welcome reception, however.)

The family moved wholesale to Ireland when I was 11, taking over Granny Ireland's house; two fences and one meadow away from the site of my debut, and opposite a small stretch of Noreside pasture known to us as the River Field. It consisted of 4.3 acres of untilled land that was liable to flood and half a kilometre of neglected, un-fished river that my father had dreamed of owning since his boyhood days, a slice of heaven whose divinity was preserved in a stratum of memories. He and his seven brothers and sisters had played, caught dinner, shat and had their annual bath in that field, and Granny had washed the family's clothes on its banks.

In 1996, he bought it from a local landlord, whose family he had known through four generations, and on whose farm he had toiled. It was the end field – the runt of their agrarian litter – but its acquisition was still a rarity. In Ireland, farmers don't sell land. His cause was aided in part by changing attitudes of younger generations of land-owners, but also by my father's generosity in youth. He never forgot Old Mr Phelan when he'd caught a few trout.

> "That was the only time he had ever used salmon spawn – or trout's heroin, as it can be known – to lure a fish, and that I was the intended prey"

Diggers respectfully tidied the bank, black sacks of household waste were wrenched bare-handed from the bed and 500 native trees were planted in a bid to restore something of the local wildlife's natural habitat.

It was in this field that I learned to fly fish, under my father's strict instruction. This, he informed me, with an elegant crack of his 12 foot split cane salmon rod, was an art form, and one to which all fishermen aspire. I was taught to tie flies in the dark. I learned to anticipate the rise and select the appropriate fly (sedges and green olives the favourites, black

gnats after 10pm). I perfected my cast and put my own spin on
the motion (born of necessity, I did not have my father's biceps)
that allowed me to present my fly to the fish with the finesse of
a silver service waitress, anywhere at all on the river. He said
that was the mark of a good fly fisher. I took his words seri-
ously, and practiced casting onto a rise in a deep hole under a
tree on the other bank with the wind against me till my hands
filled up with welts.

Summer nights by the Nore. The swish of a cast. The
cold rush of water around my legs (we never did care much
for waders). Diamond stars in a pitch-black sky. The splash of
sprats jumping. The deep tantalising gulp of big trout rising.
My rod. My daddy. And me.

———————◆·◆·◆———————

In the years that followed, life by the river changed course
and ran between us: him steadfast and oblivious on one bank,
casting away merrily, building up a fishing school, manicuring
his banks; and me, stubborn, proud and neglected, growing up
The English Kid in the excruciating glare of the Irish catholic
convent school system on the other. We diverged. I hung up
my rod and moved to the city to pursue a treacherous but ultimately successful career as a rock and roll journalist, a passion
of mine he cared not to comprehend, and I came to resent the
waters he allowed to consume him deeper than his own blood.

When at 17 I got a commission (and, later, an internship),
from the country's biggest music magazine, it took him two
years to remember the name of the title. When I moved back

to the UK at 21 to join the rest of the sprats throwing themselves against music industry's weir, he could never remember
which city I lived in. When I tried to converse with him over
the phone, he'd only ever offer the same specific phrases. I
thought he wasn't interested in me, and took his neglect deep
into my heart.

But it wasn't until he introduced my mother to me as
my uncle that I realised that this cocoon he existed in was not
by choice.

Three years ago, he was diagnosed with Alzheimer's
disease, and nine months ago was taken into full time care. For
a man who has never tasted alcohol, who has never smoked
a cigarette, who has never touched a narcotic, who has spent
every single day of his life out doors, who until a year ago could
do a chin up, flip his legs over his head and land on his feet, to
be locked in an air-conditioned ward on a cocktail of drugs is
beyond hell on earth.

Our only consolation is that he doesn't remember.

⋯•⋯

For my part, I went to India, re-discovered my heart and the
importance of family, returning just as he was taken into care. I
moved back to Ireland then and am still here, with my mother,
doing what we can. Nature is slowly consuming The River Field,
and the banks are growing over. Nevertheless, with youth and
blind ambition on my side, it is my hope to re-open the Inchbeg
Fly Fishing School – as it is known – next season, and to donate
some of the proceeds to the Alzheimer's Society.

The water has changed. My father has lost his river, and I now walk its banks alone, more than a little lost myself. But through my sorrow it gently reminds me, in the ripples and gurgles of that old familiar voice, that we each have our own course to run; that as tributaries dart from that same river seeking their own place amongst the earth, so must I. And there I find, safe in nature's glistening example and comforted by my own precious memories, that I am not consumed in a whirlpool of grief. Through these waters, my father has bequeathed to me a metaphor for peace in troubled times. And in them, I too have found what it is to be free.

Hannah Hamilton is a jack of all trades, but likes writing the most. She currently lives by the river in County Kilkenny, Ireland, where she is busy with the Inchbeg Fishing School (www.inchbegfishingschool.com). She plans to spend the off season travelling through Africa and India. Some of her favourite things include masala chai, crosswords, yoga, rock 'n roll, cycling in Cambridge, sunsets and Powers whiskey. She was born in 1982.

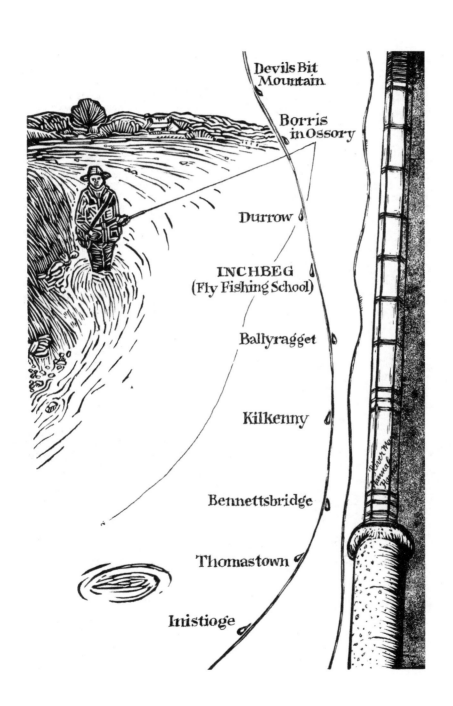

Devils Bit
Mountain

Borris
in Ossory

Durrow

INCHBEG
(Fly Fishing School)

Ballyragget

Kilkenny

Bennettsbridge

Thomastown

Inistioge

ENDLESS SUMMER

GROWING UP WITH THE RIVER OGMORE

BY
ROBIN TURNER

> *"Sometimes, if you stand on the bottom rail of a bridge and lean over to watch the river slipping slowly away beneath you, you will suddenly know everything there is to be known."*
>
> *Winnie the Pooh*, AA Milne

———————◆———————

It came as a shock the day the Ogmore burst its banks. Back in the '70s, Bridgend seemed to be devoid of bad weather and the kind of pinched, miserly nights you get fobbed off with in autumn and winter. For me, the place was locked in a state of permanent summer; spliced into an endless loop of glorious, Pinewood Technicolor where whistling delivery men called round with everything from Cresta pop on a Thursday to wet fish on a Friday. On this day though, Welsh weather delivered on its unspoken promise. Down at Newbridge Fields behind my Grandmother's house, the river had spilt over. My brother and I sprinted down to be met by a Dali-drunk-on-SA vision – one where fields of marshy, mulchy grass were covered in writhing eels; the natural world having displaced its own in a moment of madness. To us – curious and just a little sadistic as children are wont to be – this carpet of displaced elvers, each of them locked in a strange and hopeless dance, seemed more like comedy than horror. The Ogmore had given up its young as a sacrifice and all we could do was laugh at their terminal misfortune. Summer had made us entirely carefree.

As a kid, I spent every school holiday in Bridgend while my Dad toured the continent fine-tuning his palette to previously-unheard French and Italian frequencies. Mainly he was getting a much-deserved respite from my brother Huw and me – a couple of pre-teen bruisers who probably asked for too much and gave very little back. Aggy (my paternal Grandmother) was, as far as Huw and I were concerned, Mother Teresa playing Santa Claus with a penchant for Superkings and twice-weekly Bridge competitions. Her house seemed huge, echoing with the sound of footfall as you ran around it. Here, rooms were still kept "for best". I remember thinking back then that Bridgend was a town populated entirely by pensioners. There were men like Mr Blatchley who had gainful employment destroying wasp's nests (do the Job Centre still advertise for such skills?) and women like Auntie Clar, who you called Auntie as a matter of fact even though they were no relation to you whatsoever. Back then I thought Bridgend was the centre of the universe. Back then I suppose it actually was.

Amazingly, considering the generation gap, Aggy was up for anything as long as she could smoke her requisite 10 fags a day. She would selflessly look after us for weeks on end, some-times two-thirds of the school holiday. All the while, she'd be at our beck and call from the minute that Dad buggered off on the Brittany Ferry, following the lure of cheap plonk and good charcuterie. If we asked, and we usually did, Ag was always ready to fire up the car for a trip to exotic, far-flung places like Roose Airport, the Mumbles or the seaward stretches of the river Ogmore.

While Aggy was always on hand to ferry us around from place to place, Dad would sometimes take us out on mini adventures, more often than not with the express intention of him and his mates ending it with a few pints. It worked for all of us though, the perfect reward for patience and gentle exertion. Nothing would be too exhaustive or pre-planned, we weren't a sporty family that would spend a day casting off or stripping down and jumping in for a spot of wild swimming. We were the kind of family that wandered from standing stone to wrecked castle; from pub to pub. For me and my brother, the payoff was the beer garden and a bottle of coke; for adults, it was the 1970s afternoon closing equivalent of binge drinking.

Although I grew up in Newport, a proudly ugly city cleaved in two by a grimy stretch of the Usk, it was the Vale Of Glamorgan and the banks of the Ogmore (Afon Ogwr to use the local name, although you'll have scant chance of hearing it used round here) that I loved. The river made its presence properly felt as it snaked its way through Bridgend at the bottom of Newbridge Fields just behind Ag's house, already well on its way to the sea and miles on into its journey. The Ogmore is a dreamy meander southwards from its nervous trickling source (the point that Roger Deakin beautifully describes as "a tear duct in the earth") out near the cemetery mountain to the west of Treorchy to its ultimate destination at the mouth of Bristol Channel where Welsh water finally gets to meet English. On its journey, the Ogmore rarely breaks sweat. This isn't a showy river; it's not the kind you need a volume control for. Where the gaping mouth yawns open into the Bristol Channel, it is flanked on each side by sandy golden stretches that whisker the base of sleepy Ogmore-By-Sea. The closest action is in nearby Porthcawl, where the once-majestic Coney Beach funfair limps along in a state of disrepair – faded and unloved in flaking paint and graffiti, ready for the knacker's yard.

The Ogmore may now be something of an angler's paradise – its waters ripple with salmon, brown trout and sewin (sea trout) – but only through carefully monitored recovery has it gained this new lease of life. Over the last couple of centuries, these waters were used primarily as a dumping ground for wastage generated by industry up in the valleys, where the detritus of everything from coal mining to cosmetics would be flushed downstream in the hope that it would become someone else's problem. My father describes the river as having run black during his childhood.

Throughout my life the Ogmore has been a river in remission. By the 1980s, industry was starting its graceless decline in the Valleys and, thankfully, people's awareness of the natural environment was becoming more acute. Its use as a dumping ground stopped, possibly because the collieries that produced so much waste were shutting down production for good. The Valley's loss was the Ogmore's kiss of life as the unwelcome swirl of flushed-down Revlon was replaced by the fizzing blur of piscine industry.

———•◦•———

As you trek out of town, the Ogmore gets more picturesque – less channeled, wilder; sketched out in violent yellow gorse, untamed bracken and grass pastures grazed down by lazy sheep. By the time you get to the Ogmore's tourist tracks, the river cuts a crystalline path through the kind of picture-book countryside that allowed a child's vivid imagination to run riot. Beyond the fields, a little further along near Merthyr Mawr village,

was the dipping bridge. Built in the 15th century in a powdery shade, the bridge was a stone arch with low-slung holes placed along its length. A generation or so before now, people brought sheep here and pushed them through the gaps and out the other side, forcing them to take a six-foot plunge for a much-needed seasonal scrub-up and delouse. Here you could stare from the bridge into the ripples below and waste time in the way that only kids really can. In tribute to the chap from Pooh Corner, we used to stop off here on the way to nowhere in particular to play pooh sticks. This bridge was a place where the most simple of pastimes, like throwing twigs into the moving current, would take on the almighty significance of an Olympic sport. Long gone by the time I came along was the inn by the side of the dipping bridge. There, the murderous landlord Cap Coch robbed, killed and buried dozens of weary travellers looking for refreshment on their pilgrimage westwards to the cathedral in St David's. Their bodies were disposed of by the waterside, blood diluting down to a pinky nothing on its unscheduled journey to the sea.

From the bridge, noses pricked and following the tang of briny air, we would head downstream before eventually coming to a set of stepping-stones at the base of Ogmore Castle – a now decrepit memento of the Norman invasion of Wales in the 12th century. In my youth, the stones had all the mighty weight of a giant's causeway over the river – mossy boulders that spanned the raging torrent and had to be navigated with tightrope proficiency. One reckless slide in the wrong direction and you were sodden from the waist down, bawling your eyes out. That fate never befell myself or my brother… but maybe that's just hindsight kindly doing some mental rewiring, blurring out many of my more embarrassing moments as the years pile on.

Further out, past the Penybont works (a sewage processing plant that has been thoughtfully hidden away from view by time and encroaching foliage) was the biggest adrenalin rush for any child growing up around Ogmore Vale. Up past the salt marshes that flank the Ogmore were the sand dunes. Back then, a visit to the dunes was akin to being transported into the opening scenes of *Star Wars*, only by Ag's Renault 4 rather than the Millennium Falcon. Here was a little piece of Tunisia dumped wholesale next to the coast in South Wales, the closest thing that the Vale had to a natural phenomenon – a mountain range in motion, rising then sinking with each uncontrollable tempest. The morning after the night before would see a whole new range of temporary peaks, drifts that you could bomb down on your sledge throughout the endless summer. With one of us on a hard-moulded blue toboggan and the other on a decommissioned wooden surfboard, we fearlessly rode the dunes like they were Polynesian breakers. Here in the dunes, 'epic' really was an understatement. In 1961, scenes from *Lawrence Of Arabia* were shot between those shifting sands although the closest that my brother and

I would get to Omar Sharif emerging from the distant horizon would be Ag coming to collect us so she could get to that
night's tournament.

Inevitably, the dunes and the river surrender themselves
unconditionally to the sea. The near-Blue Flag beaches (well,
there are Blue Flag beaches nearby, does that count?) roll
out for miles, offering something for everyone – kite surfing,
horse riding, dog walking and plentiful opportunities for stoned
teenagers to burn stuff. Squint hard enough here and you can
see the plumes of smoke from the steel works in nearby Port
Talbot, which in a certain faded light, takes on the appearance
of *Blade Runner*'s Los Angeles. Looking out to sea on a clear
day over the widescreen vista of the Bristol Channel, you get
a good view of our English cousins on the North Devon coast,
a sight impaired only by the low-slung craggy island known as
Tusker Rock – proudly wrecking ships until as recently as the
1960s. Over the sea lay the Great Unknown, places like Weston-
super-Mare, Ilfracombe, Woolacombe, Lundy: each unfamiliar
name was like shovelled coal to the fires of the youthful imagination, as evocative as the stern proclamations of the Shipping
Forecast. For all the water that swelled up between us and
them, those places might as well have been on Mars.

My relationship with Bridgend and the Ogmore changed
for good when Ag passed away a few years back. The places
that I used to play in are barely recognizable now. Bridgend got
younger and a whole lot more serious. Roads were pedestrian-
ised, buildings uglified – market town architecture reimagined
by half-pissed Brutalists on behalf of Boots The Chemist and
Woolies (RIP). Recent history paints a gloomy picture of the

town, stunned by the unfathomable spate of teen suicides, the ghastly legacy of decades of pit and factory closures in the surrounding areas. The land between my Grandmother's house and the fields was eventually filled in and built on as over-eager developers snapped up any available green spaces. We sold her house and my ties with the town itself were severed. For me now it's simply a train station on the way to somewhere else.

Out of town, the dipping bridge is now a monument to a time gone by, one where local farmers cared enough about the well-being of their livestock to give them the occasional spot of beautification. The few thousand or so scraggy sheep that roam free around the salt marshes of the Vale do nothing other than annoy daytripping motorists with their somnambulant grazing. They all look like they could do with a wash – or at the very least a push off a low bridge in order to shake them awake. The stepping-stones are in reality just a hop, a skip and a jump over the river, something to be tipsily traversed after a couple of pints in the Pelican, the nearest decent pub to the waterside. If you're lucky, you can crouch on a stone and watch a sub-aquatic dual carriageway rolling along under the surface. Just a few feet deep by the stones, it's undoubtedly a trout tickler's fantasy... well, a printable one anyway.

These days you would drive straight past the dunes without a second glance. Sometime in the '80s, a panic must have set in that said, unless the drifts were stopped, they'd up sticks and cover up Swansea. With that, the dunes were cultivated, allowed to grow over and shift no more. What was once the biggest free fun park in South Wales is now a set of grassy verges, tethered down by a carpet of alien roots and shoots.

Still a location for film crews, nowadays you're far more likely to see the likes of Russell T. Davies filming there than any budding David Lean as the river and the surrounding areas have been co-opted as backdrops for *Doctor Who* ever since his police box was parked permanently in South Wales a few years back. Add to that the BBC production of *Merlin* – where the Vale of Glamorgan magically transforms into the Vale of Avalon for 45 minutes once a week – and you've got a veritable Taff Tinseltown right there under your nose.

Now when I look at the Ogmore and all those landmarks that nuzzle up next to it, I wonder what the wide-eyed, childhood version of me would make of the fact that the dunes, the river and the beaches he was brought up in the shadow of would years later be doubling up as far-flung windswept planets or an ancient Britain rife with witchcraft on national television? And would those outer-worldly outposts really have been any more impressive, any more tangible than the places that existed as figments of my own imagination; untethered thoughts allowed free reign to swoop and dive along the Ogmore in the perpetual summer of youth? That sounds like the kind of contemplation that needs to be done in that beer garden down by the river where the cool, cool water rolls on out to sea in front of you; the only constant in a landscape that's subtly being remolded as much by nature's pragmatic evolutionary march as by man's generational mood swings.

So, who's round is it?

Robin Turner has worked at Heavenly for as long as he can remember. He is the co-author of The Rough Pub Guide.

The
Ouse
Burn

BY
KATHRYN WILLIAMS

I've never felt right living away from water. I don't need to look out onto it, but I need to know that within so many miles, say 10, I could get there. I remember feeling really dizzy on tour in Germany because we were so far away from the sea. It's the same as my need to be near a fire exit in a theatre or venue. I think water must be my built in escape route. Maybe it's in my blood from my sea-faring grandparents?

I grew up near the Mersey. Being from Liverpool it was something to be proud of, to sing about. Our flag. We didn't see it all the time, but we felt we knew it enough. My Gran took us on it for days out. Grandad would pretend he was just coming to wave us off, and then the ferry would move. We'd be shouting "It's moving! It's moving!" and he would put a leg over the edge as if to jump, and then pull at some rope and eventually say, "it's no good, I'm going to have to come with you!" We would shout hooray, not thinking how there was always enough egg sandwiches for everyone and a flask with two cups.

Because of those boat trips, the river and the sea were always associated with them. They had a boat in a bottle on their mantlepiece in the front room. The front room that no one sat in, always smelling of polish, with all their treasures in glass fronted cabinets. Ashtrays in the shape of swans bought on their travels. A long shoehorn, in the shape of a hand for backscratching, was carved from whalebone by a pirate. Or was it actually good old-fashioned brown smoky plastic? To remember it now makes me yearn to see things through those believing eyes. I saw it as a house by the sea. I swear I smelled, and can still recall, the salty air in that street. Even their outside toilet seat looked like driftwood. My grandparents were seaside folk. At least they were to me.

Last year, in my thirties, I found out that a picture of my Gran and Grandad standing by the Great Wall of China with my uncle's first wife was actually...North Wales! This picture had been the truth to me, a silly joke to someone else. It had been an important picture. It carried with it the idea of my family as adventurers. All those years goading my own bravery to face travel because my grandparents had gone to China ("when travel wasn't easy" said the voice when I panicked about getting on a plane.) In river terms I had reached an intersection. One branch, one conversation had taken me to a new line. I knew not all history was true. A thing can change that seems fixed.

"We paddled in the water, as novel as snow, wishing we had a dinghy to float around our flower beds, a spade for an oar"

I now live in the north of Newcastle and our garden backs onto a river. The Ouse burn. Not the most romantic of names. Reminds me of something you would be embarrassed to go to the doctor with, but never the less. A beautiful meandering little thing that makes it's way to the Tyne just east of the millennium bridge. This year it flooded. I don't mean a bit. It rose 9 feet, burst its banks, running into our garden. Creeping along, combing the grass, turning it into an underwater weed. We paddled in the water, as novel as snow, wishing we had a dinghy to float around our flower beds, a spade for an oar.

It had been a sweet, romantic river. A place to contemplate, to see electric blue kingfishers fly over, the sound of it bubbling and cooling on a summer's day, but now it had taken up arms. After it swallowed the lawn its personality changed, it became aggressive and greedy. It had muscle and tone and form. It was lifting itself higher and drinking the rain faster, gaining energy. Its volume intimidated. What had been a whimsy stream was now a torrent. Virulent. Creeping with fingertips towards rock, patio and bricks. Feeling its way into long forgotten cracks, seeping into porous walls. The river has burst its banks like it was crying at a funeral. Heaving. Lapping a breath, and heaving again.

People always talk about the movement of fire. They say it's an animal, the way it creeps. Water is like a ghost. You turn around and it has come closer. Like someone moved the furniture while you blinked. What you take as the truth can change. This river wanted to be a sea. The climbing frame, the plum tree, were all shipwrecked without a voyage. The swing was pointing like a windsock from the current. We laughed to see a traffic cone, a bin and three ducks speed past us. All had a look of shock. Louis started asking the river to give us our garden back. "Why is it doing this?" he asked. I shrugged. He was shouting at it like king Canute. But it rose higher, each hour a step closer to the house.

By the evening it had come into the cellar. We sat listening to it move the furniture around. I guessed that the bookshelf had swum and then fallen while Neil tried to guess what small things were tapping and banging around. Now we were crew.

We were no longer watching water but sailing on top. It had
defied all of our expectations; it felt capable of never stopping.
It was now growing dark and still it kept on creeping up. No
sleep for water. I sweated and tossed in the night, waking to
look out of the window, wondering if I would wake floating in
a bed.

Morning came. It was gone. Football pitches, swimming
pools, thousands and thousands of cups of water had disappeared. Our own sea was gone.

I walked down to the bottom of the garden. There it was
just stream again. Like nothing had happened. A psychotic
episode now forgotten. A dream? No. Behind me was the

brown silt. All through the garden up the walls, stinking and clinging on to flowers, walls, and furniture. It was drying in the sun into a clay chalky snow. It fucking stank. All those houses, all those gardens had all been touched with the same brush, with the same paint, the same water. We had been left gifts by it of logs and pots and plastic. Matted hairy plants stuck to our plants, still leaning the way of the river. The three of us walked around the garden marvelling that yesterday we would have been over our heads in water. It didn't feel like our garden. It smelt like the river. It had taken our home once and like the unease after a burglary, we knew it was possible again. We all needed to get out of the house. To know that we were docked. We walked down by the quayside in Newcastle. The Tyne was full. Plumped up like a big brown cushion. I leaned on the cold black railing. I thought "In there is our sea".

The water that had come into our lives and touched our things. It had spent a night in our house. It had taken from us and given gifts from others. Amongst it was the water that had gone into other homes. And run down hills and mountains first, and rained from the sky and all of it, all of it was washing towards the sea where it would carry on. It would keep going on…wouldn't it? Swirling around in me, in my history was the Mersey, the Tyne and that river that I thought I owned. But I didn't own anything. Not my family now or long gone, not the house or the water. It was all passing through. And so was I.

I thought about the river and it's memories. We can never give our memories to someone else without them diluting. After all no one else sees them or paints them as bright. No one can course the route. They are ours to draw, write, paint, and talk about. But the eye, heart and head it goes into will never taste it the same as you. History is just one big sea. It looks like a whole, hugging time just as the sea hugs land. It's made from the rivers of generations pouring into it. Fragments, Streams, landscapes. Stories, houses and faces, never touched by each other, come together. My parents fell in love and changed course to their own stream. They had us and we'll do the same. Here I am standing on the pier. Knowing the sea can rise, that rivers can burst their banks, that photographs can lie. Things that are true change shape. History moves like a ghost. You turn around and it has come closer.

Kathryn Williams is a singer-songwriter based in Newcastle upon Tyne. Her second album earned her a Mercury Music Prize nomination. Her most recent release is Two, *a collaborative album with Neill MacColl (of the hugely influential folk family) which came out in the UK in 2008. She plans to release her eighth album of quiet beauty in mid 2009.*

THE
PENKILN
BURN

BY
BILL DRUMMOND

The Penkiln Burn is a small river in Southwest Scotland.
It rises in the Galloway Hills at the Nick of Curlywee.
It tumbles and turns for eight-and-a-half miles,
Passing on the way Scheuchan Craig, Lamachan,
Glen Shallock, Auchenleck, Garlies Castle and
Cumloden before it flows into the River Cree
At the village of Minnigaff.

The Penkiln Burn is also something else.

So this is the plan. I load up the Land Rover, then I drive. I drive as far as I can before the hallucinations get too vivid and I become a danger to whoever else is on the road.

I was on the M1 heading out of London by 7.30 pm. Light was already draining away. The destination was Stroke City (Derry/Londonderry) via the ferry from Stranraer to Belfast.

It is now 7.43 am, the morning after the drive up the M1, M6 and along the A75. I'm sitting on a large boulder on the bank of the Penkiln Burn staring down into the waters, letting my thoughts drift and float. Early this afternoon I catch the ferry but, for the next couple of hours, I've got time to let those thoughts drift and float and get these notes done. A few weeks back I got an email from Jeff Barrett of Heavenly asking if I would be interested in writing a piece for a book he was editing about fishing and rivers called *Caught By The River*. I knew instantly that I needed to write this. It is something I had been planning to write for some years, but I knew I had to return to where I am now squatting for me to do it. I hope I can get it all out of me in one go.

When I set off last night I assumed I was going to pull into a Travelodge somewhere up by the Lakes, get more than half the journey behind me, have a few hours' sleep and get the rest done this morning. But the three Lodges that I pulled into were all full, so I bought another can of Red Bull and kept driving. By the time I was passing the turn-off for Carlisle, it was well past midnight, so I yanked the ring pull on the fourth Red Bull and thought 'Fuck it! I may as well do the last 80 miles and get to the Penkiln Burn tonight.' I had a sleeping bag with me in the back. I could sleep on the banks of the Burn. The day had been a glorious autumn one. The temperature touched 21 degrees Celsius, according to the weatherman. The sky was clear and studded with stars, just the sort of night for sleeping out.

As I was crossing the border at Gretna, it started to rain. But I kept going, turning off the motorway to head west along the almost empty A75, passing names on signposts that began to pull me back to another age, a far-off land – one before Kennedy was president and Paul had met John, even before Elvis was King. Way back to the mid 1950s when this was the limit of my known universe. Dalbeattie, Cardoness Castle, Moss Yards, Blackcraig: on and on the names come, each momentarily caught in the glare of my headlights before disappearing back into the darkness. Sleeping villages and small Scots towns. I could almost feel a starless, bible-black, crowblack, bobbing sea moment coming on, but I was in the wrong land even if it was the right decade.

Then, in a blink, it's the Minnigaff turning. I made a right along by the Cree Bridge Hotel and then a left where the sawmill used to be, up around the Kirk, down to Queen Mary's Bridge and finally a few hundred yards along a farm track that runs parallel to the Penkiln Burn. I pulled up and switched off the engine. It was still pissing down. Sleeping out was not an option. I considered making a bivouac using the two paintings that I've got lashed to the roof rack, but even if I did that, the ground would still be soaking. I pulled my boots and jeans off and hauled myself into the sleeping bag, got as comfortable as I could across the front seats of the Land Rover, checked the time, 3.35 am and fell fast asleep almost immediately.

———◦•◦———

I woke about 20 minutes ago. Four hours solid kip. Not bad. Although overcast, it is no longer raining. And I'm sitting here on this boulder staring into the water. This is where I come from, where I belong and where I will come back to when I die. The passport in my pocket may say different but this boulder on the bank of this modest river, the Penkiln Burn, is at the core of my existence.

The boulder measures about five feet in diameter. The rock it is made from must be a few million years old. I guess it took on boulder-shape status and ended up here on the banks of the Penkiln at the time of the last ice age. By contrast, I was eight years old when I first sat on it and stared into the water flowing past. That would have been back in 1961. For the next three years until we moved south in June 1964, I would find myself back on this boulder at least once a week. Whatever the weather, whatever the season (well almost), I would be here staring into the Burn and the surrounding world.

The Penkiln Burn had been part of my life for some years before I started sitting here. My father had taken up fishing as a hobby. I guess he thought it was away of getting away from work and family responsibilities, but it was not long before my mother was getting him to take me along as well. This would have been about when I was three or four. The first time he took me to the Penkiln, we went a few miles further up from where I'm sitting now. This was my first introduction to the art. My father had a bamboo rod, a wooden reel, a linen line, a length of gut, a lead weight and a hook with a worm on it. He told me he was hoping to catch a brown trout. He was a beginner; once he had mastered this he would move on to the proper thing, fly-fishing.

We had dug for the worms in the garden before we set out. I had held the jam jar full of worms as we drove the few miles in our pea-soup green Austin A40. The worms fascinated me. I watched as he put the hook through the worm and it wriggled and wriggled in protest, He told me that, once the hook was in the water with its worm on it, a hungry trout would come along, think it was dinner and eat it. And once the trout had eaten it, the hook would stick in the trout's mouth and we could pull the trout out of the water. We then would take the trout home and have it for tea.

My dad cast his line into the water, with the still-wriggling worm on the hook. I expected that the hungry trout would be gobbling down the worm in no time. We waited. We must have waited for all of 30 seconds before I got bored with the waiting for the hungry trout, so I went off for a wander. I wandered along the bank, then I tried skipping from stone to stone on the water's edge, I slipped and fell. I ran back to my dad completely soaked. The fishing was curtailed for the day and we drove home to be welcomed by the wrath of my mother.

A few weeks later, my father was required to take me along again, and again I fell into the Penkiln Burn before the hungry trout got to eat the worm that I had dug up for him in our garden. And again we drove home to be welcomed by the wrath of my mother.

I am not aware that my dad ever went fishing again after that. As for the rod and the reel and the hooks and the sinker, he kept those at the back of his wardrobe. They took on almost mystical significance for me. There would be times when I would creep into their room, open his wardrobe and pull out this rod and put it all together.

I saw other men fishing, some in waders standing in the middle of River Cree (the Penkiln is a tributary of the far-larger Cree), casting their line again and again. I was told they were fishing for salmon. I learnt how the salmon was a huge glorious fish, revered by all and that, although born in rivers, the salmon spent most of its life out at sea and, after some years, it comes back to the river it was born in to get married and have babies.

I had never seen any of these men standing in the River Cree catch a salmon but I had seen one at the fishmonger's. It was a splendid-looking giant of a fish. I was told its meat was pink, not white like the fish we had for tea once a week. I was told that only rich people ate salmon. That it was the king of fish. This was decades before farmed salmon brought its price tumbling down and we all ate the stuff. By the time I went to school at the age of five, I learnt that some of the big boys in primary four (8 years old) went fishing on their own. I wanted to be like the big boys. Our neighbours had a stand of bamboo canes growing in their garden, so I climbed through the fence and got one. Tied a length of string to the end, got a pin from my mum's mending basket, bent it and tied it to the end of the string. Next I dug up some worms, put them in a jam jar and headed for the nearest bit of water. This was the millrace for the Cree Mills mohair factory. I fell in. I came home soaked through. My mother was not pleased.

———◆———

So that was it for me and fishing until I was given a proper cane rod for my eighth birthday in April 1961. But between the ages of five and eight, the mystery of the Penkiln Burn grew in my imagination. My father helped out with the local boy-scout troop. I would be taken along to the camps with him. One camp was in the White Lady woods up near the Penkiln. Me and the big boys were collecting wood for the campfire. I lifted a log and underneath was a perfectly-coiled snake. A beautiful black zigzag marking went all the way from its head to the tip of its tail. I stared transfixed at this snake, which I knew to be an adder, as it uncoiled itself and silently slithered away through the grass into the safety of the bracken. It was my first snake. There is nothing like coming across a snake in the wild to make you feel alive.

Sometime later we were in the grounds of Cumloden House, the home of Lord and Lady Galloway. They had opened it to the public for the day. The Penkiln Burn flowed though their estate. They had a Chinese-style bridge over it, the sort of bridge you see the lovers escape over on Willow Pattern plates. This was magic, like something out of a Rupert Bear annual. I stood on the bridge staring down into the water waiting for the magic to begin when a bolt of electric blue with a slash of orange flashed straight under the bridge followed by a repeated short, sharp whistle. Nobody else seemed to see it. But I described what I had witnessed to my father. He said it must have been a kingfisher. The following week there was a story in the *Galloway Gazette* about the Reverend Jack Drummond's wee boy seeing a kingfisher flying along the Penkiln Burn, and, if his claim was true, it was the first seen since before the war. I make no claims for what I saw or did not see, but whatever it was I knew it was something beyond the dull daily world of school and TV programmes.

Some months later, I was out on my bike along the Cumloden Road up by Glenhoise. I got off to watch a herd of deer that were between the edge of some woods and the bank of the Penkiln. From the herd emerged a large stag, with a full set of antlers. What shocked me was that he was pure white. I had heard stories about this from my teacher at school, she called it a white hart and how they were very rare and how, back in the days of heathens, people used to think they brought good luck. I looked at the stag and the stag looked at me and then he and his herd turned and disappeared into the woods. I climbed over the dry stone wall, went down to the Burn and drank some water, remembering to not lower my face to the water to drink like they did in cowboy films, but lift the water in my cupped hands. This was so that I could pass the test given to Gideon's army, in the book of Judges; this meant that I could be one of the 300.

Another time when out wandering on my own, I found myself standing on the Queen Mary's bridge, which is only a few hundred yards downstream from where I am making these notes. The Queen Mary in question is better known to the world as Mary, Queen of Scots, who had her head chopped off at Fotheringhay on the instruction of her cousin, Good Queen Bess. From the tradition I come from, Queen Mary was never looked upon with any sort of pity, but the fact that she had walked over this very bridge, or so I was told, made me feel in touch with history. Proper head-chopping off history.

————•◦•————

So anyway on this particular day, I'm leaning over the wall of the bridge staring down into the rushing waters many feet below. Just up from the bridge, the water tumbles through a narrow gap and steeply down over some rocks. The level of the water drops about 30 feet in about the same distance. There are three or four small pools between the top and bottom. While standing there watching the power and force of the water, a large salmon leapt out of the water attempting to make it to the next pool up. It failed and fell back to the one it came from. A few seconds later he tried again, and failed again. This carried on minute after minute. As I indicated earlier, I know something of the

231

life cycle of the salmon, that this beast I was watching was now attempting to return home, way up to the head water of the Penkiln Burn where the Burn would be no more than a shallow brook. He will have left the Penkiln heading for the sea, as a mere smolt, no more than a few inches long, and here he was returning, a splendid fully-grown monarch of the waters.

I kept watching and just as I was about to give up on him and the rain started, he took one great leap, his whole body pushing against the air and all the forces of gravity that were trying to drag him back down, and he made it to the next pool.

The following winter, it rained for weeks on end. The waters of the Penkiln Burn rose and rose. No longer clear and dancing but a charging swirling torrent of murky brown, ripping chunks of its banks away from where they had been since before man had set foot in Scotland. Whole branches, if not trees, came crashing down with the charging currents.

It was Mrs Monteith, our primary three teacher, who broke the news to the 47 of us in her class. The Queen Mary's bridge had been swept away in the flood. We might have been taught to despise Queen Mary for her papist ways, but she had walked across our bridge and now it was gone. I didn't dare return to the Penkiln Burn for almost three months after the news had appeared as the front-page story on the *Galloway Gazette*.

It was the April when I turned eight and got my own proper fishing rod that I made it back to the Penkiln for the first time since the floods. Where the Queen Mary's bridge stood was a gaping chasm. What had been done could not be undone. A new bridge could be built but it would not be the one she had walked over. But the waters were crystal clear again. The new leaves were out; lambs could be heard bleating in fields. I walked on up the small track that ran parallel to the Burn. I had never been up this way before. I came up the same farm track last night. I was looking for a pool to start fishing in. Between the bank and the burn was only two or three yards, but it was thick with trees, bracken and brambles. Finally there was a break in the foliage and I could get down by the water with ease. Here was a huge boulder that I clambered on to. From this vantage point I looked downstream at a large pool of calm water. This would do.

I sat there without getting my rod ready for some time, unable to do anything but drinking in the wonder of it all. Both banks, as far as I could see were blanketed in the azure of bluebells. The intensity of the colour almost hurt my eyes. After 20 or so minutes, I pulled myself from the reverie, got the jar of worms from my pocket, hooked up a big juicy one and started my first day of fishing.

How long I was there, I do not remember. I just know I spent as much time staring into the waters to the other world below the surface as I did wondering if any fish were about to take the bait. What I do remember is how the day ended. It was like this. I felt the line running through my finger, I struck. Started to turn the reel. The line went tight and then I could feel it. Something alive and pulling was at the other end. It felt strong, it twisted and turned. Maybe I'd hooked one of those salmon or a large sea trout, big enough to feed the whole family. I kept trying to wind the reel, to bring whatever this monster was into land, but he kept pulling the other way. After what seemed like ages, I began to get the better of this unseen Leviathan.

When I finally lifted that first catch clear of the water, I was shocked, disturbed and dismayed to see it wasn't a salmon or large sea trout but what I guessed to be an eel. It was no more than 15 inches in length. As I tried to grab the serpent, the rod slipped from my grasp and fell into the water. The eel wriggled free of my grasp, but he was still hooked to the line. I caught hold of line in my left hand, picked up a stone the size of a tennis ball in the right hand; pulling on the line, I dragged the eel up the side of the boulder until he was on top, still writhing and wriggling but unable to shake himself free of the large hook I could see coming out the side of his jaw. With the stone in my right hand, I bludgeoned his head. But he kept writhing. Another blow and this time his head was totally smashed to

bits. Still he was not giving in so I rained down blow after blow until his blood covered the stone and splattered my face. My hands were covered in his slime, but he was dead.

I stood on top of the boulder, took my jersey, shirt and vest off, rubbed the slime on my bare chest and roared my little eight-year-old boy voice at the world. But the world said nothing back. So I roared again. This time I did hear the world answer back. What I could hear were the bleating of distant lambs, the rustle of the spring leaves, the gurgle of the Burn and the silent tinkle of the massed multitudes of bluebells all around. I listened and I listened until the bloodlust and killing frenzy drained from me. After that, I pulled my rod from the water on to the bank. Got dressed. Put the jam jar of worms in one pocket and the battered and defeated eel in the other and headed for home.

My mother declined my offering. But she said I could eat the eel, if I cooked it myself. Using my penknife I gutted it: I had seen my mother regularly gut fish. Then I chopped it up into two-inch lengths and fried it in the pan with lard. It tasted better than any fish I'd ever tasted before or since. Eel is the most nutritious fish in our rivers – fact.

From then I made it up to the Penkiln Burn with rod and jam jar of fresh worms every week. That is every week in the season from 15 March to 14 October. And it was always to the boulder. There I would sit holding my rod and thinking my thoughts. These thoughts were not just about the elusive big fat brown trout that I might catch one day. Most of the thoughts were vague and unfocused, about the call of a distant curlew or the rattle of an angry wren in a bush on the opposite bank.

Or I'd compare all the shades of green on the different trees, but mostly I'd just stare into the water at the parallel universe beneath its surface.

As for the fish that I caught over the next three years, they were mainly parr (baby salmon or sea trout) and young brown trout, none more than eight inches long. And of course there were many more eels. It was always just a worm on a hook, a lead weight, and cotton line with about 12 inches of gut at the end of it. Fishing with a fly was for men, a mystery to be learnt at a later stage in life. Maggots as bait were unheard of, and as for floats, they were just seen in storybooks about English boys.

Everything I caught, however small, I killed on the boulder. They would all be taken home to be gutted, fried and eaten by myself. As far as I knew back then, brown trout, sea trout, eels, salmon and of course the mysterious sparling, were the only fish to live in fresh water. I once found a strange-looking eel that had sucked itself onto an underwater rock. It was some years before I learnt it was a different fish altogether called a lamprey. When I was 11 and we moved to England, I discovered there were all these other fish but hardly any were worth eating.

Sometimes I would take a break from the boulder to explore further upstream or climb a tree. The trees I chose to climb usually had a branch that over hung the Burn. Once while sitting on a branch, staring down into a sunlit patch of water, a large brown trout swam into the light and stayed there for some time gently holding his own against the current. I say large: he was probably 18 inches at most but a giant of a brown trout in these parts. And when I say brown, these fish are anything but dull in colouring. The sun highlighted the reds and blues, yellows and greens that the brown trout has around his speckles. His colouring dies almost as soon as he is pulled from the water and is nothing like the bland colouring of the rainbow trout you find in restaurants.

I stayed up there on the branch watching this wonder for an eternally long time for a restless young boy. I knew even then that I was watching something of extreme beauty and, in the intervening 45 years, I feel I have yet to experience anything more beautiful. Nothing since has triggered complete awe for the whole of creation in the same way.

———•·•·•———

So we moved away in 1964. The years tumbled by. I learnt to fish in muddy, slow-moving waters. Learnt to appreciate the majesty of the chub and his daring comrade the dace, the colour of a rudd's fins, the humour of a perch and the cold cunning of the pike. But fishing and the call of the river slipped down the ranking compared to the electric guitar, the open road and all that messy relationship stuff that happens. My rods gathered dust, my keep net hung dry for decades and the worms lived peaceful lives. But as those years went by and the decades took their toll, I could not stop that longing for the Penkiln Burn growing and growing inside my head.

The first return to the Burn was in the summer of 1972, when I dragged my teenage sweetheart away on a camping holiday to Galloway. I took her to the boulder; I was probably still too young at 19 to weep for my lost innocence.

Through the 1980s the myth of the place grew in me. It was becoming my Garden of Eden, my paradise lost or maybe if I'm lucky, my heaven yet to be reached. It became a place to be visited in moments (or months) of crisis.

As you edge deeper into life, mortality beckons. Question like, should I be buried or burnt are framed in the mind. Well, the answer to that one was decided by the thought that, if I was cremated, at least I could have my ashes scattered into the Penkiln Burn from the boulder. While on another camping holiday, two of my older children were taken by me to the spot and shown where I would like my ashes flung. They were probably too young at the time to take it in or care about what I was saying; their here-and-now lives being vastly more important than whatever their father was going on about.

At some vague time in the late 1980s or early 1990s, the notion started to evolve that, if I was ever to have my own book-publishing imprint, I would call it The Penkiln Burn. That notion became a reality by the end of the 1990s. But this Penkiln Burn was not just content with book publishing; it embraced everything I have ever done or am likely to do in my creative and working life.

On its success as a strategy to regain paradise, the jury is still out. As a branding exercise, calling your company The Penkiln Burn is a total failure. It is too long, nobody can pronounce it and is meaningless to anybody but me.

What about the coiled adder, the flash of kingfisher, the leaping salmon, the white hart, the brutally-slaughtered eel, the silently ringing bluebells and the brown trout forever caught in the sunlight? How much has my own myth-making tarnished my memories? Does it matter? Did Jesus actually turn the water into wine? All those creatures did exist. I am certain of that. The bluebells will rise and blossom again next spring, like they did last. But was the eel caught on my first time? Was it from the Queen Mary's bridge that I watched the salmon try and try and try again like Robert the Bruce's spider? Is there a Chinese bridge over the Penkiln Burn or is that my childhood love of Rupert Bear annuals seeping into my 'real' memories? As for the brown trout caught in the dancing sunlight, over the coming years I spent many an hour sitting on branches that overhung streams, brooks, burns and rivers, to watch the fish living their lives below. Have those memories just merged to make one shimmering and unfocused whole? Snakes, salmon, kingfishers, white harts all feature heavily in the myths of many peoples and traditions. Over the years, have I allowed my memory to stay focused on the above, giving them prime place, because I've subsequently learnt of their importance in other more validated myths than my own?

Sitting here on this boulder in the here and now as the grey morning brightens, I can feel the first pangs of morning hunger. After I have finished these last few paragraphs, I will head off in search of breakfast, before leaving to get the ferry from Stranraer to Belfast, and then to Derry before nightfall.

Looking around, I'm amazed at the variety of trees and bushes there are. I count them: rowan, silver birch, wild cherry, hawthorn, alder, hazel, ash, sycamore, holly, scots pine, oak, beech and rhododendron. Us blokes love a list. Then there are the ferns, the ivy and the brambles still with blackberries to be picked. I listen to the birds: pheasant, jackdaw, wren, robin, crow, blue tit, great tit, nothing too out of the ordinary but welcome all the same. I stare into the water – on the bottom among the pebbles and the stones, I can see a small parr darting about, no doubt a distant relative to the ones I caught from this spot 45 years (and counting) ago.

My hands stroke the top of the boulder. I notice someone has carved a heart with an arrow through it. There are two names but the lichen has grown over them and, however I try, I am unable to read the letters. I never noticed this when I was a lad. Do I share my glimpse of heaven with others that have come after me?

There is another whole story that I thought I would tell while sitting here. One that involves me finding a human skull on these banks and Robert the Bruce, but time is running on.

But before I leave, one last thing, some years ago I set up a site – mydeath.net – this is a web site where you can, in as many or few words as you wish, set out for all the world to read, how you want your funeral and what you want done with your body. I was inspired to set it up because I'd been to a couple of comrades funeral's that didn't live up to what I think they would have hoped for. On setting up mydeath.net, I always assumed I'd put up my own entry on it. Somehow I never got around to it, maybe now is the time. But breakfast first.

Bill Drummond was one half of the pop group KLF and famously burnt a million pounds. He is the author of 45 *and* 17.

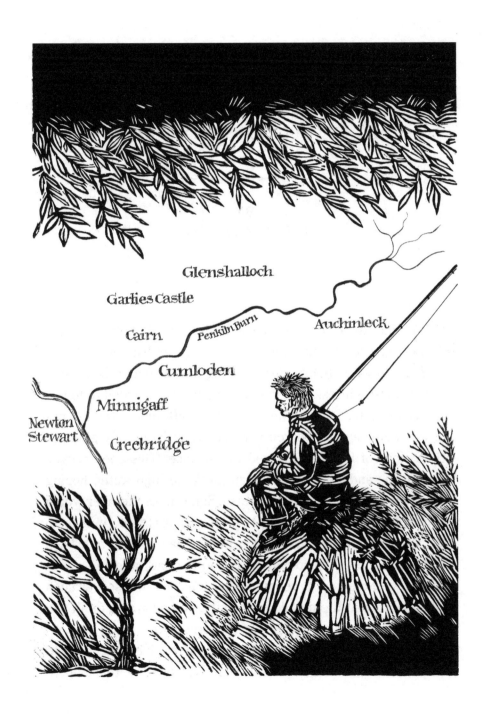

Glenshalloch

Garlies Castle

Cairn   Penkiln Burn   Auchinleck

Cumloden

Minnigaff

Newton
Stewart

Creebridge

ACRYLIC AFTERNOONS

BY
JARVIS COCKER

The River Porter is visible at the side of Sheffield's train station. It runs through a concrete channel for about 20 yards before disappearing into a tunnel. Sometime in the mid-Eighties, myself and some friends decided to follow the river as far as possible. At first we attempted to stay out of the water as it appeared very polluted: large, oily globules the colour of ketchup covered the surface. This soon proved impossible and we waded though the knee-high water, hoping not to contract an industrial disease. Sometimes the river would run through a dirty brickwork tunnel for a quarter of a mile or so (which was quite scary, seeing as no-one had thought to bring a torch) and then it would emerge in another part of town – never where we expected. It seemed quite amazing to discover such an adventure in the middle of the city we had grown up in and which we all professed to be totally bored with.

I suppose this discovery must have given me a taste for river exploration, as next year I attempted to navigate

Sheffield's largest river, the Don. This flows mostly above ground, though it has many weirs along its length which make it slightly treacherous. I had purchased an inflatable dinghy from a jumble sale, so this trip had an altogether more official air about it. I was living in an old warehouse in an area known as the Wicker and the river flowed directly past. One summer afternoon, myself and a friend blew up the boat and set off on our adventure. And an adventure it was.

After a couple of close calls with weirs, we began to relax and enjoy our journey. We were traveling downstream so we didn't have to do much rowing, and somehow drifting past familiar landmarks from a different angle seemed to fill us with excitement. At one point we were enveloped in steam from a neighbouring factory and I began to have a feeling that maybe we were involved in some kind of South Yorkshire re-creation of *Apocalypse Now* – it was like the river had decided where it wanted to take us.

The journey continued and the landscape began to get less familiar. We saw some gypsy kids using a bread crate to kind-of 'sledge' down a weir. Some parts of the river were almost stagnant, with large, evil-smelling bubbles rising to the surface. We had seen quite a few fishermen along the route, but, as we approached Rotherham, we came across a man attempting to shoot fish with an air rifle – whilst uttering the immortal words 'Stitch that, you bastards!' Maybe this scared us slightly; anyway, soon after that we deflated the boat and got the bus home but not before marking our end point with a pile of stones and vowing to finish our journey at a later date. Of course, this never happened and the boat got punctured in a later incident

– but that day has stuck in my mind as one of the happiest of my life, so I couldn't entirely rule out going back to continue it one day – even this long after the event.

WICKERMAN

Just behind the station, before you reach the traffic island,
a river runs thru' a concrete channel.
I took you there once; I think it was after the Leadmill.
The water was dirty & smelt of industrialisation
Little mesters coughing their lungs up & globules
the colour of tomato ketchup.
But it flows. Yeah, it flows.
Underneath the city thru' dirty brickwork conduits
Connecting white witches on the Moor with
pre-Raphaelites down in Broomhall.
Beneath the old Trebor factory that burnt
down in the early seventies.
Leaving an antiquated sweet-shop smell
& caverns of nougat & caramel.
Nougat. Yeah, nougat & caramel.
And the river flows on.
Yeah, the river flows on beneath pudgy fifteen-year olds
addicted to coffee whitener
Courting couples naked on Northern Upholstery & pensioners
gathering dust like bowls of plastic tulips
And it finally comes above ground again at Forge Dam:
the place where we first met.

I went there again for old time's sake
Hoping to find the child's toy horse ride that
played such a ridiculously tragic tune.
It was still there – but none of the kids seemed
interested in riding on it.
And the cafe was still there too
The same press-in plastic letters on the price list
& scuffed formica-top tables.
I sat as close as possible to the seat where
I'd met you that autumn afternoon.
And then, after what seemed like hours of thinking about it
I finally took your face in my hands
& I kissed you for the first time
And a feeling like electricity flowed thru' my whole body.
And I immediately knew that I'd entered
a completely different world.
And all the time, in the background, the sound of that
ridiculously heartbreaking child's ride outside.

At the other end of town the river flows underneath
an old railway viaduct
I went there with you once – except you were somebody else –
And we gazed down at the sludgy brown
surface of the water together.
Then a passer-by told us that it used to be a local custom
to jump off the viaduct into the river
When coming home from the pub on a Saturday night.
But that this custom had died out when someone jumped
Landed too near to the riverbank
Had sunk in the mud there & drowned
before anyone could reach them.
I don't know if he'd just made the whole story up, but
there's no way you'd get me to jump off that bridge.
No chance. Never in a million years.

Yeah, a river flows underneath this city
I'd like to go there with you now my pretty & follow it on
for miles & miles, below other people's ordinary lives.
Occasionally catching a glimpse of the moon,
thru' man-hole covers along the route.
Yeah, it's dark sometimes but if you hold my hand,
I think I know the way.
Oh, this is as far as we got last time
But if we go just another mile we will surface surrounded
by grass & trees & the fly-over that takes the cars to cities.
Buds that explode at the slightest touch,
nettles that sting – but not too much.
I've never been past this point, what lies ahead

I really could not say.
I used to live just by the river, in a dis-used factory
just off the Wicker
The river flowed by day after day
"One day" I thought, "One day I will follow it"
but that day never came
I moved away & lost track but tonight I am thinking
about making my way back.
I may find you there & float on wherever the river may take me.
Wherever the river may take me.
Wherever the river may take us.
Wherever it wants us to go.
Wherever it wants us to go.

Jarvis Cocker has been making music for two-thirds of his life. Two dozen of these years (1978–2002) were spent in Pulp, a group with whom he enjoyed both commercial and critical success. At the end of 2006 he released Jarvis, *his first solo album, which was greeted with open-armed goodwill. His second is due this year.*

BITTER LIMEN

THE EAST SUSSEX ROTHER

———— ◆ ————

BY
DEXTER PETLEY

Your first river is like your first anything; it haunts all life's other rivers. You hanker for its simplicity, that childhood-scale vision of rivers when even a ditch had greatness. Every stretch of moving water held a full day's entertainment, enough fish to exhaust the meagre rations of your tackle box, enough mystery to invent a thousand and one lies. A river to a boy is a storybook for the rainiest of days. It's the only poem you need know by heart; the only homework of any point. And rivers come with parental clamour; bad company for a schoolboy. A pike-filled paedophile, Greek Tragedy practical. That boyhood naivety magnifies the river. Myth and mystery by nature, nightmares or insomnia, rivers carry an essence of what comes your way in the adult world. Rivers will be everywhere. You won't have to scrounge the bus fare or beg lifts from miserable old baggots in pokey black cars not assembled for boys or fishing rods. No need to lie about your muddy bootful or your fanciful pike. But these grown-up rivers are easy-come. No need to imagine. They trickle disappointment under the bridge. The mystery is abstracted, the nightmares shallow. Concrete knowledge, experience; your fingers no longer tremble as you bait a hook. Only in old age will you come back to mine that lost awe on your deathbed, on your river of death.

I was lucky with my parent river, though a boy's river is probably an aunt pensioned off on hard times, or a unisex missionary returning from Heathenville to teach Sunday School. Such rivers make the rules, but you only need stick to the ones that keep you alive. With the river at your feet, you didn't need people at all.

The East Sussex Rother was three miles south of village life, but three miles measured by a twelve-year-old consciousness, which itself is only three yards wide. So you did the leap of consciousness on the No. 84 bus to Hastings, a wooden-floored, smoking rattler, those snub-nosed Leylands you mounted like the first step up a lighthouse. You paid your explorer's fee, and Mr Stamp in his peeked Maidstone & District cap wound off a pink ticket from a machine like a football rattle, his conk twitching at last weekend's pong coming from your keepnet. You propped your Empire Made boat rod or mixed-cane plonker on the tartan seats and got excited about eels and bream slime and the wedge of apple pie wrapped in greaseproof paper inside your gas-mask haversack. You stepped off at Bodiam (Bodge'm to those in the know) outside the village shop and walked down to the sandstone bridge where the Romans crossed. Leaning over the parapet, you squinted into a river the colour of your old man's tea and imagined the chub swaying pewter-backed in the bright green slip-weed. And there you had it; the river was a force of hope worth more than your life would ever be worth; it could change your luck, things come and go, it has an ongoing life that stagnant, village iron ponds and their stunted, lipless rudd didn't have. If you caught a fish, it was like catching a falling star, or stopping a whole minute from passing in its tracks. And maybe you had an inkling, as you were there to outwit the unseen, that life wasn't just a broken reed floating by at the whim of tides. You'd better get on and make it all count, this stolen minute, this day, this river, before it all flows away into the sea.

I must have made that river count because it marked my growing-up as no pencil scratch on the kitchen wall ever could. It made an angler of the boy, a man of the teenager. It gave me my first flood, pike, fight, fag, in-bra fumble and first ever crime. My only ever dab, first eel, first celebrity, first "bigg'n" and last ever tuppeny bus ride. My first nightmare too. What more can you ask of a river?

It began one Sunday afternoon when we stood in the lane below Burgh Hill at Etchingham, gazing over the fields with plastic telescopes and Brownie cameras. The black family saloons, perfumed and Turtle Waxed, all parked in a row along the hedge. I was five and I'd been brought to meet the Rother for the first time. She was in full matinee dress and not taking kindly to us gladraggers. A river in flood, the history of its life, the sick aunt if you like, in extravagant flow and not about to suffer fools gladly. Troublesome, the bane of English Kings in fact. In those days you went to visit the Rother Valley floods of a Sunday afternoon to feast your eyes on the drowned, but this was the great flood of 1960. The year when enough was enough and things had to change. The water came all the way up to the five-bar gate. Oilskin tourists waded across or swooped down on bikes into brown water deeper than welly tops. I clung to the landlubbers. There were no foetal flashbacks to explain the panic in my hand-knit wollen soul. My scanty knowledge of horror swelled in that flood and the nightmares began; I stood alone in those fields of flat calm sick and semolina on all sides. One move and I drown in this migrating sea, no warning line of bankside trees spell out the river within. For thirty years, 1 had that Rother dream. Like a memory of the dead, the river is only sleeping, its wrinkles are smoothed in a spreading repose. It only stopped when I learned to swim.

"You'd better get on and make it all count, this stolen minute, this day, this river, before it all flows away into the sea"

Aged six, I knew Dad was no fisherman before I'd seen him fish. The way he toe-punted the football and called it footer. The way he'd no relatives and Mum had dozens. He fetched the fishing rod from the village shop in a Saturday swelter, the kerbs like breakers shifting in the heat. We were going to fish that Rother now it was in a better mood.

The coming of the fishing rod into a family like ours was one of those moments like a black death flea leaping the threshold, or a book on the sofa instead of the TV Times. An upset followed by doom. Dad's winter blakeys silent on the melting pavement. The way he carried the rod, uncertain, hand too far along it, walking-sticky, a thrashing-switch from a hedgerow. Nothing to get sentimental about. And he was no fisherman most of all because he'd had to go buy the rod from a sweet-shop just to fish with Uncle Bruce sometime. "Nothin' fancy Mac", Bruce'd said, "in case fishing doesn't set your jelly."

Ma Pullen who kept the sweetshop only had the one rod in stock. A boy's rod she called it. The old man called it a Hong Kong lawyer. With curtain rings whipped on, it did for quelling riots or yanking pike for pot and cat out of meres. And we were going roach fishing at Etchingham with Uncle Bruce.

He wasn't really my uncle. False uncles came and went. Once gone they were never heard of again. They were all called Bruce, these ex-shipmates, fellow Kiwi demobs. But in Bruce's hands, our boy's poker dignified itself in sunlight with its red silk whippings, mottled tonkin smooth under yacht varnish, bottle-green wood handle, brass fittings and a rubber button. He tackled it up for us beside that same five-bar gate, only this time I could see no petticoats of water anywhere.

"There y'are Mac, abracadabra."

"Get on with it," Mac said. "Haven't got all day." And he wandered off, bored already.

Bruce called him back, said he'd show us how to walk to a river. Dad punted a shredded object towards us through the grit.

"Someone's gorn an lost their fanbelt."

As the men fished, I looked down the windswept Rother

from a high bank. Dad standing up, rod skyward, trying to grab his hook as the breeze sent it whiplashing out of reach. Bruce downstream, stock-still on his wicker basket, orange quill riding the current. Black-fingers Mac couldn't get his bread to stay on the hook so he pinched a sultana out of our scones and nicked it on the point. It fooled a one-minute roach, a silver object spinning in the wind.

Our last trip with Bruce was in November, where the Hexden Channel joins the Rother at Newenden. Cold yellow grass, first thick winter muds, the hewing wind across our bobble hats. Dad tried two half-hearted casts then handed me the rod with no instruction. I'd never been allowed to touch it. A wind knot in the line kinked into a bird's nest. The rod blew out my clutches before the float came out the sky.

"Nay goot," he said. "Pack it in."

Bruce stayed catching livebait for jack pike. Back home our gear was dumped under the bench behind the dog's box in the shed. The Rother was "that blinkin river" again, best forgotton unless it came under the front door.

———•◦•———

The Romans named the river Limen, latin for threshold or entrance. It became known as the Rother, or the East Sussex Rother, in the 13th century. Rising in the High Weald at Rotherfield, it runs 35 miles east-west to its mouth at Rye Harbour on the Channel coast, through the villages of Etchingham, Robertsbrige, Salehurst, Udiam, Bodiam, Newenden, Appledore. Almost treeless its entire length, the great forest of Anderida long gone to the Wealden iron industry, from Bronze Age hoes to the last canon cast in 1813, (canons so heavy they took five years to deliver by cart to the gunners of the Napoleonic Wars). A river once so wide you couldn't be heard shouting across it to your fellow Saxon, it is these days reduced to a torpid, treeless, brown silt-filled ditch you can all but leap where once the Roman pig-iron barges moored and the Flemish timber traders turned their medieval ships for home.

———————————

The Limen is an index of English history. It stood at the threshold of passage or invasion for anyone crossing the channel from mainland Europe. The Beaker Folk three millenia before Christ, the iron workers of Northern Europe a thousand years before the Romans. They settled in the forest along the riverbank to work the iron ore deposits in the clay and sandstone layers of the Hastings Beds. Trees fell to fire bloomery and forge, land was cleared and cultivated. Southern wealth owes much to the Limen. The Romans first sailed up the Limen soon after the invasion of 43 AD and assimilated the Wealden iron industry into the Imperial system. The Limen was tidal as far as Bodiam, the Roman's most inland port. They constructed timber wharves and built roads through the forest. The iron went downriver in flat-bottomed barges, along the coast to Dover where it crossed on its way to Rome. In a post-colonial age, it is easy to forget that the Roman Empire was burnished thanks to Wealden ore, and that Medieval Flanders was built of Wealden oak.

As the Empire crumbled, Saxon pirates sneaked up the Limen undercover, gathering intelligence for a full invasion. They inherited what was in effect a nationalised Britain with functioning systems, squandering civilization in what was probably the world's first mass privatization. Roman roads fell into ruin as the Saxons blundered along impassable muddy tracks.

In 892 Haesten's fleet of two hundred and fifty black Viking longships came up the Limen to Appledore and reduced it to ashes. Danelaw in Britain came to an end when Harold's main army, marching to Senlac in 1066 to engage with William of Normandy, probably crossed the Rother at some point, fording at below-flood levels, with the stragglers crossing by ferry at Bodiam. Their pay probably did come downriver, but the paymaster buried it beside the River Brede which runs into Rye Bay alongside the Rother.

<hr />

The Rother Valley is below sea-level and, for a thousand years, the fragile shingle coastal defences ensured that every Roman governor, Saxon king, Viking bloodaxe, Norman conqueror and British monarch made the Limen their business. Britain's most unruly subject, untrustworthy gateway to invasion, vital exit of wealth, this river was silting up so rapidly that navigation would become impossible and the iron industry would be choked lifeless. Its geological evolution makes the struggle against flooding and silting heroic but doomed. When the ice age glaciers melted eight thousand years ago, the sea level rose a hundred metres and the land bridge between France and the Strait of Dover was submerged in what geologists term a "catastrophic breakdown" giving rise to the mass of shingle deposits in the English Channel. The instability of this shingle kept the Limen in a state of constant flux.

The Limen is the result of ongoing catastrophe, always at the mercy of storms. The 1200s was a century of huge storms along the Rye/Pevensey/Winchelsea coastline, the effects of which are felt to this day. The storm of 1250 put the Limen out of all control for 800 years. Eye-witness accounts exist, but Hollinshed captures the freak nature of it in his *Chronicles*:

"On the first day of October, 1250, the moon upon her change, appearing exceeding red and swelled, began to show tokens of the great tempest of wind that followed, which was so huge and mighty both by land and sea, that the like had not been known, by men then alive. The sea, forced contrary to his natural course, flowed twice without ebbing, yielding such a roaring, that the same was heard (with great wonder) a far distance from the shore. Moreover, the same sea appeared in the dark on the night to burn as it had been on fire, and the waves to strive and fight together after a marvellous sort, so that the

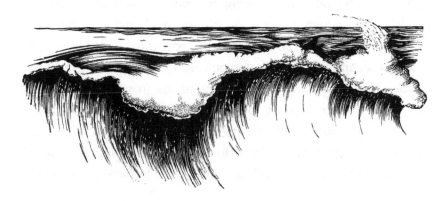

mariners could not devise how to save their ships where they lay at anchor. At Winchelsey, besides other hurt that was done in bridges, mills and banks, there were 300 houses and some churches drowned with the rising of the water."

The river simply moved its mouth to the weakest points in the shingle. The Romans had fought the same battle. Wharves silted up overnight, whole ports were abandoned. By 1562, the River Rother was changing for the worst. 2400 hectares was flooded every winter from Reading to Robertsbridge. Between Reading and Rye, the river had narrowed from 60-90 metres to 5-7 metres according to fishermen. All the safe harbouring of the Camber had gone. Much of the Rother valley was "summer lands" or permanently "drowned lands".

Even in my own childhood, the Rother was tidal as far as Newenden. Everything was tried to keep the sea out of the river. Dykes and sluices, locks, canals, drainage, sea defences. All swept away at the next storm. The Rother was even diverted through marshland to the north of the Rye into the Tillingham at enormous cost and labour. That failed after one winter, in 1610. Until the 1950s, parts of the Rother levels were wholly unproductive and known as "duck country".

———◦—

My first encounter with that river marked her flood of tears. In November 1960, the entire Rother levels in flood, all patience was lost and it was decided to put the sick aunt into a home. The Rother Area Drainage Improvement Scheme was formed and deadly engines were took to water; dredgers. The entire river was dredged, ditched and denuded, leveed and shored up to above flood level. In 1969 a 7.14 cumec pumping station near Union Sluice drained Walland Marsh into the tidal Rother. Then 20 Archimedian screw electric pumping stations were installed to drain the marsh areas and deal with the upland water. 245 hectares were set aside as the "wet level" for flood storage where water is penned in the valley below Bodiam and discharged through sluices when conditions permit. It is still dredged annually, the excavated alluvium piled on the levees to stabalize the flood banks. A new sluice and loch system a mile north of Rye means the Rother is only tidal as far as Scots Float. It still floods, one step behind global warming. December 1999, October 2000, right up to the five-bar gate. A Rother more restrained maybe, but there is no getting shot of the bane of Kings without knock-on catastrophe. From 1975 to 1997, Rother Valley agriculture also drained away. Cattle declined by 60%, pigs almost vanished, the agricultural workforce reduced by 23%, permanent grassland declined by 10% and set-aside was about 10% of tilled land. Urbanisation is now viable. The new Folkstone to Honiton motorway plan in the neighbouring Brede valley; green field development, expanding Gatwick and Manston airports. Roads need traffic, traffic begets connecting road improvement. The houses will need water. Anglers claim the fishing has suffered from lack of flow too. Thriving carp bear witness to that. In my childhood, there were no carp in the upper reaches. Now thirty-pounders are common below Newenden. My one dab is no more.

And what of my one Bodiam dab? The rod passed into my hands when I was nine. By age eleven, I was on the bus to

Bodiam or Newenden most Saturdays. My childhood Rother, for all its last days of ebb and flow, was the sedated, half-stagnant stream on her deathbed, de-silted like an invalid on an iron lung, the colonic irrigation of a once-fierce bowel. I fished those new high banks, those Newenden bolsters. I slid down the grass of widow's perm on my arse to do hand-to-hand combat with eels, the only foreign invaders I knew. But Bodiam became the centrepiece of my freshwater dramas. I knew of nowhere more exciting. A river with a castle.

They filmed a 1967 Hammer version of Robin Hood there, with vapour trails visible above the battlements. They shot one valve-blowing TV episode in the 1950s, the one with Richard Greene. He drove a three-wheeler and lived in Sandhurst, the village on the hill above Bodiam, built to survey the flood plains in case the French Invaders came to cut down

> "Everything was tried to keep the sea out of the river. Dykes and sluices, locks, canals, drainage, sea defences. All swept away at the next storm"

their church bells and behead the rustics as they had at Rye. Bodiam Castle was the dramatic part of our family fortune too. It was built in 1385 by Sir Edward Dalyngrigge, possibly for show as there are doubts about its capability as fortress. Lord Curzon, last Viceroy of India, bought the castle and restored it for the nation. Itinerants after the war, my folks strapped their laquered trunks to the Morris tourer roof and sought fortune in Bodiam. Hop-picking for Guinness, mole trapping, hanging crows for nobs with grass tennis courts. One of them was Lord Curzon's widow, the Marchioness, living above the Castle at the Castle Dower House. My parents went into service for her and were sacked, as drudges were, turned out on the spot after the drunken housekeeper sabotaged the boilers, blew the heating pipes to smithereens, my old man getting the blame as conspired. Lady Curzon discovered the truth sometime later and wrote a letter inviting them back. In Robin Hood fashion, the old man tore the letter into shreds. The Castle was bequethed to the National Trust, the Marchioness sold up and went back to her seat in Keddleston.

I fished below the castle, the Curzon scandal giving me a scanty root and that edge over futility. In sleepy villages like Bodiam you can dream, though I never gave its history a proper thought. I was of its present; the Castle Inn, the General Stores & Post Office, summer tea garden at rear. The Tunbridge Wells/Hastings bus stopping hourly. The Rother flow slowing at each new turn of Archimedes' screw. Bodiam Station closing when Beeching axed the Branch Line from Robertsbridge. Guiness selling up the hop farms. Old Holborn using a gatepost behind the castle for a magazine ad. The summer visitors passing by with picnic rugs on sunny days, their long struggle uphill through sheepshit and thistles, just to put their faces into arrow slits. The castle keeper with his 6d tickets; he knew we sneaked in and up the towers while he was out in his old green punt. Our sweaty palms, the dizzy views down river, or down-moat, into the gaps between the lily pads to see what snouted there. My sister's boyfriend came seventh in the annual Bodiam Hill Climb. My godfather dug up this Heinkel

III in a field, pilot bones still in their flying jacket. I catch my dab, my first pike, and my first fish on a fly.

Rother days, no misery memoir there. Days which spanned whole length of river, from Rotherfield to Rye. The old man became an insurance broker in Rye when I was 12. It beat exterminating pests. Emlyn, Hughes & Petley. The Petley brokerage opened a shabby brown linoleum office above an apothocary shop just off the High St. To keep the nipper out of mischief, I was sent downstream to this brokerage, on Quink days, only to roam Rye's cobbled streets unseen by the old man's Fire & Theft eye. First crime; the nicking of floats and hooks from Woolworths. First fight; beside the river itself, watching the fishing boats come in, some Rye-boy pinned me to the dirt over a girl. First eel from the estuary on a compost worm. First and only celebrity too.

We stood beside a rough plank shed, that Rother silt behind us at low tide. Another Bruce was there, fellow Kiwi, saying to my old man: "that kid of yours know how to keep schtum? This is top secret, Mac." Padlocks and chains undone, there's a car under a green tarpaulin, gently unpeeled for titilation. "There she is Mac. Can you do it?" The man was Bruce McLaren. It was 1964. We were looking at the first ever McLaren Elva in a garden shed stinking of creosote beside the Rother. "You want that fully comp?" my old man said. First bathos too? My old man tried to sell him life insurance. He'd gone back to motor factoring when Bruce was killed at Goodwood in 1972 testing his M8D.

⸻ ◆ ⸻

It was a still, summer afternoon in Bodiam. I'd eaten my cream crackers and cheese, swing-tipped up a breamish looking thing and some pokey roach which christened the new keep-net from Mum's catalogue. They'd hardly been in the net ten minutes when a ruction in the water left a rip in the mesh and a wounded roach. I had a jointed plug in my tacklebox, home-made, off-cuts from the village coffin-makers. The plug was a green wooden diver with silver trebles and a minimum of rust. The first pike I'd ever hooked in my life clamped it second cast not a yard from the keepnet, into which it was duly imprisoned. I was 13, the golden age of lies. It was a twenty minute bus-ride from my mates down All Saints Road. The jack weighed in at 4lbs 4ozs. They wouldn't believe me.

I was a thorough, organized angler at 13 and always had a small towel in the gas-mask bag. The pike's long journey home began, wrapped in the wetted towel, curled like a banana into the gas-mask bag, jaws poking out one side, tail the other. Pike travelled free on the number 84 in those days, and, even though the bus was three-quarters empty, an old lady of the Sunday School kind just had to sit beside me and ask what all the twitching and dripping on my lap was. William Brown would've said he was taking the family pike to the dentist for his sister Ethel. I was too proud and fearful to draw attention to it, but when the jaws grinned at Miss Winterbottom's smelling salts, she got off the bus in Sandhurst to have a reviving cup of tea with her sister at the vicarage. By then the pike had been out of the water for over 45 minutes.

Mr Weller was driving the bus that day. He wound the seat up to the top and still had to sit on a cushion. If his feet weren't size 12 kippers he couldn't have worked the pedals. Up the bus sheds they called him Squadron Leader for creaming his hair flat and waxing up his pencil 'tache. He went in Wally Nun's the Barber's every Friday for: "me tube o'usual, Wally please." This nerve-wracking driver of my pike stopped in laybys to count the change, stopped at Ted's to fetch a cabbage, picked up the Sunday joint from old Farnworth, checked his watch every hundred yards and finally swung into the bus station at the regulation 3 minutes to. The pike's driest hour was up, so I legged it down the road yelling to any one in earshot: "poike, oi god a poike". The yell went round. Petley's godda poike! Seven of us made it to the pond at the bottom of the road, and even I couldn't believe it when the poike shot off like an arrow fired through the castle slit. There goes Bruce, I said, not knowing why.

It's 1975 already. The Rother is about to lose its innocence. At nineteen you take the easy road to self-deception, there's no hard one in any case, just a smooth freeway. It was probably the desire to get out of Hawkhurst on a Wednesday afternoon, away from the parents all worried sick, the blinds drawn on closed shops, the British Legionaires and their dewdrops taking flowers up the cemetary. In this good year, you could still buy cane rods in tackle shops for a fiver, but adolescence had abruptly tumbled into a heap of brown terylene flares which wouldn't get off the bed. Childhood wouldn't quite give me up. There was always the river at Bodiam, so off we went, me, the new wicker basket and the ugly blue roach rod with a handle wrapped in ceiling tile cork, thick as a pole-vault, a swing-tip screwed in the top eye like a broken chicken leg thirteen floppy feet away. Team Leo Sayer. I decided to leger without conviction, preoccupied with my old man's next move to make me get a job in that workaday world of his now I'd left college, my spots had cleared up and I'd become a layabout treating the house like a hotel. Jobs meant the petrol pumps, the lawn mower showroom, the woodyard... It was February, and by sheer fluke I pounded the breadflake on a shoal of hungry, unscrupulous, unemployed chub. Fourteen over two pounds, that kiddies keepnet bulging like a Christmas stocking. And it was a gift. It changed things. I'd become an angler when least expecting to. I went home and got a job, in the woodyard, and fished for chub at Bodiam on the days I rang in sick.

Dexter Petley is a contributor to Waterlog *magazine and the author of four novels.*

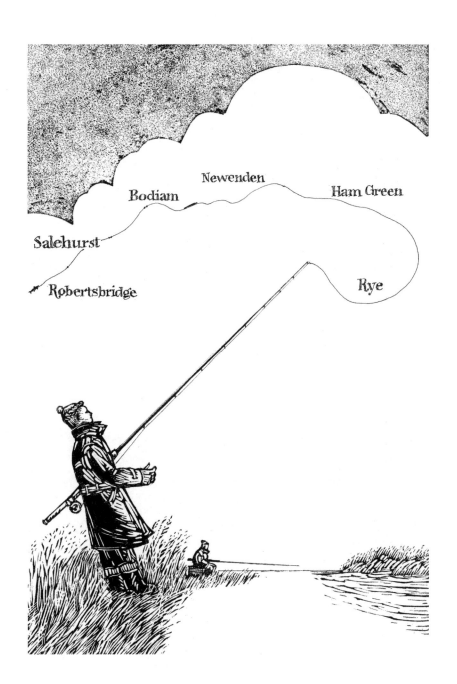

Salehurst

Bodiam

Newenden

Ham Green

Robertsbridge

Rye

SEVERN
BY
SEVERN

———◆———

BY
KARL HYDE

One day, my Dad came home from the factory and announced, "we've got a canoe!" Stuff like that never happened in our house – this was an amazing thing. The kind of thing that could kick off a life of "fabulous possibilities".

Dad and his mate (Dad had lots of mates he did unexpected things with) acquired a section of the riverbank (this is still a family mystery) on the east side of the river at the back of the old chocolate factory that used to be the old pop bottle factory. Clearing that riverbank was magic. I felt really important like we'd been given special privileges that nobody else had: that never happened to us. It was summer, and the smell of the nettles and weeds as we hacked them down and the aroma of the earth as Dad exposed it with his spade to cut steps down to the water's edge was rich and heady. We uncovered loads of old pop bottles – the kind without stoppers that had little glass balls in their necks and dad showed me how to smash them so I could use the balls for marbles.

Owning a kingdom, even a tiny thing like some dirt steps, was a radically new experience to a family more concerned with where the rent money was coming from. To make sure everyone in town knew this was our plot so "keep off", Dad, in an unprecedented display of wealth, bought a roll of barbed wire and nailed it to a barricade of bits left over from making 'The Raft'.

The Raft? Oh my god – we had a raft! Dad acquired six large steel drums from the factory, the kind that contain toxic chemicals, and lashed them to the underside of a floating stage of virgin pine. He called this, "our landing stage" and tethered it to wooden pegs up against our dirt steps.

The canoe arrived at the river on a borrowed roof rack (the one that carried our suitcases on holiday to Porthmadog). Everything smelled great – the canvas canoe, the gleaming white wood raft, the sweet-stinking weeds that grew along the bank and my new friend the river. I had never been so close to it. Dad held the canoe tight to the side of the raft as I climbed in between him and Mom and got that first rush of floating out to midstream. We were airborne. The impossible was suddenly graspable. My family was cutting loose and floating free from the bottom of the pond.

Dad took us under the bridge and it felt like we were sliding under the belly of a giant stone lizard. I looked down into the water, following the pillars until they disappeared fearing the bridge might raise them out from the mud and squash us. I felt the depth of the water beneath us and it gave me goose bumps. We were explorers with privileged access to places ordinary people couldn't go.

As we floated beneath Thomas Telford's river crossing, I watched the whirlpools kicked up by the rivers flow between its pillars and the fears returned. Everybody told us: don't go near the whirlpools. They will drag you under and, days later, your body will be found downstream. There was legend that someone had fallen in and been sucked down into an underwater cave where he waited for weeks to be rescued but when they eventually sent divers down there was no cave and the body was never recovered. Still – the legend of the hidden underwater cave and the possibilities of worlds concealed within the mundanity of our own lit a fuse.

Bodies being lost and bodies being recovered from the river were stories we grew up with and now, as we floated serenely downstream, I began to see the town from an entirely new perspective. It looked a lot smaller and I felt for the first time that it would inevitably become too small for me. This was the 1960s, time of hope and regeneration – the land of the future-now. We didn't care much for the past, we pulled it down and covered it with hardboard, but a lot of things about the lunatic old architecture of this town started to make more sense when you saw it from the river. I felt connected to a bloodline that went back through the generations of all of us who'd lived and died in this backwater. It was a feeling that would come and go and eventually stay gone until I was long gone and far away but longing for something simpler and familiar.

I realised for the first time that we lived in a valley and not on a series of flat plains – some that went down and some that went up. I heard the sounds of the town echoing between the riverbanks, the screams and shouts of children playing, of heavy lorries changing gear as they squeezed their pig iron between listed buildings (yet to be listed), of doors slamming and couples quarrelling, of mothers yelling 'time for tea!' and the 'thump' in your chest as steam trains pumped and hauled coal from the pit along the valley rim. I heard steam whistles howling and the midday rumble of the rocket engines tested somewhere hidden underground deep in the forest and transistor radios in 1960's sound-clash and I was floating through a Ray Bradbury novel. This was my *October Country*, my *Dandelion Wine* and I wanted to never have to step back on land again.

It was also the first time I saw 'the pigs' – the ones that had fallen in upstream and drowned. They would float down and get caught in the weeds where they'd blow up like skin balloons. Later, when I was older, I learned you could bounce rocks off their bellies and burst them with pointed sticks and that when you did, it really stank.

The day my dad launched our canoe was a magical day. A day of imaginations that stretched beyond the confines of the valley to rivers in other parts of the world where stuff you only saw on telly happened.

As we headed back to the landing stage I even got to have a go at paddling myself. Dirty river water ran down my arms soaking my vest till my armpits stung but I didn't care. Dad held the canoe tight against the raft as we crawled out and wobbled, getting our land legs back. I looked around at the water and smiled.

Everything was going to be amazing now.

That winter, the landing stage disappeared in the floods and the canoe ended up on top of the carport where it rotted under a tarpaulin. The barbed wire rusted and the barricade became overgrown with weeds, but I saw it every time I crossed the bridge on the way to school and it reminded me of that day. A day of the endlessly possible and how I, for the first time, had peered over the wall.

Karl Hyde is one half of Underworld & creative partner in Tomato. He exhibits as a painter with the Underworld off-shoot 'Artjam' & has published two books: Mmm Skyscraper I Love You *&* In the Belly of St.Paul*. When not touring he lives in Essex & writes worldwide...*

RIVER
AT THE
END OF
AUTUMN

BY
CHRIS YATES

There was a mist in the valley when I first looked out this morning, though I could not see anything until I'd wiped the misted glass. Then I opened the window and immediately caught the metallic, slightly sooty smell of frost – the first frost of autumn. Everything in the garden was grey with it, and beyond, in the fields, everything was grey with mist, except along the ridge of the hill where there was a blush of amber telling me that, behind the house, the sun was rising.

Had I not have already organized with a friend to spend this day fishing on my favourite river, I would have said it was more suitable for an ambitiously long walk through the local woods. We had planned to fish for perch, but though they are hardy all-weather fish, even perch can become a bit sullen at the first sharp foretaste of the coming winter. However, I reasoned that, if the sun shone all day, the fish might start moving and feeding by evening, and, whatever the fish were doing, it would be good to see the river in its autumn colours.

Mick arrived at mid-morning, which meant that he didn't have great hopes for the fishing, either; it also meant that, instead of the usual urgency to get to the water, we could be civilized and spend an hour over a pot of tea, discussing the recent river news – the floods of the previous week, the monster chub caught from somewhere near Wimbourne, the huge trout seen near Blandford, the reappearance of salmon in the tidal reaches, near Christchurch. We were going much further upstream, where the Dorset Stour is no more than a winding overgrown brook, almost narrow enough to leap across in places. But, despite its size, there are very deep pools at some of the bends and an astonishingly large, varied population of fish. Furthermore, there is a wonderful sense of wilderness in the scrubby, tangled woods and small tussocky meadows.

The sky was still completely cloudless when, at a little before noon, we finally got down to the riverbank. The water was carrying only a tinge of colour and was running maybe a few inches above normal autumn level, which was what we were hoping for. It meant the Stour had settled down after the monsoon of the previous week, though the storm had evidently had its effect: All the lily beds and most of the midstream reeds had been swept away, leaving the river looking more open, more accessible than it had been on our previous visit, only a fortnight earlier. We dumped our gear at the upstream end of a long sweeping bend and went for a stroll along the waterside, looking to see how each familiar pool had changed, hoping for a sign that might tell us where to cast.

"Birds often reset their systems to courtship and nest-building mode just because an autumn day is exactly the same length as a spring day"

The chill that I had felt at first light was not even evident in the shadows under the trees; the sun had done its work and my uncharacteristic pessimism soon vapourised in its steady beam. Moreover, the day felt more like spring than autumn, especially as there were a few snatches of unseasonal birdsong in the air. Also a crow flew past with a bunch of dead reeds in its beak; and a pair of buzzards was showing off to each other, high up in the blue, making wonderful dives and loops, their wings completely folded as they flipped effortlessly on the backward curve. But then, birds often reset their systems to courtship and nest-building mode just because an autumn day is exactly the same length as a spring day. Fish, on the other hand, would never behave so irrationally!

———•◦•———

Mick decided he liked the look of a sheltered pool bordered with young willows, while I had a sense of something in the deep water beneath a leaning sycamore. I set up my tackle – a slender cane rod, a centre-pin reel and a red-tipped porcupine float – and watched the current for a while, trying to see where it would take my quill once I had cast. If I dropped it in close to my own bank, the float would saunter slowly into the gentle eddy under the tree and hopefully not get drawn beyond it. Midstream, the flow was too strong, but alongside the reedbed on the opposite bank, there was a quiet perchy looking slack – though I would have to fish standing up, holding the rod high to keep the line clear of the centre current. I prefer to sit down out of sight when I'm fishing, so I decided to concentrate on the pool under the tree.

The quill sailed down towards the downreaching boughs and was caught in the slowly-revolving eddy beneath them. It was a classic perch hole – deep, dappled, sheltered and perfect for ambushing any small fish who might flit by.

Settling back in the long grass, I prepared to wait for however long it took for the float to disappear, not that this

would demand my patience as there is something uniquely mesmerising about float fishing which makes even a bite-less day entertaining. The eye remains fixed on a miniscule point of colour that, despite its size, shows up vividly against a shifting background of ripples and reflections. At first there is the mad expectation that it is going to vanish instantly, but as the minutes pass, you relax and fall into its gentle swaying rhythm. Everything in the waterscape is just a vignette for this small central image – and yet at any moment it might mysteri-ously dip and slide as some unseen fish takes or tests the bait. Despite the steady focus, I am usually aware of other things that might be happening on the edge of vision, like today, when something fluttered into hazy view and I registered a wagtail, sitting on a nearby reedstem. Then a single spark showed for a moment in midstream and I glanced sideways to see a curled-up floating leaf that was cupping a drop of water. As it turned in the current, the droplet gleamed in the sun.

In the clear air, sounds were sharply defined, especially the sound of the river itself, which is mostly too quiet to hear unless I am sitting absolutely still. The Stour is not a quick-flowing stream, like its sister, the Hampshire Avon. The Avon sweeps majestically along towards their shared estuary, but the Stour meanders idly and unhurriedly. Where there are no bends or shallows and the water runs deep, it has no voice at all, except in a spate, but where it ripples across shallows, through the roots of a tree or round the outside of a bend there is always a constant subdued susurration – a sound which seems good for the heart. Today there was also the occasional birdcall and, in the stillness, the delicate clatter of large dry leaves tumbling out of the chestnut tree just upstream, the early frost having finally loosened their stems. For hours, there was a golden flotilla of them gliding past me on the stream.

Apart from a few little dips and quivers – small fish tweaking the worm – my float hardly moved until mid-afternoon, when it was slowly dragged down. I picked up the rod and tightened into a fish which seemed to merely roll across the riverbed, sending a series of strange bumping vibrations up the line. I brought it steadily in, but it kept to the bottom and I had to wind the rod tip down to the surface then, taking care not to strain the cane, heave the thing inch by inch to the surface. I stared down, wondering what I'd hooked – not a fish, not anything alive, just a big knobbly stone. When I'd netted it and swung it ashore, I found the hook, still with worm attached, neatly lodged in a hollow recess. I hoped I hadn't offended the river in some way. Why else the stony response?

I decided to stop fishing for a while and go and see how Mick was doing, walking down towards him through the tall yellowing grass, enjoying the wider view which seemed so much more expansive after the close shadowy images under the sycamore. Quietly, I crept up to the place where my friend had chosen to fish, a pool hemmed in on either side by high willow-covered banks. I knew there was a narrow grassy ledge down at water level where I presumed he would be sitting, but when I peered over the edge, I was surprised to see that he had turned into a heron. The heron was also surprised to see me and it leapt forward, its big grey wings flapping furiously.

Though heavy and ungainly, a heron can move quite fast when startled. It swept up and over the far bank, emptying its bowels as it went, leaving a white diagonal trail across the river.

Though I always thought there was something heronish about him, Mick hadn't shapeshifted. He had given up on his original choice of pool some time earlier and wandered a few hundred yards downstream where I eventually found him, sitting below an ancient willow, smoking his pipe and watching his float sailing down the outside of a long reedy bend. He was looking happy, having just caught a rather fine perch of just under two pounds. However, he had earlier lost another which he said had been much larger, but the tragedy had not affected him.

"Have a sandwich," he said, and, with a freshly-made cup of tea, I sat down in the dry reeds to enjoy a late lunch. We discussed our recent experiences and generally enthused about the look of the river and beauty of the day.

"Did you see the kingfisher?" asked Mick.

"No, but I spooked a heron."

Eventually I headed back upstream, across the fields and then, after collecting my tackle, through a boggy thicket above which I discovered a lovely slightly sinister-looking pool, where the stream abruptly narrowed and deepened and a half-drowned alder reached almost halfway across from the far bank. The current was quicker just downstream where the water shallowed and quicker upstream where it flowed between three sedge-covered islets. The alder pool, in contrast, was almost still and I cast my float across to the opposite side so that it rode at anchor a few yards from the drowned branches.

As I settled down into the atmosphere of the place, gradually absorbing those more subtle characteristics that a momentary glance can never reveal, I decided that the reason I love this stretch of river so much is because of its intimacy. Unlike many other, grander rivers, that sweep along with an expression of cool remoteness, these few miles of narrow stream seem to whisper all kinds of promises – promises not only to do with the fishing. Any reasonably-experienced angler would recognise the potential in such a variety of glides, eddies, bends, shallows and deeps – a variety made so much more attractive by the amount of natural cover along the banks – but there are other less obvious qualities, perhaps more to do with the general direction of flow through this gently-undu-

"Though I always thought there was something heronish about him, Mick hadn't shapeshifted"

lating landscape; and I like the way the light effects certain stretches, and the way the river seems to disappear down tunnels of reflected trees. There is also a sense of sanctuary, not so much for an angler, but for the diverse natural life that furtively exists here.

The sun, lower in the southwest, was now shining through the trees behind me. The dappled glow on the opposite bank was mirrored by the dark surface, but the reflections didn't obscure the red-tipped float. It swayed and drifted gently for a few minutes, then, just as I began to stare at it more intensely – had it twitched a moment earlier? – it suddenly wasn't there anymore. I flicked the rod tip, which curved over as I hooked something that at least was not an inanimate object. It jagged. It felt like a perch – it *was* a perch. The fish rolled on the surface, then dived for the upreaching branches, making the reel sing, but I steered it away from danger and gradually teased it over the waiting net.

The colours, when I lifted the perch out of the mesh, were all the colours of autumn – the crimson fins, the yellow-green mottling around the head, the ochre, amber and pearl along the flank. The fish was like a symbol of autumn – the dark vertical stripes like trees backgrounded against a field of gold leaves, which were the overlapping scales. I thanked it for being such a marvel, apologised to it, and slipped it back.

Perhaps a shoal had begun to feed. Perhaps one of the river's patriarchs would start prowling around. Though my fish had not been much above a pound, at least it confirmed that Mick's perch was not the only one unaffected by the dip in water temperature and I cast with new hope. However, after I'd recast, the float did not move again. Also, there were no small fish rippling on the surface, something that usually occurs as the evening draws on.

I needed to get back through the willow bog before dark or risk a dunking in waist-deep mud, but I decided, anyway, that I should return to my original pool and see if anything was stirring. Picking my way through the thicket – never easy when carrying a rod and net – I noticed a strange glow beyond the last tangle of boughs and realised it was a faint cloud of mist rising up from a more open stretch of river. The temperature was falling again and I felt the chill when I stepped out from under the trees. The deep hole under the sycamore was looking much darker and even more fishy than before, but once again there was no response when I cast into it. I sat on my rolled-up raincoat, peering at my float through a narrow gap in a bed of dead reeds and willowherb. I must have been completely invisible from upstream because a kingfisher came arrowing up the river and swerved through the reed gap, taking what I presume was a familiar short cut across the bend. Hearing his high-pitched whistle as he approached, I had lent forward slightly to see him and was startled by a blue blur flashing inches from my nose. There was an audible *fzzzz* and the faintest draught, a little puff of air bulletting past.

The mist was pooling into the hollows in the surrounding fields as I went on down to find Mick. As I walked, I looked towards the high hills in the east, hoping to see the moonrise, but, a day after full, it still had another hour to sleep. The grass underfoot was already heavy with dew and as I swished through it I could just see the familiar silhouette of a fisherman, still sitting by the old willow. But before I went to ask if he'd caught any more fish, I had to have a last cast in a lovely glide just upstream of him. Once again, I settled down amongst a bed of matted reeds and, without a float, because it was nearly too dark to see, I cast a freelined worm into midstream.

It had been still and quiet all day, but there was an intensity about the twilight calm that made me want to hold my breath for fear of disturbing something. Feeling the line for bites, I waited expectantly for maybe ten light-sinking minutes, and then noticed the inky reflections wobbling and breaking up in front of me. There were no sounds, just the slow heavy rippling that appeared to be spreading from somewhere upstream. Finally it was as if something was drifting down invisibly under the shadow of the far bank. I stared into the quickly reforming reflections, but nothing else happened.

Reeling in for the last time, I went down to tell Mick that it was surely late enough now, and cold enough, to be thinking about a pint by the fire in the village pub.

'I think an otter went past me just now,' he said.

Chris Yates was described recently by the Independent as 'the master'. He has just published his second book with Hamish Hamilton about sea fishing called Out of the Blue.

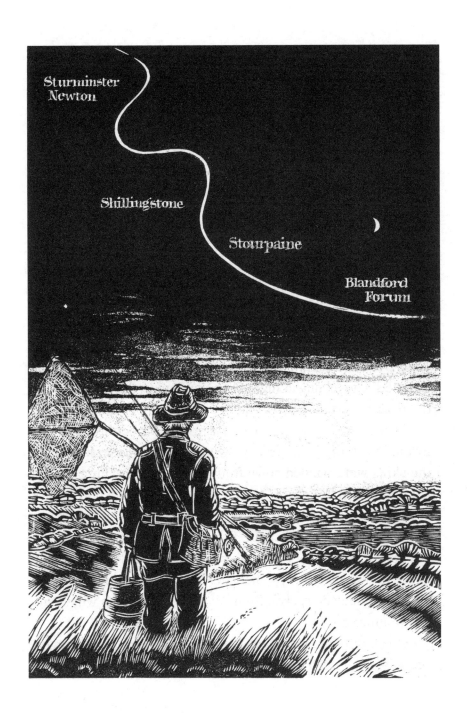

Sturminster
Newton

Shillingstone

Stourpaine

Blandford
Forum

CORACLE MAKER

BY
BERNARD THOMAS

M y name is Bernard Thomas. My father was a coracle man, but because of the war and then bringing up children I didn't start making them until I was about 52. I go fishing at night. The number on the side is B1. In the dark the bailiff comes and sees the number and says 'Oh, that's Bernard Thomas'. The nets are now made from jute or nylon, but in my younger days we made them from horsehair, the skills were handed down from father to son. There is such a tranquility in the gorge – yes it's beautiful. When it gets dark you can look up into the sky and count stars. Once you know it is dark enough so that the fish can't see the net, then you can fish. Fish are very scarce now these days. It's because of modern ideas, fertilisers, insecticides and pesticides, but also sheep dip; they do reckon from where it is used fish will die up to two miles away.

I can tell you, many years ago when I started I was averaging 5–6 salmon a night, and a load of sewin. Now last year I caught one salmon all season. I catch mostly sewin these days. A sewin is a sea trout and you get them up to about seven pounds. Eels don't come up here so much anymore. They work on a seven-year cycle and come back to where they came from. Up the Gulf Stream they hit fresh water, millions of them – and they go across land at night. Between 7 and 12 years later they start coming back to breed.

I make coracles between October and January when the frost means the sap is down. I soak the willows in the river for five days. Then I make the frame. The willow is all split and chamfered before, so the frame only takes five hours to make. I keep it out until it loses all its water before applying oil and preservative. The frame is covered with linen, which is then sealed with pitch and linseed oil. I had an argument with someone in a pub once about how man arrived on these islands. I said 'well, it must have been in a coracle' and they said nobody could cross the ocean in a coracle. So I did it. In 1974 I went to a place called St Margaret's Bay. It took three attempts but eventually I crossed in thirteen and a half hours before finally landing in France.

Reprinted by permission from the good people at Howies.

Way
Across
The River

HAMMERSMITH BRIDGE
TO THE ISLE OF HARTY

———— ◆ ————

BY
JON SAVAGE

Ray Davies for The Kinks, *See My Friend* (1965)

———————◆·◆·◆———————

Water cutting through earth, the river is a potent source of wealth and life. It is a conduit, facilitating communication and trade. When not polluted, it teems with life. Yet it has a dark side: it can overflow and flood the land, killing all that lives there. Flowing water, it symbolises the free expression of emotion, whether anger, sorrow, murderous rage, regret and loss.

There are river songs to cover every mood: the frightening depth of obsessive love (*River Deep Mountain High*); a rush of fluid that drowns sorrow (The Rising Sons' *If The River Were Whisky*); a prelapsarian idyll (Creedence's *Green River*); a mystical force (Nick Drake's *The River Man*); the location of what the Welsh call hiraeth, home and roots (The Stone Roses' *Mersey Paradise*).

During the mid 1960's, Ray Davies wrote two extraordinary hit singles that used the river as a metaphor for memory and loss. The first was *See My Friends*, issued in early summer 1965, when the Kinks were coming off four raucous sound-alike hits and a comparative flop – all within a year. The pace of pop was killing, even more because nobody thought it would last.

Determined to break the Kinks' template re-established by *Set Me Free*, Ray Davies dug deep and, inspired by a visit to Bombay early in '65, recorded one of the first UK 45's to explicitly source the drones of Indian music. (The other was the Yardbirds' *Heartfull of Soul*. Although both sought to reproduce the sound of the sitar, neither record featured one).

The result was a cyclical masterpiece as allusive and elliptical as *Sally Go Round The Roses*. Like the Jaynettes' hit, *See My Friend* is all about loss, hurt and emotional distance – a subject that Davies would return to again and again. Are the singer's friends replacing the lost 'she', and does the river mark a journey into male bonding and its outer reaches – even homosexuality?

'It's about being a youth who is not sure of his sexuality,' Davies told me in 1983. 'I remember I said to Rasa (his wife) one night, "if it wasn't for you, I'd be queer". I think it's a horrible thing to say to someone of seventeen, but I felt that. I was unsure of myself, and I still find it hard to relate to guys who are out with the lads. The song is about acceptance: that's the way the situation is'.

Eighteen months later, the Kinks delivered the song that they are still known by. Beginning with an explicit evocation of the Thames, *Waterloo Sunset* continues Davies' observer stance with an arrangement – worked out with Rasa and brother Dave – that delivers both subtlety and punch. The mundane becomes mysterious, and life is transformed – a very 1967 obsession.

During 1983, I was doing interviews and researching for the book that would eventually become *The Kinks: The Official Biography*. It was a strange experience: I was learning on my feet – it was my first book – and was spending a lot of time with the troubled group. Dave Davies was fine, no problem, straight-ahead and forthright, just as you might expect, but his brother was foxy.

Ray was then living at Maida Vale, in the Sutherland Avenue house that he shared with Chrissie Hynde. For a few months, I conducted long interviews with him and patched them straight into the MS. Ray was going through a turbulent patch – his marriage with Chrissie was on the rocks – but I didn't catch much of this turmoil. There was a definite mood, but this was a sixties rock star.

Proceeding chronologically, I'd got to 1966 just at the point where Ray checked himself into the Priory. The book deadline demanded that the interviews continued, so I picked him from Roehampton one winter day and we settled on an anonymous pub, the Castlenau, right near Hammersmith Bridge. It was the best single interview I did in the whole three months.

We covered the Kinks' killer 1966 album, *Face To Face*, and those great singles, *Sunny Afternoon, Dead End Street/ Big Black Smoke*. But Ray was most fulsome about *Waterloo Sunset*: 'there's no memory of that song that isn't a pleasure,' he told me. 'I woke up singing it in my sleep. I used to put a notebook by the bed, which made things impossible for poor Rasa.

'I woke up singing it like Frank Sinatra. It was in a swing mode – that's how I first heard it. It was so different for us I thought twice about doing it. I wanted to write a song about a Liverpool sunset because of the death of Merseybeat and all that. Then I thought, "I'm a Londoner, why all the tributes to

Liverpool? I have a real passion for London, and it was also a very personal song'.

'I was in hospital, at St.Thomas, for an operation when I was a kid. I nearly died. I had a tracheotomy and the balloon burst. I was attached to a machine and pulled all the things out of my arms. Then two or three days later I couldn't speak because of the operation. Two nurses wheeled me out on to the balcony, where I could see the River Thames. It was just a very poetic moment for me'.

This candour was too good to last. A couple of months later, Ray suddenly turned on me during a dinner at L'Escargot. It quickly degenerated into a shouting match: the f-word and the c-word were freely bandied about. Luckily, the book was almost done. Ray then threatened to stop publication, but after a couple of lawyers' meetings, it was all ironed out.

I didn't take it personally. I felt that Ray had to have total control, and that – despite his contractual rights – he could feel it slipping away as the book neared completion. Perhaps I'd got too close. When I met him a couple of years later, he was fine and so was I. It certainly didn't stop me from being passionate about the Kinks, whose sixties records enlightened my adolescence.

As a Londoner born and bred, I've found that the river Thames threads through my past. There are the embankments – Chelsea, Battersea – and the bridges: with Battersea Power Station, on which my grandfather worked as a sub-contractor, looming in the background; Waterloo Bridge, with its unbeaten views; Tower Bridge, at the outer boundary of my known city.

What follows then are a few memories evoked by the river Thames: a couple are documented on video, others remain simply in my head. Now that I no longer live in the city of my youth, it's as though these events occurred to another person, in another life. Like Ray Davies, I'm standing on the other side of a watery barrier: see my friends, way across the river.

1 : WESTMINSTER PIER

It was supposed to be secret: a boat trip held by the notorious Sex Pistols – high in the charts with *God Save The Queen* – on the evening of the Queen's Silver Jubilee. My friend Steven Lavers told me about it on the day. I was determined to go, so I called up the Sex Pistols' urbane PR, Al Clark, from the *Sounds* office and threatened to tell everyone unless he put my name on the list.

Al submitted to these cheap blackmail tactics with his customary charm. A few hours later I was jostling to walk up the plank of the "Queen Elizabeth", which was moored at Westminster Pier. It was the usual fight to get into a Sex Pistols event, with the ever-present threat that you wouldn't get in, just like at the Notre Dame Hall in March – their first gig with Sid.

By this point, the Sex Pistols were well into their mythic, paranoid stage. They were carrying too much baggage: the repository of England's hopes and fears, depending on which side of the divide you were. They hadn't played in London since April, and that was another last minute private party type of event at the Screen on the Green. So the whole thing was fraught from the start.

This Monday was the bank holiday, the climax of the Queen's Silver Jubilee. This anniversary was a huge national event and the Sex Pistols had become the standard bearers for everyone who thought that the whole thing was a rotten lie. This was not the majority view. As the only obvious refuseniks, Punks were public enemies: to be on the boat at all was to step outside the law.

Once the boat set off, the actual party was grim: the weather was awful, people were speeding their brains out, the Sex Pistols were grumpy and aloof. The atmosphere was uptight. Like the Jubilee as a whole, it was supposed to be fun but it wasn't. We were stuck there, going up and down the Thames, from Battersea to Rotherhithe, waiting for something.

The river was threatening that day. There weren't any other vessels around and very little sign of life on the embankment or other parts of the riverfront. It felt like the boat had cast off into a psychic black hole. As Derek Jarman wrote that summer, in the script for *Jubilee*: 'now is the time of departure. The last streamer that ties to what is known parts. We drift into a sea of storms'.

Things started to hot up when day-glo banners advertising the Sex Pistols and *God Save The Queen* were hung down the ship's sides. The captain had been told by Virgin Records that a German synthesizer group would be playing. When he saw what was actually going on, he was not happy and was looking for any excuse to terminate the event as quickly as possible.

When the group finally appeared there was a tremendous sense of excitement and release. They were shoehorned into a small covered area at the back of the upper open deck.

Conditions were far from ideal: the wind whipped away the
sound, already hobbled by dreadful feedback. Sid Vicious didn't
do very much, so Steve Jones and Paul Cook worked very hard
to keep everything going.

That left the burden of performance on Johnny Rotten. He
did brilliantly, but you could see what an effect the whole weight
of expectation was having on him. It was all too much for his
young shoulders. I was a few feet away from the group and all I
could think about was that Iggy line from the Stooges' *Gimme
Danger*: 'there's nothing left of life/ But a pair of glassy eyes'.

The Sex Pistols began by playing *Anarchy in the UK* as the
boat went past the Houses of Parliament: a fantastic moment
of theatre. It felt as though they were dramatising our rejection
of the false consciousness of the Jubilee. Instead of facing the
realities of recession-hit England in 1977, most of our coun-
trymen were dreaming of empire and post-war glory, were
partying like it was 1947.

But the whole thing felt volatile, unsafe. There were
photographers and a camera crew, getting in the way, and irri-
tating an audience that was already impatient and primed for
aggression. The footage was eventually edited into a short
called *Sex Pistols Number 2*, as part of McLaren's plan to get the
group into films. I saw it years after the event, and it captures
the atmosphere.

The whole area is windswept, grey. The group is cornered,
the audience is sparse and – like many punks – they took pains
to disdain the camera. Nobody is smiling. The camera focuses
on Helen Wallington-Lloyd, with hennaed hair, who looks
suitably disgusted. I'm standing behind her, leaning on a pillar:

the instant that I come into focus, I turn away. Blink and you'd miss it.

The inevitable happened. A few songs in, a photographer got too close to Jah Wobble and there was a fight stage front. The captain had found his excuse, and called the river police. Two launches started to circle the Queen Elizabeth, giving a particular charge to the group's manic cover of *No Fun*. The power was turned off. Paul Cook continued to beat his drum-kit, but the show was over.

As the Queen Elizabeth turned towards Westminster, there were serried lines of police waiting on the dockside. Nobody wanted to leave. While Richard Branson argued furiously with the captain, there was a tense stand-off. This was quickly broken once some of the guests, bored and cross, started throwing bottles and cans. Things quickly degenerated.

While the Sex Pistols – then public enemies number one, and prime targets for a good kicking – were spirited up a small staircase at the other side of the dock, the crowd were forced to run the gauntlet as they emerged on dry land. A pitched battle ensued: the police were determined to show no mercy to these anti-monarchic punks, who in turn were spoiling for a confrontation.

Twelve people in all, including McLaren, Vivienne Westwood, Jamie Reid, and my friend Zecca Esquibel, were slammed into waiting Black Marias – a fate that I narrowly avoided. Shocked by this police overreaction, Tony Parsons, Peter York, Steven Lavers and I went straight along to Bow Street Station to see if we could help anyone. We were firmly asked to leave.

The night ended with us walking nervously around Covent Garden trying to make sense of it all. It was the Jubilee week-end and the pubs were decked out in Union Jacks and it was Jack Warner time, the war that never ended: Rule Britannia, mustn't grumble, have another cup of tea. In our non-standard, if not actively punkish clothes, we were easy targets.

I had to spring Zecca the next day. If he was to be released, he had to present his US passport. He was staying in the art-critic Mario Amaya's flat in Earl's Court. So I had to rush there in my lunch hour and break in – there was nobody home – then rush back to Bow Street to get him out. When he'd signed on as Cherry Vanilla's keyboardist, he'd never imagined this would happen.

It's very hard to think that such a small, chaotic rock show could have such a political and an emotional charge. But England was very polarised that summer. The Sex Pistols offered the only coherent, popular anti-Jubilee protest – the organised Left fumbled the opportunity – and we were showing solidarity by being on the boat. I thought they were very brave that day, and still do.

But it taught me to never go on boat trips. Nine years later, I broke my rule and attended the filming of the Boat Trip sequence in Alex Cox's *Love Kills*. It felt very weird to be recreating an event that I had witnessed: the younger punks – including a pre-S-Express Mark Moore – were having a great time experiencing what they had missed, while the production staff worried about authenticity.

Even so, the shoot caught some of the original event's flavour: it was claustrophobic and bad tempered, and it reminded me of why I don't enjoy being on a river-boat: the wind is very cold when it rips off the water; the event always goes on for far too long; alcohol + river swell = nausea; and you can't get off when you want to leave. I haven't been on the Thames since.

2: THE ISLE OF HARTY

London owes its position and its historical wealth to the fact that it was a major port. The Thames offered a safe harbour for the transport of goods – one of the foundations of Victoria prosperity. The Docklands stretched out for miles eastwards along the river – from Tower Bridge past Rotherhithe, Millwall and North Woolwich out to Beckton, the point where the Thames really starts to widen.

This huge area constituted – as it still does – a city within a city. The warehouses of Wapping, the narrow streets of Limehouse, the vast spaces of Royal Victoria, George V and Surrey Commerical docks, the workers' communities at Silvertown and Cubitt Town – all of these were hidden from the great majority of Londoners. This was a world unto itself: proud, independent, inward-looking.

During the Second World War, Docklands was the area of the city worst hit by German bombers: not just because of its strategic importance, but because lying to the East, it was directly on the bombers' flight-path. The river was not blacked out, and provided the perfect navigating tool. Whole districts were flattened: the bomb-sites prevailed until the early 80's.

The inner reaches of Docklands were badly hit by the move towards containerisation during the 1960's: much of the trade moved out to Tilbury – further down the Thames, in deeper water – or to Europe, the port of Rotterdam in particular. Within twenty years, all of London's docks were closed, leaving many unemployed and at least eight square miles of East London totally derelict.

During the 1970's, Docklands was in a sorry state. Jah Wobble was born and raised in Stepney. He remembered that time: 'I went to the London Nautical School. I wanted to go to sea. I had a little bit of a seafaring tradition in the family. I'd go down to the docks – there again, the butt end of the docks, it was when they were closing, it seemed like the butt end of everything'.

'The future was, go east, young man, to Dagenham, and have 2.4 kids. Everyone moves out of the East, right from the fifties. It was Labour who kept that going right through the 60s. So if you're in Stepney or Poplar, you go east. If you're from south, you go to Bromley. For their days out they go to Brighton, for ours we'd go to Southend. A huge expanse of mud'.

As elsewhere in London Punk, these empty spaces and blank places – while redolent of human misery – offered breathing space to the young and fearless. London seemed empty then, with whole districts left to rot – not just Docklands but whole swathes of North West London, North Kensington, Covent Garden, even parts of Chelsea around Lots Road.

Riverside dweller Derek Jarman caught this paradox in his film *Jubilee*, one of the few cinematic records of London during the high summer of 1977: 'The source of the film was often autobiographical', he wrote in his memoir *Dancing Ledge*; 'the locations were the streets and the warehouses where I had lived during the previous ten years'.

In the opening scene, the camera pans from a row of destroyed houses and the customary rubbish fires to a brick wall on which is inscribed the graffiti: 'postmodern'. Filming in Docklands, particularly Rotherhithe, Jarman saw the dereliction as both indicative of social breakdown and offering a paradoxical kind of freedom. It was an interzone: the past and the future all at once.

Jubilee is a state of the nation film that embodies these paradoxes. Nobody cares, so you might as well do what you want, as state brutality rubs up against alternative lifestyles: the gay couple Angel and Sphinx, the homicidal girl gang led by the reincarnation of Queen Elizabeth I. The resolution is, in part, prophetic: punk turned spectacular by big business.

In 1981, the Conservative Government decided that something should be done: then Secretary of State for the Environment, Michael Heseltine, formed the London Docklands Development Corporation to upgrade the whole area. The LDDC was very unpopular with locals, particularly in the early years when clearance was pursued more assiduously than affordable rebuilding.

A couple of years later, I explored this landscape in transition with Derek. I'd met him through our mutual friend Chelita Secunda – an extraordinary person who deserves a book to herself. When I moved back to London from Manchester in early 1983, I started seeing more of him: he was living in the centre of town, at Phoenix House on the Charing Cross Road.

That was a good summer. I'd just moved back to London from pre-regeneration Manchester and, despite the chaotic nature of my job at TV-am, relished the freedoms of the city. The soundtrack was a mixture of Electro and first wave Psychedelia, as I'd found at my parents' house all the West Coast albums that I'd squirreled away. You weren't allowed to listen to them during Punk.

It was hot. The city didn't seem crowded. One evening I turned up at Phoenix House. Derek was alone – a comparative rarity, as there was always someone there, a mix of the great, the good, the bad and the ravished. We smoked a joint and decided, on the spur of the moment, to go for a drive. And so a pattern was set that lasted through that summer into the next couple of years.

That first derivé took us out East on the North side of the river. We passed through Wapping – not yet disfigured by the

News International building. This was familiar territory, the location of the B2 Gallery and the Prospect of Whitby pub. We pressed on through Limehouse and round the Isle of Dogs – then a deserted spur with run-down housing estates and terraces.

Here you could just sit and look at the river as it stretched out around Blackwall Point. London here began to straggle out into low level industrial installations: empty wharves, derelict factories, and power stations – all presided over by Greenwich Observatory on the south bank. There was very little traffic on the water, and it felt peaceful.

It became a regular event. Each time we'd press further on, through the A13 bottleneck at Canning Town down through Silvertown and North Woolwich, and then Beckton Works – a huge gas works closed in 1970. Before regeneration, it was a vast, blasted space: used for film locations – including the Bond film *For Your Eyes Only* and Stanley Kubrick's *Full Metal Jacket*.

At night it was spooky. The whole area was desolate, on both sides of the river. In the south, the huge Plumstead marshes stretched out. In Beckton, there was just the street lighting, no houses. We got back onto the Barking by pass and went down another road that ended up on the other side of Barking Creek: it was empty except for a single pub at the water's edge, 'The Crooked Billet'.

This was like the landscape of the 1952 John Mills film, *The Long Memory* – a noirish story of injustice, endurance and revenge set in river locations. There was nothing except industrial detritus, wooden posts, and mud stretching into the distance. The road then turned off the river: the next stops were the ruined Barking power station and the Dagenham Ford works.

So we started exploring the south side. The start was easy, turn left at Rotherhithe and explore the little knot of roads around St. Mary's Church. A quick stop at the Mayflower pub and then on over the bridge around the peninsula, taking the road that skirted the Surrey Commercial Docks – Rotherhithe Street, one of the oldest and longest in the capital.

In 1983, the whole area was trashed: full of deserted water and corrugated iron. Derek knew the area intimately: here was the house – now boarded up – where he had shot Max's garden of gnomes and plastic flowers in *Jubilee*; here was the square of roads around the Redriff Estate where, in the sixties, he'd picked up sailors from the teeming pubs. No more: it was a ghost town.

Surrey Commerical Docks felt like a black hole. It was easy to get lost without a map: many times we found ourselves retracing our steps. Hugging the river was impossible after Greenland Dock, so it was back on the main road for a bit and then left into Deptford. Again, blank space: few small estates, high brick walls, scrap yards, beautiful old churches, twisting roads.

Then there were the lights of Greenwich, a major focal point with the Cutty Sark, and the river walk past the Royal Naval College, Christopher Wren's baroque masterpiece. We'd smoke a final reefer and contemplate the building: huge, imposing and empty. Lights flared from only a few windows of the many hundreds in the façade – a relic of England's seafaring supremacy.

Greenwich was a bit of a psychic barrier. One night we eventually pressed on, through nondescript Charlton, but this time there was a definite end in sight. Both of us were obsessed with Antonioni's *Blow Up* – the definitive account of high sixties London – and I knew where the film's principal location was: Maryon Park, just outside Woolwich.

So we parked in Tamar Street, just off Woolwich Road. The corner shop where David Hemmings buys the propellor was no longer there. Nor were the passing queens who give him a thorough appraisal. Instead, there was low density modern housing. It was daylight, but the park was nearly empty. It was quiet, except for the rustling of leaves that you can hear in the film.

We spent the next hour recreating the film. The factories were still there, looming behind the hill – called Cox's Mount – where Hemmings witnesses or doesn't witness a murder. We ran up and down the steps, and toured round the circular lawn where the kids drive their mini-moke and, at the end of the film, play an imaginary game of cricket.

'We walked through its deserted and secret glades half-suspecting to find the body under a May tree,' Derek later wrote. 'As we wandered our footsteps fell into the rhythm of the put put of two boys playing tennis. The park meanders across ridges, with different views of the city. The silence is broken only by the trains which run through a cutting at its southern edge'.

'The park is a blaze of colour, the tulips form perfect pink and red battalions, inclining slightly to the setting sun. Both of us feel this park has a special intimacy, it's so silent. Years ago I queued with my friends to extra in the film, and Ron, my first love, appears subliminally dancing to the Yardbirds in the nightclub sequence'.

After Woolwich there was another riverside barrier: the old Royal Arsenal, and the road turns inwards, through Plumstead, Abbey Wood, Belvedere. You can only access the river again once you get to Erith, a fascinating old port village with crowded streets around the dock area. But eastwards are more barriers: the river Darenth and Dartford Salt Marshes.

As a West Londoner, I'd always followed the impulse to go West: to Heathrow when I was a child, watching the planes with my father, later to the Chilterns where my friend David Chipp lived. I took Derek to his house in Ibstone that summer, to work on his film that was never made, *Neutron*: we spent most of the time playing croquet with obsessive, stoned competitiveness.

On these trips, the impulse was to go East, further East into what was for me totally undiscovered territory. One day in April 1984 we forgot trying to hug the river and leap-frogged from Erith past Dartford and Greenhithe to Cliffe in the Isle of Grain. It was hot and sunny. Derek shot some super 8 images of an electronic tower that later found their way into *Angelic Conversation*.

We pressed on past the Power Station back to the A2, before turning left over the Kingsferry Bridge – with its mono-lithic, concrete pillars – onto the Isle of Sheppey. It felt like stepping into a time warp: the main town, Sheerness, was deserted and depressed, so we found the river bank – hidden by a huge concrete barrier against the tides. Derek later gave me the VHS he shot there.

It was the first day of spring. There were hardly any leaves on the trees but it was warm enough to enjoy the sun and the sea air: for Sheerness is where the Thames opens out to became salt water. Derek did a couple of 360 degree shots: from the Isle of Grain power station, with a plume of smoke in the South Wind, the line of the concrete sea wall, the nothingness of sky and sea to the East.

The next stop was Minster Abbey, one of the oldest churches in England, where we happened upon a wedding. Derek shot the bride and groom coming out of the church, and all the accoutrements of a ceremony that then was not available, or even thought of for gay people: the bride fussing with her hair, the parents and parents in-law, the best man, the tired and emotional bridesmaids.

Feeling like two Peter Pans, with our noses pressed against the window of secure normality, we drove East into Leysdown, a holiday village at the NE tip of the island. It wasn't a place to linger, with holiday camps (the Paradise Club), caravan parks, rows of bungalows. If only we'd known, there is a naturist beach on the coast there, but that was not then our preoccupation.

Derek filmed me driving. I had a Mark II Jaguar then, a beautiful but impractical beast: 871 DLA, gold exterior, white leather interior. First registered in 1961, it had trebled its natural life of about 7 years, and was always breaking down. That day, however, it did sterling service and seeing the walnut dash in the VHS reminds me of how much I enjoyed driving that lump of heavy metal.

It certainly rolled round the corners of the single-track road that took us out Leysdown southwards, to the Isle of

Harty. There were no holiday camps here, just empty fields, old-fashioned layer hedges, and one line of telegraph poles. The road twisted and turned until it eventually petered out at the edge of the Swale, the strip of water that divides Sheppey from the mainland.

This was the end of the line. There were no houses nearby, just mudflats, wading birds, the remnants of wartime fortifications, and a single vessel sailing in the near distance. You could see the hills of Kent rising across the water. This was as far as we could go before the Thames became the sea: an island off an island off an island. 871 DLA gleams in the sun. The VHS cuts there.

During the mid 80's, Derek obsessively returned to Docklands for film locations: an empty warehouse in Canary Wharf for *Caravaggio*, Surrey Commercial Docks for the video of Marianne Faithfull's *Why Don't We Do It*. You can see these ravaged landscapes in the promos he did for The Smiths: they dominate his extraordinary visual rant, 1987's *The Last of England*.

Our Docklands wanderings wound down after then. Derek bought Prospect Cottage in Dungeness and that became the new axis for a while. From that time on, he became progressively more and more ill with AIDS related symptoms: at the same time, he upped his work rate, frantically producing films, manifestoes, broadsides, books, to squeeze in everything before the inevitable.

He died in 1994, and left a huge hole in the lives of those who knew him. He is still very much missed. Derek was a catalyst: immensely generous with his time and his friendship. He was a leading figure in the cultural resistance against Thatcherism – it's easy to forget how many people turned New Right in those years – and the full extent of his life and art has yet to be appreciated.

It's starting to happen. During 2006, Colin MacCabe disinterred a fifteen-year old interview that he had conducted with Derek in Dungeness. With direction from Isaac Julien and narration from Tilda Swinton, this illuminating dialogue became the spine of the film *Derek*, premiered at Sundance in 2007 and commercially released during 2008.

By the time that Derek died, I was spending much of time in North Wales – the area where I now live. In our different ways, we had solved the problem that our Docklands derivés had posed without us knowing it: how to find mental and physical space and peace within a huge, sprawling megalopolis, where the nearest open countryside is at least an hour away.

Those drives would be impossible now. Twenty-five years later, there have been waves and waves of regeneration. What was once wasted space is now full of life, as the pressures on

London grow ever greater. It is, of course, much preferable that housing should exist where bombsites and dereliction once stood, but it also means the disappearance of the city within which I grew up.

When I return to London now, the population density in West London, for instance, is probably three times what it was when I was a young man. A lot of money has been spent on eradicating the worst inner city slums, but there is a downside that goes beyond property prices. (Even at the height of the boom, London was still the same old London: dirty, tough and bad-tempered).

Much of what occurred during the punk and post punk periods made a virtue out of necessity, but London was easier to live in then. It wasn't jam-packed, nor was its infrastructure strained to the limit. Open spaces are necessary for cities and their populations to breathe, and one of the reasons that I left compelled to leave London was that they were slowly being filled in.

Even so, the Thames remains London's forgotten lung, offering plentiful bird-life, clean air, and a sense of perspective and depth. There's a moment in the VHS of the Isle of Sheppey when I take in a long breath of sea air, and stretch my arms and body in the sun. It's great to escape into the open spaces, and they are still there in London, if you take care to find them.

Jon Savage is the author of Teenage *and the definitive history of punk* England's Dreaming.

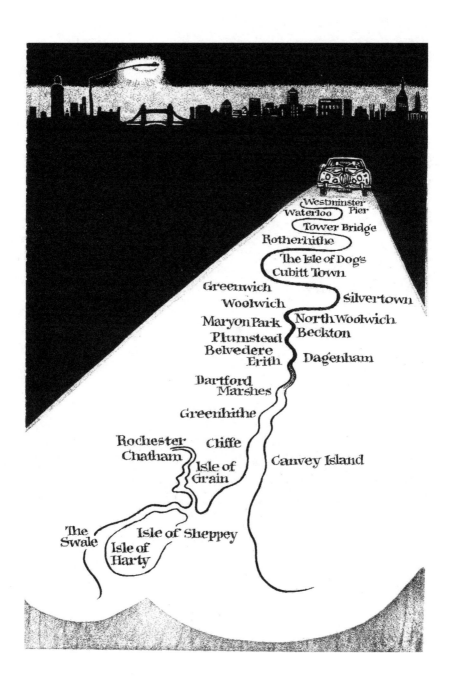

THE
POETRY
OF SMALL
AMBITIONS

BY
PAUL KINGSNORTH

Sir John Spelman wrote his *Life of Alfred the Great* during the English Civil War. An avowed Royalist, Spelman had a point to make with his lengthy and in some places fantastical biography of the king he called the 'first founder of the English monarchy.' Spelman wanted to shore up the position of the Stuart monarchs by glorifying 'the line of their famous ancestors'. He had a vested interest in glorious doings.

In their pursuit, he claimed that Alfred had not only founded the English monarchy (he didn't: Alfred was only ever King of Wessex) but England itself (though it didn't exist as a nation state until the time of Alfred's grandson Ethelstan). Spelman also firmly believed that Alfred founded Oxford University (also highly unlikely). And then there was this:

'...there were some Assembly of the Chief of both Orders of the Kingdom called together at Sifford (or Seaford) in Oxfordshire ... the King there consulted with his Clergy, Nobles and Others, about the Manners and Government of the People...'

Spelman was claiming that Alfred held, at 'Sifford', what was effectively an early form of parliament – an institution which would, he goes on to say, become a tradition amongst his successors, who would 'hold assemblies of their Bishops and Nobles continually thrice a year, in solemn consultation of the affairs of the Kingdom.'

If Spelman is right, then Sifford – or Shifford, as it is today – ought to be both more notable and more noticeable than it is. The tiny village is just visible from the footpath that winds its way along the south bank of the Thames, through empty meadows of grass and cornflower. Shifford's farm, small church and brace of houses lie just downstream from its quiet nineteenth-century lock, one of the last constructed on the Thames, in an artificial cut which changed the course of the river. There's a small wooden footbridge across the narrow, lazy channel. And that's it. Nothing to suggest that a founding event of English history may have taken place here. Nothing to suggest that anything has ever taken place here at all.

If Shifford was the site of some great gathering during Alfred's reign (and modern historians seem to think otherwise), you would never know it today. There has been a settlement here for well over a millennium, but you would never know that either. The upper reaches of the river Thames are like this: they conceal and envelop and remake. This river, more than any other, has been central to English history. Even above Oxford, where it shrinks and meanders and seems so unprepossessing, it is a palimpsest of power and significance. Much has been concealed, and remains so – even today, Viking swords are dragged from its depths. Walk the banks in high summer and you have to look, and know what you are looking for, to understand what has been.

Here is Bablock Hythe, an ancient Roman crossing point; now an unprepossessing pub. Here is Shifford, possible seat of one of the earliest precursors to our much-vaunted 'Mother of Parliaments'; now one of the smallest villages in Oxfordshire. Here is the beautiful yellow stone of Newbridge, built by monks in 1250 to service the burgeoning wool trade of the Cotswolds, then the prime engine of England's economy; now, like the Cotswolds themselves, a prettified tourist attraction. Here is a crumbling pillbox, hidden in the reedmace, smelling inside of urine and beer cans; once one of 5000 built along this river, together making up 'Stopline Red', the last-ditch defence against Nazi invasion.

Hidden histories, hidden places: for years the upper Thames has been my own private Brigadoon. While down through London, the wide tidal river becomes the world's business, above Oxford, somehow, it is only mine. Ancient Bablock Hythe is today a chalet park: woodchipped mobile homes are scattered across the fields like wheat ears and the riverside pub's car park is rammed with shining silver vehicles every summer weekend. Somehow, though, I am the first person to have discovered this place since Matthew Arnold's Scholar Gypsy was ferried slowly across, his fingers trailing in the moonlit waters, his lap full of wild flowers picked from the ash woods. Edward Thomas's Lob, 'as English as this gate' and as sentimental too, guides me through William Morris's landscape of beautiful, doomed revolution. The upper Thames is poetry between banks of poplar and bullrush, and, on a summer evening, it can stake a serious claim to being the best place in the world.

I'm no Bruce Chatwin – though for a period in my twenties I wanted to be – but I've been around a bit. I've travelled by klotok up the rivers of Borneo in the early evening, when fruit bats swarm from bank to tree-dark bank, and gibbons come to the waters' edge to call. I've swum with giant otters in Guyana's brown Rupununi. I've helped create a makeshift log crossing of a raging white torrent in the highlands of New Guinea. I've driven across the Golden Gate and ridden a donkey across the freezing Himalayan currents of Ladakh.

I've traveled a great deal in England, Britain – homeland to myself and the Thames. At the insistence of my father I spent much of my childhood tramping the long-distance paths of this island, from the east to the west coast and from Land's End to John o' Groats. I've laboured up and down the coastal cliffs of Pembrokeshire and Cornwall, Northumbria and Sussex. I've slogged across the South Downs and the Cheviots, the Yorkshire Moors and the Pennines, the Black Mountains and the Flowerdale Forest. I've seen a fair number of rivers. But never a river like the upper Thames.

Why? The Thames – especially its higher reaches – is hardly the most magnificent river we have: think of the Severn's annual bore, or the foaming waterfalls of the upper Tees, or the broad sweep of the Forth as it slews into the sea. In comparison, the Thames is sluggish and unassuming. And for sheer beauty, there are other rivers, or at least stretches of other rivers, that can easily compete. There is nothing spectacular about the upper Thames. And this is precisely the point.

——•◦•——

This stretch of river wends its way through the heart of one of the most overcrowded regions of one of the oldest, most over-crowded, and most industrialised nations in the world; a nation in love with all the dirt and danger that advanced capitalism brings. Yet in winter you could sit in the watermeadows east of Old Man's Bridge for days and see only foxes. Sometimes you can't even hear the traffic; just the breeze in the top branches of the poplars, the nervous chatter of dunnocks, the clattering of dragonflies. If you are lucky, there will be no mobile phone signal. If you are lucky, the world will leave you alone.

If the lower Thames – the docks, the capital, the estu-ary, the tide – is the world, the upper Thames is home. If the London wharves and the Cutty Sark represent the England of bombast and conquest – Empire and redcoats and capital-ism and the White Man's Burden – then Northmoor Lock and Tadpole Bridge represent an England that is older than that, and perhaps embarrassed by it. The England of the tenant farmer, not the landlord; the villein not the baron; the pressed not the commissioned. There are lock keepers up here who have been working the gates and the sluices for fifty years, landlords whose grandparents ran the same pub, farmers still working their ancestral ground.

This river is old: 58 million years old as a discrete drain-age line, and around 450,000 years old in its present course.

Older, in other words than the English who now claim it, and older than the Celtic British who named it. It has been used and utilised, named and exploited, crossed and harvested and channelled. It has turned the water wheels that made merchants rich and millers a living, provided water for canals and enough draught to take waterborne cargoes all the way from Lechlade to the sea. The strip lights and strip malls of contemporary England are easily reachable by car, but the river banks can be seen only from a smallish boat or a pair of boots. Even a bicycle, as I've discovered myself, will be soon short-circuited by the endless stiles.

There is magic in this landscape, the kind of magic you only find in a few places in modern Britain: the magic of a place which has, somehow, retained its essence in the face of everything we have thrown at it over the last century. The upper Thames, unlike so much of the landscape of southern England, remains stubbornly human-scale; and this is the key to its character.

For fifteen years I've lived in Oxford, where the Big Thames becomes the Little Thames. I can shut my front door, walk for ten minutes to the river bank and not stop until I reach the source. I've done that, twice, and spent many days and weekends in and on the waters. I have written poems and a novel about this stretch of this river; slept on its banks and camped in its woods, canoed, swum and kayaked its inlets and its tributaries, explored its medieval churches and crossed its medieval bridges, caught pike and perch in its weir pools, slumped drunkenly on the tables of its riverside pubs.

And still, this is my river and nobody else's. It saves up secrets for me and distributes them according to its mood. It

gives me restored medieval churches, the foundations of abandoned villages, quicksand-rimmed lakes, tall, silent poplar groves,
secret pools, tiny osier-studded islands, disused canals, Bronze
Age mounds. It gives me reed warblers – tiny brown birds you
rarely see but often hear – and startling blue damselflies with
black wingtips. It gives me water voles and banks of reedmace,
meadows of snake's head fritillary, herons crouched like sculp-
tures on the branches of dead elms. It gives me paddle-and-rymer
weirs, abandoned houseboats hidden behind the rushes, old toll
bridges and the ancient, evocative names of its tiny tributaries
– Windrush, Evenlode, Cherwell, Glyme.

A few years back, bored and tired of words and writing, I spent
a summer working as an assistant lock keeper on the Thames
in Oxford. I worked with an experienced keeper, manning three
locks. I learned how to operate the gates and the sluices, and
how to open the weirs when the signal was received from
upriver that the levels were rising. I weeded and watered the
flowerbeds and drank a lot of tea and smoked a lot of rollups.
Like most of his colleagues I had come across, my keeper was
garrulous, cynical, unambitious and well-learned about the
ways of the river. You had to be, because, if you got your job
wrong, you could sink a lockful of boats, or flood a streetful of
houses. It was best to know what you were doing.

Our three locks were a contrast. Furthest downstream
was Iffley, at the south end of the city, just above the ring road.
Passing by in a narrowboat or a skiff, Iffley looks picture-

perfect, with its riverside pub, pair of weirs, punt rollers, ice cream kiosk, 1930's lock keeper's cottage and the top of the tower of the Norman church, one of the oldest and most beautiful in the country, just visible above the trees.

You had to work there, though, to know about the city's special gifts to this part of the river: the gangs of pissed-up-teenagers who occupy the riverside benches after the families have gone home at night; the car thefts; the used needles in the copses. Iffley lock is just around the corner from the Rose Hill estate, which has some serious problems with long-term unemployment and crime. Iffley is where the tourist image of the upper Thames meets the reality of urban 21st-century Britain. Live-in lock-keepers at Iffley don't always last very long, even with the newly-installed CCTV system.

Osney lock, in the centre of Oxford, just around the corner from the train station, hides different kinds of secrets. Osney Island is on a flood plain, and its pricey little houses are still regularly doused with river water at least once a year. Before the houses were here, the island was home to Osney Abbey, one of the greatest in the region, dissolved by Henry VIII. No sign of it remains today. Now, Osney is also a declining industrial centre. Like so many English cities, Oxford has decided that industry, especially small-scale industry, is a passé embarrassment. What is needed is not production but consumption. Opposite Osney lock is the shell of an old mill, dating from the twelfth century, which burned down finally in 1940. Some of the locals can still remember the fire. For years, the shell of the mill has stood opposite the lock, hung with creeping ivy and elderflower. If the local authority have their way, it will soon be replaced by the kind of bland, soulless housing development that has already killed off the character of most of the old Oxford canal, just up the river. Times change, the city grows and the past will never be allowed to stand in the way of the future.

Finally, north of the city, beyond the great medieval common of Port Meadow, on which the commoners' horses still graze, is Godstow Lock. Godstow is the gateway to the upper Thames: its lock cottage lies a few hundred yards from the ruins of the 12th-century nunnery, in the grounds of which, somewhere, are buried the remains of Henry II's mistress, Rosamund the Fair. The geese that nest on the bank opposite every summer, waking the keeper up at 5 am with their cackling, and have done so for centuries.

And it's when the sun rises above Godstow and burns off the white dew from the grasses of the meadow that you know you have arrived somewhere special. This is where the upper Thames springs to life: this is where, for the first time, it looks, feels, smells like the river it will become as it leaves the city under the concrete ring road bridge and meanders under the scarp of ancient Wytham Wood, off to the west. This is where the magic is first evident. It is where the secrets will start, if you are slow enough, and interested, to show themselves to you. This is where it begins.

Paul Kingsnorth is the author of Real England *described by* The Independent *as 'a crucially important book.'*

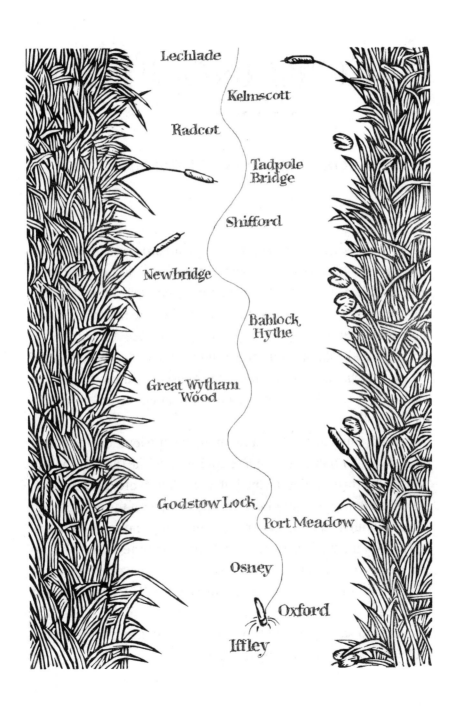

Lechlade

Kelmscott

Radcot

Tadpole
Bridge

Shifford

Newbridge

Bablock
Hythe

Great Wytham
Wood

Godstow Lock

Port Meadow

Osney

Oxford

Iffley

TICKLING FISH

BY
LORD PEREGRINE ST GERMANS

As a boy, I wormed for the abundant brownies in the Tiddy, the local river and part of the Tamar Estuary system. To call the Tiddy a river is rather extravagant as for the most part it is hardly ten feet wide and not quite three feet deep. Yet passing through it, I could see the migrating sea trout and salmon of up to six pounds. I was told they could not be caught on rod and line, yet everyone knew they were there because a 16-pounder had been caught in the wheel at the sawmill.

Years later an enthusiastic fisherman friend came to stay on his way to fish the Tamar. I told him about the fine fish in the Tiddy, three fields away, but that they were uncatchable. He ignored me, and set out to try his hand with fly and spinner. After an hour, utterly exasperated, and to my sheer amazement, he took off most of his clothes and jumped in the water. Fifteen minutes later he had tickled three lovely sea trout onto the bank – one of them at almost four pounds. He was reluctant to explain to me exactly how he did it. As much as he was prepared to say on the matter was. "Just get in the water and feel about and catch 'em by the tail."

I was determined to emulate his success. After many fruitless attempts I began to get the hang of it and, though I say it myself, I eventually became an accomplished tickler.

There was a time a decade or two ago when driving about the English countryside that I would regularly stop at small rivers, one of them a famed chalk stream and try my luck, more often than not successfully. My best day with a friend was 23 sea trout averaging 1.5 lbs whilst the largest fish I ever got to grips with was a 12 lb salmon – it took two of us to get it onto the bank.

I am happy to share the secrets of my technique which combines stealth, dexterity, and brute bloody force. Contrary to the orthodoxy of tickling, I work downstream kicking up the riverbed as I go. By doing so I benefit from working in muddied waters. As I move I also splash about and slap the water. This panics the fish into darting for the imagined safety of the banks. It is then a matter of very, very cautiously feeling about under the lip of the bank amongst the roots and reeds. Some of these recesses can be a foot or two deep in which case, depending on your level of commitment, you have to get down on hands and knees, take a deep breath and ease yourself into the crevice. Sometimes a fish can be found and tickled on the margins of the reed beds that swirl about midstream.

However warily one approaches a fish on first contact with it, it will frequently flit away but, should it not, the tickling process can begin. Slowly. Very slowly, as if you are caressing a lover, move your fingers along its flank and underside. Keep in mind the original meaning of the word tickle, which was not so much to make laugh, as to delight, or thrill.

Firstly you have to determine which way the fish is lying and exactly where it's head is. Everything depends on finding the head and the gills. You must constantly and very lightly keep stroking it. Astonishingly, unless you make a clumsy movement, the fish will become quite docile. If the tail is the only part of it that can be reached it is quite possible to hold it and pull it quietly back towards you. On a number of occasions, unable to reach the head of the fish with my hands, I have reached in with leg and foot and slowly manoeuvred it back to within arms-reach to get a hand on it.

Having stroked and caressed the fish into a trance-like state, the next step is the kill. The surest way to hold onto a fish is to get your forefinger and thumb into its gills. This sounds impossible, but, as you are feeling around its head, you will detect that the gills are constantly opening and closing a little. Just sufficient so that when you make for the strike, you can drive your finger and thumb under the gills and into the opening and the furthest recesses of its gills. Ideally your finger and thumb should end up locked together from opposite sides. Your other hand should be round its tail as you pull the creature towards you in a lethal hug. When you go for the grab, it is no good imagining you are merely going to catch it, you must really want to KILL it. Using all the force you can muster, as if your children's life depends on the outcome – KILL it. At this moment you are doing something brutishly atavistic: killing with your bare hands. Not with a spear, club or gun nor a hook, net or dynamite, just with your bare hands. If you can't face doing this, don't try tickling it because if you miss, the fish will get away in a horribly damaged state.

There are caveats to consider when you go to a tickling. Firstly it is illegal and not all the creatures in the river are as benign as a fish. Several have teeth some even have fangs coupled with vicious reactions if cornered. There are rats and mink to contend with. These live at the back of the banks and, if you put your hand in their domain, you'll get bitten and God help you if it's a mink. There is another creature you'll encounter that feels filthier than anything you have felt before and has teeth – backward facing teeth – namely a live eel. Apart from its fascinating life cycle, I can find nothing about eels that endears me to them.

So the next time any of you are seeing rises all around you, and been hitched several times on the same snag with only the mosquitoes biting, jump in the water and try a little tickling. When you get back to the lodge or the pub with a basket full of fish and tell them how you got them, they will just think it's another fisherman's tale.

Peregrine Eliot, 10th Earl of St Germans, is co-founder of the Port Eliot Lit Festival.

THE
LOWER
TRENT

BY
J W MARTIN

Whether we look at this river from a mere fisherman's standpoint, or whether we look at it from a broader or more historical point of view, it is full of interest for everybody – the tourist, the antiquarian and the naturalist, as well as the wandering angler. Is not this district famous in song, legend, and story? The historian has connected it with some of the earliest and most thrilling episodes in English history; the poet has sung its praises in deathless language; while the story-teller has woven around its waters and its villages stories based on old legends that will live as long as Englishmen live to watch its gliding stream and its leaping fish.

Over thirty years have slipped off time's reel since I had my introduction to that grand old river, and received my first lessons in the famous Nottingham style of stream fishing from men who were as famous in their day and generation as the very river itself – men who, alas! have gone to that bourne from which no traveller returns. At that time the fishing from Newark down to Torksey and beyond was very fair indeed, although a few years later it began to show signs of deterioration; then I had the great advantage of having angling friends who knew every inch of the water, and had constantly fished it for twenty, thirty, and in one or two cases for even forty years. I need only mention the names of such well-known Trent men as Thomas Bentley, James Chatterton, Frank Sims, Andrew Broughton, Thomas Sunman, William Bailey, George Holland; Owen, the old Newark tackle dealer; Corby, the rod maker, who lived in the old Northgate Almshouses, that used to stand close to where the brewery offices now are; not to mention other well-known working men anglers; to show that the information I was able to glean in those days of the fish and fishing in the river was varied and extensive.

Among the better class anglers of that time, mention may be made of Dr Waterworth, Mr Cafferata, Henry Norledge, Harry Weaver and Mr Hibbert; every one of these famous anglers has now joined the great majority. There are few of the old school left, but not many; perhaps Robert Dale, the old verger of the parish church, is the oldest survivor of the old brigade.

It must be more than thirty years since the Newark and Muskham Fishery Association was first formed to take over and preserve the waters that up to then had been rented by Dr Waterworth and Mr Cafferata. Sunman used to look after the water a bit for the gentlemen just named, and I have heard him say that the place swarmed with all sorts of coarse fish,

"The story-teller has woven around its waters and its villages stories based on old legends that will live as long as Englishmen live to watch its gliding stream and its leaping fish"

chub and pike being especially numerous. It was no unusual thing for his patrons to get a dozen or more of the latter fish, running up to fifteen pounds apiece, during a single afternoon; a favourite place for big fish being in the eddy opposite Crankley Point, just at the junction of the two rivers. At that time there was a famous run of water containing quantities of large chub alongside an old willow holt that stretched from that point up stream in the main river, to the brick and stone bridges that carry the Great Northern Railway across the valley. Under those old boughs there was an average depth of five or six feet of water, with a sandy bottom and a nice steady stream. Many were the bags of fish of nearly all kinds that Sunman captured in those days of long ago from there.

The willow holt has long since disappeared, the stream itself has silted up, and changed completely in its character; no one who knew it then would recognize it as being the same place. On the opposite side of the main river were some famous shallows that used to contain a fair sprinkling of grayling. I can just remember one or two fly fishermen who used to wade for those fish there; but even then the glories of the place had waned, and it was only occasionally that a brace of grayling were brought to creel. I believe that they have now disappeared altogether from that part of the Trent.

The piece of water known as the Dyke, running from the bottom locks under the iron suspension bridge and joining the main river at Crankley Point, was in those days a famous haunt for coarse fish, particularly roach and bream, the stream being nothing like so rapid as it was in the main river; also it was of a good average depth, and fringed along the sides by flags and bushes, this no doubt being the cause of the abundance of those two fish. I heard the old anglers say that forty or more years ago any of them who cared to fish there only had to go

down after tea on any afternoon in August or September, with a handkerchief full of brewer's grains and a handful of stewed wheat or malt, and catch as many roach and bream during the evening as they cared to carry home.

Coming down still later to my own recollection of the same stretch of water, I can remember the Newark and Muskham Fishery Association, to celebrate the taking over of the water and starting the society, fishing a sweepstakes match: one Saturday afternoon I think it was. There were about a score of competitors, and in three hours the winner had something like twenty-eight pounds of fish, while the last man of all had a bag that would be considered a very good average first prize catch nowadays.

Those palmy days have vanished, but whether they will ever return is another question. The streams and eddies lower down the river to Winthorp, with its once famous Corporation fishery; the stream known as the Rundalls, Denman's Marsh, the celebrated Holme waters, right along to Collingham Wharf and Carlton Ferry, to say nothing of the Meerings and Sutton Holmes, were waters much patronized by that famous Nottingham angler William Bailey and his equally famous friend George Holland. The chub that swarmed down all those reaches at that time were something to be remembered; it was no uncommon occurrence for those two fishermen to be out for a week together, living on the proceeds of the sale of their fish to the neighbouring villagers; very frequently they would get two or three four-pounders out of one hole in as many swims. Bailey and myself got as many as from twenty to forty pounds of chub during a single day; and once I knew forty-two chub to be taken in an afternoon from one meadow alone. Most assuredly we shall never see the like of that again, although there is some talk of the Navigation Company building a new lock and weir some where opposite the village of Cromwell, which will hold up a lot more water and improve the fishing prospects to a very great extent; because the constant dredging of the channel, and the drawing away of the water from the banks and bushes, has spoiled the fishing without any doubt.

The famous hole at the corner of Foottits Meadow, between Collingham Wharf and Carlton, used to yield very big bags of bream; but I hardly ever hear anything about that place now. Down those lower waters barbel used to be met with, sometimes in considerable quantities, a Newark angler named Robert Wells once getting no fewer that a hundred and twenty-three in a single day. I thought the days of the huge bags of barbel were past; but councillor David Slater, fishing in the Muskham or Holme waters, as recently as August, 1905, got as many as ninety seven in one day, and something like three hundred of those fish within ten days, so hopes still run high.

All down that reach opposite Carlton, and past the mill to the corner known as the Sentry Box, is some capital deep water, where barbel are sometimes got. A good deal of this water for miles and miles is free, Sutton-on-Trent being a good place for any one to make their head-quarters. From here they can go down stream as far as they can walk and find good water nearly everywhere; while by crossing the ferry at the Meerings they have a long range and choice up stream. I might add that miles of this water can be spun over, the fishermen taking care to select the bends and corners where the stream is a lot steadier; pike being occasionally got of a good size. I remember two that were taken on sprats from the Sentry Box eddy that weighed nineteen pounds and sixteen pounds respectively. Flounder-fishing used to be a favourite game of mine in those days; these fish swarmed nearly everywhere then, and a catch during the summer was almost a certainty.

An extract from the book My Fishing Days and Fishing Ways *by J W Martin (Trent Otter) Published in 1906 by W Brendon & Son (Plymouth). Republished in 2004 by Medlar Press.*

THE
RIVER
WANDLE

BY
ROY WILKINSON

Brian Wilson of The Beach Boys collects Toby Jugs. All around us there are things that don't necessarily have to be where they are. Around 10 billion miles from Earth, out on the verge of interstellar space, you'll find recordings of a tractor, a sheep and of Chuck Berry playing *Johnny B. Goode*. They're all on a record aboard the space probe Voyager 1, there for the interest of unknown alien life forms. Will they have a record player? Maybe, but they should have water. If there are extraterrestrial beings out there, it's generally accepted their biochemistry will have needed the stuff to fizz and spark in. It could be true. Down here we have water – and all kinds of things that don't necessarily have to be where they are.

The River Wandle is around 11 miles long, originating on the North Downs in Surrey, by Croydon and Carshalton. The river ends when it flows into the Thames at Wandsworth, sluggishly easing in beside a gasometer and the now empty Young's brewery. Unlike most Thames tributaries, you can actually see the Wandle. It lacks the subterranean mystery of the Falconbrook and Tyburn, but the Wandle's flow and flood-plain still brim with the unexpected.

These waters hold whole scooters from Tuscany; elaborately-decorated metalwork all the way from Silesia. Admiral Nelson lived and fished on the Wandle – having relearnt his angling skills with his left arm after losing his right at the Battle of Santa Cruz de Tenerife. Cliff Richard has also lived by the Wandle. The young Cliff arrived from his birthplace in India to attend Stanley Park Road Primary School in Carshalton. His tan led his his classmates to demonstrate the strange blend of ignorance and innocence that held in the 1940s. They nicknamed him Nigger.

Cliff's school days show the olden times weren't always for the better. The same applies to this river. The Wandle is a chalk stream and, these days, its waters are often limpidly clear. The upper reaches have the restful, bucolic atmosphere you'd associate with Hampshire or Dorset rather than the suburbs and industrial estates of South London. Green fronds of water crowfoot sway in the current while pollution-sensitive brown trout hold their position alongside. The mood seems immemorial. But it hasn't always like been this. For much of the previous two centuries, it was nothing like this.

Nelson fished on the Wandle for a few months in the early 19th Century. At that time, the Wandle wasn't as filthy as it would become. But there was industry on the river even then. The Wandle's rapid flow made it an attractive power source and the Domesday Book says there were 13 mills here in 1086. Industry, population and pollution increased. John Ruskin occasionally visited an aunt who lived by the Wandle. In 1890, he wrote of the river's increasingly blighted state: "Just where the welling of stainless water, trembling and pure, enters the pool... The human wretches cast their street and house foulness; heaps of dust and slime, and broken shreds of old metal, and rages of putrid clothes." Trout were effectively extinct in the Wandle by the early 20th Century.

Walk along the upper stretches of the Wandle today and you'll find a burbling stream – sometimes not much more than ten feet wide and often less than a foot deep. It flows through varied surroundings – council estates, woodland, warehouses, parks. There are both mock-Tudor terraces and the authentically Tudor Carew Manor and Dovecote. A van from

Nutkins Pet Store makes a delivery at the wildlife hospital in Beddington Park.

The rain can't help but flow down to the river. Sometimes it seems we're equally compelled to head down to the water – drawn there by things other than a desire for transport, power and something to drink. On the Wandle's banks lie an array of exotic, brightly-hued objects. They're things that don't have to be there, things that remind us how having a drink often involves more than just slaking a thirst.

Empty aluminium cans litter the greenery. Most are unprepossessing, both in external design and the liquid they once held: "FOSTERS EXPORT. Premium Quality Lager. ALC 4.9% VOL." But there are other, more bewitching exemplars of joy-in-a-tin. Another empty can nestles among the alder leaves. It's a gilded, florid thing – gold, white and red with a crown and antique lettering: "TYSKIE BROWARY KSIAZECE A.D. 1629." Metal, language and lager, all the way from the Silesian voivodeship. Alongside lies an empty can of Scrumpy Jack. Brought to us by Bulmers of Hereford, it lacks the alien allure of its Polish neighbour. But there's still a kind of magic. The print on the can details how the now-gone cider was enhanced by the Dabinett and Chisel Jersey. Alongside the Foxwhelp and Slack-My-Girdle, these apples give our ciders the bitter edge we love so well.

The empty cans are a mess. But they also hint at the special qualities we find in rivers. We include them with the things that are so good they need to be made even better. As with romance, music, sport, it seems rivers are wonderful enough to be accompanied by alcohol. But, fear not, there is increasing awareness that it's possible to have a drink by the water and then remove your rubbish when you're done. And, even for those who don't yet know this, there is help at hand.

The Wandle is far from a natural thing. Concrete channels occasionally run down its centre and its current course is almost entirely a product of human engineering. Snuff, gunpowder and flour were all milled on the Wandle. There was other industry, and agriculture too – brewing, textiles, watercress beds, leather production. Discharge of untreated effluent continued into the 1960s, when the river was officially listed as an open sewer. Even a decade later, locals would watch as the river turned red, pink, brown or blue, according to which dyes were being used by the tanneries. But, in the last ten years, the Wandle has once again become a clean measure, a revivifying draught adding life and lustre to the city.

The new, clean Wandle is the result of inspiring local action. On the lower Wandle, work began around 2000. Initial work was undertaken by the local man Alan Suttie, an illustrator and angling artist, with help from the environmental charity Thames 21. Suttie sat his dream of a clean, fish-filled Wandle under a spectacularly contrived acronym: The JETSET Club. Here was a match, perhaps, even for 1959's Exposition interRnatiOnale du Surrealism (EROS). Or the time the British Army decided to name an anti-tank gun the WOMBAT (Weapon Of Magnesium, Battalion, Anti-Tank). JETSET stands for Junior Environmental Taskforce, Senior Environmental Taskforce. But beneath the goofy nomenclature, good work was begun.

A key initiative was carried out under the more self-explanatory title of Trout In The Classroom. The JETSET

Club has since mutated into The Wandle Trust and its angling offshoot, The Wandle Piscators. The Trout In The Classroom project has continued – with local schools hatching trout and then releasing the young fish into the river.

There is, of course, a paradox in the way fish quite often owe their lives to fishermen – the same people who yank them from the water with a bronzed, barbed hook. Maybe of a lustrous, curved design called something like Sproat, Sneck, Kendal or Viking. But, as with with Tammy Wynette hiding George Jones's car keys lest they lead him to the liquor store, sometimes short-term cruelty equals long-term kindness. Unlike George, however, the fish couldn't overcome the immediate inconvenience by jumping on the lawnmower and riding that to town...

The Wandle Trust organises monthly river clean-ups. I go to one of these mass river-sprucings, on a stretch of the Wandle a little to the east of Wimbledon Common. Perhaps Tomsk and Tobermory and the other forward-thinking greens in the Womble burrow were looking on approvingly.

If environmental action can sometimes suggest mind-numbing labour, this Wandle clean-up isn't like that. There's excellent organisation, some tea and cake and the chance of an invigorating encounters with eel and vole. Around 40 people materialise by a bridge in South London. Here the water is deeper, sometimes over head-height. There are waders for everyone who wants them – bringing the great pleasure that comes when cool water flows over your still-dry thigh. There's also the satisfaction of dragging a lot of stuff up out of the water.

Previous clean-ups along the Wandle have turned up a complete fitted kitchen, a selection of bronze antiquities and a wrought-iron spiral staircase. Today the accent is on two-wheeled transport. We pull out two scooters, a bike and the remains of two motorbikes. One of the scooters is a modern Vespa with space-age silver curves, its manufacture overseen from the company's HQ in the Tuscan town of Pontedera. The scooter is nearly new, seemingly ready to respond to a kick-start once it's drained off a bit. It's clearly been nicked, used for a brief joyride and then launched into the river.

It sometimes seems a river can draw in anyone or anything. Eels have pulled themselves away from the great vortex of the Sargasso Sea, swimming here from their birthplace out by Bermuda. A Vespa has come splashing in from Italy, brought here by petty criminality and the water's concealing depths. A river can also draw people from afar, as is illustrated by the case of Ziggmunde J Sinnette.

I meet Zigi, as he's known, at a National Trust cafe by the Wandle in south London. With his lurcher Isabel and his Scottish longdog Oscar lying placidly under the table, Zigi tells of distant origins. He recounts how he was born during the

Second World War in Nazi-occupied Ukraine. He now works as a water bailiff on the Wandle, based at Morden Hall Park, an 18th Century National Trust estate at the southern end of London Underground's Northern Line.

Zigi is in his late sixties, but his camouflage-clad frame would he tricky to age unassisted. A couple of trout flies – a Klinkhammer and bumblebee pattern – sit on his baseball hat. But he also sports one lime-green fingernail and a bushy goatee beard – somewhere between 1960s Captain Beefheart and the abrupt facial eruptions favoured by today's heavy-metallers. His favourite band are the grunge-era Seattle rockers Alice In Chains, whose singer Layne Staley died from a drug overdose in 2002. It's not exactly *Fly Fishing* by JR Hartley.

Zigi explains how his grandmother brought him to Britain from the distant east. His interest in fishing began in his adolescence, after which came National Service, then an Army career. He finally ended up in South London, where he discovered the Wandle. With a few confederates he began to remove abandoned cars and other wreckage from the river, unaware The Wandle Trust were doing the same kind of thing a little downstream.

Zigi is, to some extent, poacher-turned-gamekeeper. Until recently, the local authorities actively discouraged fishing on the upper Wandle. Zigi was involved in the occasional mass-protest fish. But, such modest riverine insurrection – fuelled by a pint of maggots rather than a Molotov cocktail – meant Zigi understood the local angler's mindset. His work cleaning the Wandle eventually led to work as bailiff at Morden Hall Park.

Visit Morden Hall and you find a cosy Utopia. What was once exclusive now offers sport for all – or at least fishing with the Morden Hall Angling Club or a run around these tree-lined acres. You don't even need National Trust membership to enter the grounds. The Wandle meanders through the park, its well-oxygenated waters adding life to its surroundings. By the bookshop, a shoal of chub hang mesmerically in midstream. Once, Morden Hall's snuff works added their waste to the Wandle and the river is still prey to chemical contamination.

Zigi has photographic evidence of the Wandle's abundant piscine population. But, the fish are sitting so calmly for the camera because they're dead. In September 2007, someone made a calamitous mistake at Thames Water's Beddington sewage works. Concentrated sodium hypochlorite – bleach – flowed into the river. An early alarm was raised and flow-management allowed much wildlife to be saved. But the photos show seemingly-endless mortality – an expanse of dead barbel, a mass of dead dace, about 40 dead roach around the 3lb bracket.

"I'd never seen anything like it," says Zigi. "We were laying out yards of dead fish, which we needed to do for evidence. Then I got a call from someone from the Environment Agency. She said, 'I'm stood on the weir at Bennett's Hole looking down the river and I can see a mile of silver.' I just burst into tears."

There was also a silver lining to this chemically-induced cloud. Thames Water admitted their responsibility and promised £500,000 toward restoration and conservation on the Wandle. And pollution hadn't quite rendered the river lifeless. Blocking flow into backwater channels saved a lot of fish at Morden Hall and soon the bleach was diluted to non-lethal levels. It was after this pollution that Zigi says a remarkable animal first appeared on the river – an albino coot, all-over white in place of its normal black-grey. As Zigi points out, various American Indian cultures see the appearance of an albino animal as an auspicious sign. This particular coot has since disappeared, but an equally albino descendent is still there.

"I see it as very good sign," says Zigi. "I, for one, feel fortunate to be here at all. There was nothing to say that was going to happen. But, here I am, every day in the best back-garden in the world and getting to spend my time on this river."

Nelson was a keen fly fisherman. He provided his mistress Lady Emma Hamilton with the funds to buy Merton Place near the Wandle in 1801. She called her residence Merton Paradise and diverted the Wandle to create her own private canal – named The Nile, after Nelson's victory at The Battle of The Nile. Nelson did get to fish the Wandle, but only fleetingly. For most of his last years he was pursuing French ships across the seas, from the Mediterranean to the Caribbean.

Nelson, of course, died after being hit by a French musket-ball during the Battle of Trafalgar in 1805. His body came back to Britain in a barrel of brandy, myrrh and camphor, this booze-filled temporary coffin lashed to the mast of his flagship HMS *Victory*.

It's now all but impossible to imagine the French and British smashing up each other's powder-monkeys with cannonball and splintered wood. Sing hosanna! As with the Wandle, things sometimes get better. Yet, Trafalgar, that remote headland in south-west Spain, remains one of the most evocative names in our history. And these distant Spanish seas now have a modest but moving connection to the waters of the Wandle.

On the 200th anniversary of Trafalgar, in 2005, the UK's Salmon & Trout Association marked the Wandle's Nelson connections with a fund-raising dinner for The Wandle Trust – or The JETSET Club as it was still known then. The dinner took place at St Paul's Cathedral. It was decided this was an occasion to be marked with appropriate traces of Wandle history. Those attending the dinner was presented with reproductions of trout flies Nelson might have used on the river.

Two fly patterns were located – the Carshalton Cocktail and the Carshalton Dun. The flies were then constructed by the ferociously dedicated fly-tyer Roy Christie. The names of trout flies conjure some of the marvel and poeticism crammed into these tiny devices: Gold-Ribbed Hare's Ear, Snipe And Purple, Bracken Clock, Spanish Needle. When I meet Roy at his home, he's surrounded by feathers, filaments and fur – the raw materials of his craft. Roy personifies the entrancing arcana and the adept's fervency that make up this world. Originally from Northern Ireland and now in his early fifties, he's intense and evangelical on behalf of a realm that fills his mind but doesn't provide his living. "This is a just a hobby," he says deadpan, "this roomful of dead foxes and minks and pheasants and parrots and peacocks..." He works shifts for

British Airways, partly because the staff flight rates allow him to travel to overseas fishing events.

The 19th-century fly recipes Roy dug up to for the Trafalgar dinner read like ingredients for a witch's potion: "Blue dun fur mixed with fur of hare's ear... The dark feather of the starling's wing made spare and short." He gives me examples of the flies tied for the Trafalgar dinner – beautifully subfusc things, with the subtle greys and browns of the Carshalton Cocktail offset by a spiral of silver. Roy is clearly lost to the rivers and isn't afraid to consider their importance in the widest terms. "They reckon oil is worth fighting for," he says. "Well, water is worth killing for. Oil rights makes you money, but you need water to live..."

<hr />

Back on the Wandle, the bohemian cafes and shops of Merton Abbey Mills offer a model in cosmopolitan capital living. There's a Belgian Brasserie and the Ting N Ting Caribbean Cafe. A musical-instrument shop offers numerous guitars in child's sizes – perhaps all the better to prime youngsters for a shot at the BRIT music school in nearby Croydon. Graduates include the singers Adele, Katie Melua and Cleopatra Royer. The latter appeared on Andrew Lloyd Webber's Saturday-night TV show *I'd Do Anything* – trilling in committed style for the chance to play Nancy in a production of Lionel Bart's *Oliver!*

As intimated by a pub called The William Morris, Merton Abbey Mills have long had connection with the arts – specifically with the Arts And Craft movement in which Morris was a prime mover. He began producing his textiles at the Abbey Mills in

1881, the river providing power and water. Morris paid homage to the river by naming one of his fabric designs 'Wandle'. Calico, stained glass and gun-turrets for the Second World War bomber the Bristol Blenheim have also been made at Merton Abbey Mills. Coincidentally, *Calico* is the name of a track by the pop group Saint Etienne, an outfit with Croydon connections. Saint Etienne are the creation of Bob Stanley and Pete Wiggs, who both spent their teenage years in Croydon. As the band formed, the pair mirrored the Wandle's course, moving from Surrey into London. With their lyrics voiced with wondrous weather-girl tristesse by singer Sarah Cracknell, Saint Etienne have often detailed the everyday poetry of London and Britain's south-east. Wiggs and Stanley would occasionally visit Merton Abbey Mills – Pete for a quiet pint after a loud night out in London, Bob to visit a record shop and expand his ever-proliferating collection. He's currently accruing examples of every UK number one single. When I meet him, he expresses some satisfaction at having acquired a copy of the first ever chart-topper – *You Belong To Me* by the Californian singer Jo Stafford, from 1952.

As with a river's unpredictable flow, Saint Etienne often place things where you wouldn't expect them – sampling some guitar by the Canadian prog-metallers Rush and adding it to a track named after the Spanish tennis player Conchita Martínez. Or writing a heart-meltingly pretty tune and naming it *Hobart Paving*, after a surfacing contractor based in Croydon and Burgess Hill. "We thought it sounded exotic," says Bob.

Saint Etienne aren't the only musicians to have followed the Wandle's course toward the bright lights of London. The Wandle is generally too fast to allow much silt to deposit, but the glam rockers of Mud formed by the river's source at Carshalton. The late Kirsty MacColl began her musical career in Croydon, in a punk-era group called Drug Addix. But the most significant musical mind to have coursed from Croydon to London is Malcolm McLaren.

McLaren attended Croydon College Of Art, where, inspired by the riots and Situationist slogans of 1968 Paris, he organised a month-long sit-in. The revolting long-hairs were fortified by cupcakes and rolling tobacco. Malcolm, of course, went on to become manager and cultural architect to the Sex Pistols. He also became so much a part of London that, in 1999, he campaigned to become mayor of the city. He canvassed the metropolitan mass-mind with a range of ideas. There would be increased adult education – in "anything from belly-dancing to the bassoon". Holograms of the much-loved BBC1 bobby *Dixon Of Dock Green* would line the streets – so the people would know where to go for travel directions. In the midst of this energetic campaign, I was lucky enough to be able to quiz McLaren on his transport policy.

As he unveiled a mayoral platform encompassing trains, buses and planes, the mind was drawn helplessly to an image on the Sex Pistols' *Pretty Vacant* single – a pair of coaches with their destination-boards given new and punkish directions. Was it true, I asked, that Malcolm's London would feature only two bus services – one going to Boredom, the other to Nowhere? "No, no, no!" he shrieked, heroically oblivious to any nuance outwith his own mind. "That was a record sleeve for the band the Sex Pistols! I am no longer managing the Sex Pistols! I am standing to be Mayor of London!"

Malcolm eventually pulled out of the mayoral race. It's easy to forgive him his slight confusion on transport. After all, who among us can be sure where we came from or where we're going? A river's fascinations and reassurances include the way we can often see its beginning and end. This isn't the case with many of London's underground rivers, but it is with the Wandle. Peer over from bridge and bank and you can see and hear clear water rinsing mellifluously over the rocks, see a trout or dace flicking at the surface.

By some measures, the Wandle can be seen as the most industrialised river in the world. But, even though 80 per cent of the Wandle's current flow is treated output from Beddington sewage works, the river is now far from the chemical-laced, junk-clogged channel it was for decades. It only took a few individuals to decide it didn't have to be like that – people who were, in effect, composing their own version of the Situationist slogans which inspired Malcolm McLaren. Not so much "Under the paving stones the beach." More "Under the shopping trollies a river."

If you walk by the Wandle, spare a thought for Alan Suttie, the original JETSET instigator. Today, his rubbish-removing, trout-releasing initiatives are being continued The Wandle Trust and The Wandle Piscators – variously aided by bodies including the Environment Agency, The Riverfly Partnership, the Wild Trout Trust, Thames Water, local authorities and the Sofronie Foundation, a grant-making organisation that supports work with children from disadvantaged backgrounds. The appropriately named Theo Pike is heavily involved with both The Wandle Trust and Wandle Piscators. Theo is in his mid thirties, a writer for commercial and charity campaigns and for fishing magazines. He came to angling relatively late in life. When asthma got in the way of a planned career in the British Army, his father suggested he go away for a spot of fishing. An enthusiasm was born – one that, in turn, led him to the Wandle. Theo became so fascinated by the river he moved to live near its source in Carshalton. He represents The Wandle Trust at public meetings on the river's future – or takes a turn overseeing health-and-safety at Wandle clean-ups. At these river restorations you can see things other than scooters and sinks emerging from the water.

"I remember one clean-up session," says Theo. "It was in January on a stretch of the Wandle in Merton. Snow was falling when, suddenly, these little iron blue dun flies started hatching from the river and spiralling up into the snowstorm. It was unforgettable. The whole scene was beautiful, cold, stark. It made me think of some Oriental print. And it was all the more amazing because of the amount of rubbish we were pulling out of the river. It was without doubt one of my most memorable moments on any river, anywhere."

Blue duns are flies of the order Ephemeroptera. As this name suggests, they don't stay around forever. During the Wandle's dirty, derelict years, there were long periods when they wouldn't have been there at all. Blue duns, brown trout and an albino coot can now all be seen on the Wandle. Here are things that don't necessarily have to be where they are – a scenic spectrum that says anything can happen.

Roy Wilkinson is a well-meaning part-timer in the fields of journalism, birdwatching and music management.

THE DIRT
WATERFALL

BY
BEN MYERS

A hole in the wall of trees signalled the beginnings of a well-worn path that dropped away from the car park, away from civilisation, and down a bank towards the river.

The River Wear. Prime waterway through the industrial ghostland of the North. Sculptor of red sandstone and granite. Supporter of lead mine and shipyard. Silent witness to our teenage indiscretions.

The Wear. Our river.

Centuries of feet had compacted the earth so that the steep path now looked like a waterfall that had had all its water stolen, or maybe a waterfall made out of dirt.

Dirt waterfall to the Wear.

We walked down it with baby steps, a clattering tangle of rods and backpacks. The dirt waterfall path plunged down into the gorge at the bottom of which sat the river. I couldn't see it yet, but I could sense it.

The close proximity of silently shifting water is something that can often be felt – its silence is deafening and its impact on its surrounding landscape tangible.

Because the river – any river – is the centrepiece of the landscape through which it forges its way armed only with a chisel called time, and anything else – trees, flowers, footpaths – are merely visitors, there to bask in its calming presence and graze on its banks like idle cows in the height of summer.

So I felt the river first, sensed it. And sure enough after ascending the dirt waterfall like nineteenth-century adventurers in barrels over Niagara falls and down into the tree-lined gorge, it all suddenly opened out in front of us. There below lay a snake-bend of the river, brown and thick with the silt and slurry of spring, its borders alive and moving with constant growth.

This movement of growth was imperceptible to the human eye, but it was easy to see that it was taking place. We were in the midst of an explosion of plants, flowers, weeds and dispersing seeds. Each day down here would be different as life crept down to the water side.

We walked on towards the river, attracted, like all the other life forms, by its magnetic pull. All creatures move towards water, because water is the source of life.

I could see more of the river now, distinguishable from the surroundings by its flatness and consistency of colours. All around it were the crude angles and chaos of nature as branches, grasses and plant life fought for their patch of sun-space and created a scene painted entirely from a palette of greens.

It was strange to think that only two or three months earlier these plants were nothing but seeds imprisoned by ground frost and the trees skeletons against a white winter sky, that this wooded gorge was remarkable for its barrenness where now it could barely contain the recent burst of activity in its plant life. Stranger still to think that only weeks ago, snow would have hidden the many ancient pathways that cut through the gorge and linked up to follow the river in both directions.

We had had just reached the bottom of the gorge when Davey James dropped his bags and let out a sigh.

"I left the maggots in the car."

While Davey James went back up to civilisation – to locate the bait he had been given the responsibility of buying that morning in an airless shack some eight miles away along country roads

– I found a spot on a familiar bend and set up using sweet corn as bait. I rolled a rock down the bank for a seat and perched myself over the water

This river was an amorphous creature that slithered off in both directions, an ever-changing entity capable of shedding its skin or wearing a different mask to suit its moods, yet at the same time utterly permanent, a reliable fixture on a rapidly-changing landscape.

Who could really know what stories and secrets the river held? Who knew the things it has seen over thousands, maybe millions, of years, and the lives it had supported and the lives it had taken? And who knew what really lay beneath its surface – what strange creatures dwelt within it, what skeletons it held in its watery river-bed closet? The river held so many stories and buried them in its bed like old shopping trolleys, like elephant bones.

The source of this river was some forty miles south-west of here, inland and – of course – uphill, though far less as the crow flies. For the changing gradients of the landscape are the river's friends. Without them the river would be stagnant and land-locked, nothing more than a pond or lake or swamp-land, those lazy half-breed cousins of the river that has gone from inception to death at sea continuously for thousands upon thousands of years.

Day after day for thousands of years, fresh water from springs and rainfall have conspired to carve a path down through fields and woodlands, valleys and villages, past great monuments of history and beneath busy shopping streets observing cathedrals, churches, ruined abbeys and the changing face of contemporary architecture, past the crooked rusted remains of the industrial age wastelands then cowering troll-like under ugly iron bridges and finally widening past sand flats and rushing forth to meet the sea.

This part of the river was much wider than the tributary we had fished the previous day, which mainly exists in one valley before joining this river about ten miles upstream from here. Yet still, in the grand scheme of rivers it was geographically small and insignificant; it was one seven-thousandth the length of the Nile and not much more than forty or fifty feet in width for most of its length.

What it lacked in awe-inspiring magnitude, it more than made up for in areas of beauty. The river's main strength though lay in its maturity and endurance. Even sitting there, rod in hand, it was obvious that the waters were much stronger than they appeared. It was a strong river of good heart and character. It had watched empires, regimes and dictators rise and fall with not so much as a shrug.

I knew from past excursions that the river begins in pools and springs way up in the valley between two remote villages that sit like moss that has grown upon the grey slate of a sky, before flowing for forty changing miles through one old historical city then further on to an economically-deprived city – the river's largest – that encroaches upon either side of its mouth like cold sores. Then, after that, a short widening swirl into the North Sea, which itself is fed on different sides by many other rivers, including the Weser at Bremerhaven, the Ems at Emden, the Meuse at Rotterdam and the majestic Rhine.

A mere twenty miles downstream from where I sat, the river opened out to waters that lead directly to Scandinavia.

From tiny springs in empty valleys to mingling in the seas with rivers they once wrote great symphonies about, it all linked up. Everything. Existence may be random in its beginnings and chaos still reigns, yet if you trace the world's waterways, you'll find they all link up.

Every last drop.

For two-thirds of the planet.

From the corner of my eye, I caught sight of a movement upstream and behind me, inland. I turned my head in that direction. It wasn't the movement of a human or an animal, but was something more expansive.

I saw it again – a sudden shifting, a flurry of activity, a flash of blue low down in amongst the densely-compacted trees.

With the line cast out across the river, I carefully laid down my rod and optimistically placed a rock upon it in case something big was to suddenly bite.

I left the little shore and went up onto the riverside path and followed it fifty metres or so upstream, then turned off into the wood.

Then I saw it again, a sweeping ripple across the ground as a wave of blue shifted from left to right.

Bluebells.

Hundreds upon hundreds of them.

I walked into the trees and came across a thick closely-contained, recently-blossomed patch of them. They were growing in a clearing beneath a heavy canopy of leaves through which the sun's ray shone down and bathed them in shafts of undiluted and highly-theatrical light, as if choreographed by a lighting director just out of shot. Many of the younger, smaller bluebells nestled in the shadows of the trees. Together they made an aromatic and exotic new carpet for the woodland floor.

As I approached this secreted bluebell patch, a light breeze swept across its surface causing the hundreds of stems to shimmer and undulate like a flag on the brow of a warship, like a Mexican wave of people at a sporting event.

As I got closer, the bluebells collectively transformed themselves from a flag into a pool of pale blue water. I waded into them as if they were a fresh spring bubbling up through layers of chalk to reinvigorate an ailing stream, as if from the pen of Gerard Manley Hopkins: "And azuring-over greybell makes / Wood banks and brakes wash wet like lakes."

The bluebells were virginal and untouched by man. They had probably opened up early this morning while I was sleeping, while we were all sleeping. For that is the magic of bluebells: like daffodils they appear from nothing, seemingly growing from zero to sixty centimetres in the blink of an eye.

Each fresh bluebell crop heralds a change in the weather, the dawning days of the warm season – a sign perhaps to dust down your fishing nets and start your mad worm dance again.

Across the land and across the generations the Bluebell has been given many names – Calverkeys, Culverkeys, Auld Man's Bell, Jacinth, Ring-o'-Bells – but has only ever had one face, that blue visage that tilts itself to the sun before silently bowing and genuflecting come nightfall. So popular and perennial are bluebells that most areas in the country have a quiet corner nearby called Bluebell Woods, each different in landscape and geography, yet constant in their covering of these much-loved flowers. If you doubt this, then I suggest you go to your nearest and most respected local elder and ask them the way to the Bluebell Woods. They are sure to reply, not with a look of puzzlement, but with some clear and concise directions.

I walked amongst the clearing, knee-deep in bluebells as if knee-deep in the purest spring water somehow turned blue by the sun's light. I fell into them collapsing to the floor. I let the bluebells pull me under as I lay on my back examining the intertwining branches above that formed a chaotic matrix of silhouette lines against the sky. I lay there, under imaginary blue water, bobbing slightly as the next incoming flicker of a breeze swept across me – across us – for in a bluebell wood you may be the only human, but you are never alone with all these nodding and bowing new friends for company.

Somewhere in the far distance, like gunshots on land heard far out a sea, a series of noises broke the silence.

Sneezes.

It meant one thing: the return of Davey James.

I could hear him a half-mile off, tramping his way back down the dirt waterfall and through the gorge, sneezing and groaning in sympathy for himself as leaves rustled and twigs snapped underfoot.

The sneezes echoed down the gorge and across the water, bouncing off the wall of trees at the other side. A few hundreds yards upstream, a grazing cow lazily raised its head and looked in my direction before resuming her cud-chewing business.

I felt something on the back of my neck. I slapped it dead.

Half an hour had passed since Davey James had left and the temperature was rising. With it came the proliferation of hatching flies; the very best time to fish.

Davey James' sneezes came closer, then suddenly he appeared from the woods, shaking his head in distress, a human smudge of snot and burst capillaries.

"Bloody hay fever," he said. "It's getting worse."

"Did you get them?"

He wearily held aloft a carrier bag which I took to be full of the prized maggots.

He sneezed, put down his bag, then flopped down in the dirt. He was sweating, his eyes glazed, bloodshot and red around the edges.

He sneezed a couple more times and then let out a woeful groan.

"Any luck?" he said.

"No, not yet. I saw some nice bluebells though."

———————•◦•———————

They're fascinating creatures, maggots – and very much maligned. Anything that provokes so much disgust, and which thrives upon death and decay is bound to be.

While on the one hand they metamorphosise into flies that dine on shit and which have, for hundreds of thousands of years, been the bane of human and animal alike, on the other they have been great benefit to man, not only as bait, but in the practice of debridement, the technique in which maggots are used to remove dead or infected tissue from in or around wounds.

The use of maggots in wounds has been going on for centuries and has been particularly well documented since the American Civil War, when field medics with impressively-maintained moustaches would remove the lid from a tin and tap a few fresh maggots into the three-day old wounds of a Union soldier who has recently had his ass peppered with buckshot by a Confederate patriot who would later go onto to be a key member in the Ku Klux Klan. Happy days.

With a bloody, muddy war raging around them, the maggots then got to work, eating away at the decaying tissue and cleaning the wounds while the soldier lay prone, his britches around his ankles as he whistled a tuneless song and dreamt of his dear old Ma,

Soon enough, in time, the wounds would start to heal and the soldier would return home to his small town and his childhood sweetheart, and he'd be greeted as a hero. He would receive a medal for his valour and rumour would have it that it had been sent down the line directly from the top, from the man himself – Ulysses S. Grant.

And for a while, everywhere he went, people would offer to buy the young solider a tumbler of good whisky to thank him for his part in helping win the American Civil War, and to gently persuade him to tell tales about what it was like out in those fields, dodging buckshot and living off tasteless biscuits. And though the soldier would accept the whisky, he would bow his head and say in a low voice "I don't like to talk about it," and everyone would assume he had seen things too despicable to ever talk again. They would respect his decision and leave it there – they wouldn't even ask about those tasteless biscuits – without ever once realising that the real reason he didn't want to talk about it was because, deep down, he knew his contribution to the war effort involved getting his ass wounds eaten by

maggots in a tent in a field during a battle that he never wanted to be a part of in the first place, biscuits or no biscuits.

"God bless America."

I baited my hook and, after a quick cup of coffee each and a hastily-smoked joint passed backwards and forwards as if it were going to self-destruct after five minutes, Davey James walked upstream slightly, around the bend some ways, but still in view.

We were finally fishing. After all the delays and with a new-found confidence in the maggots, we went at it with quiet determination.

It was our first fishing trip as adults; the trip we had planned for years but had been far too lazy to get round to doing.

And now the flies were fully hatching and swarming in halos across the surface of the river now. The light breeze of earlier dropped so that everything became perfectly still and the sun at its highest point in the sky. Even the river appeared to breath a languid sigh of relief, stretching and yawning like a cat basking in the afternoon glow. I tried to relax with it. I tried to become part of the scenery, as immoveable as the trees, as fluid as the water, as expansive as the sky. I attempted to become part of nature, rather than the visitor or plunderer that I was.

These woods and river were full of history – my history.

A mile or so downstream there sat a huge but little-known viaduct that straddled the valley, peering from the tree tops like the sails of great galleon that has taken a wrong turn in time. The viaduct had long since served its original purpose, which was to provide a link from the coalfields and quarries of the northeast to the burgeoning rail networks. But there was a sadness to this viaduct that was now closed off to vehicles and public alike. Sad because it was in fine shape and a mere 160 years old, maybe less. And sad because, remarkably, it couldn't be seen from the surrounding areas. Hidden in the trees with its roots at the foot of a gorge that plunged itself deep away from passing roads, it had simply disappeared from view. Many locals knew nothing of it.

What the viaduct now lead to on either side merely highlighted its sense of isolation. On the one side were farmer's fields, on the other there were tracks and a wasteland that lead to one of the city's two prisons, this one infamous for the notoriety of its inhabitants, all of them serving long sentences. Even these wastelands had stories to tell though. Within them was a pond a quarter of a mile wide that I had fished with my dad as a child, without luck, while written records in the local equivalent of the Domesday Book, which date back to the 12th century, mention a farm that once sat there.

Fixing my rod into the crook of a branch I had stuck into the ground I wandered down to the viaduct and was awestruck by its towering presence. The engineering was impeccable, the brickwork flawless and the condition very good and now it just sat there, alone and immoveable like a totem pole, like a deep-rooted gravestone.

We used to come here as teenagers in the early '90s, Davey James and I, and other friends too. The barbed wire tangles and KEEP OUT signs were of no consequence to us. We'd walk the couple of miles along roads and across the fields down to the river, then follow it downstream until we came to the viaduct. Then we would scramble up the dusty banks to the top of the gorge, climb over a fence, slip through the barbed wire and walk out on to the viaduct and suddenly find ourselves above the tree line and in the lap of the Gods. Here we would smoke cigarettes and take turns pissing over the edge or, if we were feeling daring, hanging suspended from the rusted and loose iron railings using only the strength of our arms, the river so far and away below that it appeared to be still and not made from water at all, but rather an open artery in the top soil.

Up on the viaduct we were temporarily elevated above our surroundings, higher than the river, the trees, the housing estates that were red dots in the distance, higher than anyone for miles around as the wind whistled through our flapping clothes and we wondered whether the viaduct was closed to the public because it could collapse any moment.

I used to have dreams about that viaduct. Each time it featured, it seemed to increase in size until it reached epic proportions in my imagination; it grew until it blocked the sky, until it became so huge it couldn't possibly have served a purpose as a bridge for no track, road or railway line could ever have met it at either end. It grew until it was no longer a once-functional relic from the past but instead became something else. It increased until it became personified, a huge brick creature, a giant of stature beyond comprehension, a sky god, until it eventually broke itself free from its foundations, shook off its railings and KEEP OUT signs and the birds that nested in its arches, shook off the dust and the dirt and the weeds that grew from the cracks within its mortar, and it took off into the night, across the slow rolling hills, maybe north towards Scotland, maybe to the sea, but either way never to be seen again.

With the bridge over my shoulder, I walked back to our spot where the fish kept leaping. As I arrived back at my spot, a sizable brown trout leapt through the air then splashed noisily back, sending ripples nearly all the way across the river to both bank sides. A silence followed that made me wonder whether it had even been there a moment ago.

Then: two more in quick succession. Splash, splash.

Then, twenty seconds later, another fish leapt, slightly further downstream towards Davey. It looked like a chub, though it was too far away for me to be able to tell. Less than a minute later, one leapt out the water and over my trailing line.

Ha, said the fishes' splashes. Ha, ha. What a terrible fisherman you are. Watch as we perform a gymnastic display for you. Watch as we leap over your sagging line and laugh at your pathetic hook and bait. Watch as we mock your every move. Do you not think we don't see you standing there on the bank?

"Just shut up," I found myself snapping. "Cocky little fuckers."

Along the bank, Davey James turned to me.

"You OK?"

"Yes," I waved back. "Fine. I'm just arguing with a chub."

I reeled in my line, skewered two fat maggots and cast off, the whir of the reel followed by the jolting click as the line reached full stretch. I had cast to within inches of the opposite bank, my float hanging in the black water of an afternoon shadow. And there it stayed.

At that moment time slipped away. It crumbled like a pillar of salt. One minute stretched to an hour, an hour was the length of a leaping fish and the entire planet fit neatly into the mouth of a maggot.

In that moment, life felt good.

If I said that the fishing was good that day, it would imply that we had some degree of success on the bank of these lush brown waters. In fact, it was the opposite – we had not so much as a nibble, yet nevertheless: "the fishing was good". The weather was perfect, the coffee was strong, the weed was stronger, the fish were leaping and even the cheese sandwiches we hastily scarfed down seemed to please the palette in new ways.

I was starting to understand for the very first time what it was that had made man fish for thousands of years, and would continue to do so for many thousands of years more. It had little to do with fish, and a lot to do with everything else: nature, philosophy, love, contemplation, physical exertion, the sweat on the back, your new T-shirt suntan, the dirt underfoot, the sky up above.

Fishing was the religion that welcomed everyone, excluded no-one and only served to make us better human beings. I was beginning to get it. But more than anything I was just glad to greet an old friend. This old silent friend the Wear, a timeless constant in a changing world.

Ben Myers is a poet and novelist.

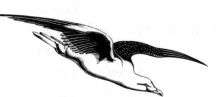

UNDER
WATER

———— ◆ ————

BY
MATHEW CLAYTON

In the winter of 2000 a strange thing happened. The Wellsbourne, a river no-one had ever heard of, let alone seen, began flowing through the centre of Brighton. It rose a few miles north of the town in Patcham and then ran down to the Old Steine, passing St Peter's church and the Royal Pavillion, before it reached the sea at Pool Valley. For the last 150 years it had lain dormant, buried in the Victorian sewage system, forgotten, except to those that had read the history books and knew the damage it had caused in the past. The Wellsbourne is that rare thing – an uncelebrated river. The problem child of a town synonymous with water. Forever causing trouble, exacerbating bad weather by flooding or letting in the sea. A lithograph of a thunderstorm that took place 17th July, 1850, shows the Wellsbourne flowing freely through Pool Valley to a depth of 6 feet after just one hour of rainfall. And it wasn't just the sea it let into the town. In 1723 "a pretty large vessel was by ye violence of the wind and tide carried in the Pool".

Rivers are not permanent features of the landscape: they expand, they silt up, they meander. These changes can be swift and dramatic. In the 1579, a single storm east of Brighton changed the course of the River Ouse, moving its mouth from Seaford to a village called Meeching. Overnight Seaford stopped being a bustling port. Meeching was renamed Newhaven and became the busiest harbour in Sussex. And so it is with the Wellsbourne. We know at one point it was a far more commanding part of the landscape as the Doomesday Book records that Brighton lay in the Whalesbone hundred – a hundred being a parcel of land within a county. The venerable tome also records a mill at Patcham which, to function properly, would have needed a constant and considerable current of water.

What brought the Wellsbourne back to life in 2000 was not a single storm but a sustained period of rainfall over the whole year that kept the soil wet and the water table high. The chalk aquifer, a gigantic underground reservoir that runs beneath Sussex, was already full when it started raining in November. It was uncommonly wet 178 mm of rain fell, compared with 21 mm in the same period in 1999, but this year it had nowhere to go.

In nearby Patcham, furniture floated on ceilings, toilets gushed water and the London to Brighton road was closed for days. The front page of the local newspaper declared, 'Floody Hell' and rushed out a special supplement to record the misery. More serious damage to Brighton was prevented by hydrobreaks – chicanes built into the sewage system designed to slow down the flow during storms. Without them the sheer weight of the rushing water would have washed away parts of the town.

"Rivers are not permanent features of the landscape: they expand, they silt up, they meander. These changes can be swift and dramatic."

It was also a test of the recently installed stormwater tunnel – a gigantic concrete barrel 6 metres in diameter and 3 miles long buried 30 metres underneath the seafront. The sewage system in Brighton, like most cities, is a combined system. The drains collect domestic waste as well as surface water. The danger of this system is that, under extreme conditions, the drains can't cope and they bring to the surface not just rainwater but also human waste. The stormwater tunnel is a gigantic overflow tank designed to stop this ever happening. It reached three-quarters full.

The tunnel also offers some protection to the immediate coastline. The city's sewage is still pumped into the English Channel, albeit three miles out to sea. This is actually an improvement. For many years there was a sewage outfall just off the beach near a spot where each summer teenage boys prove their manhood by leaping off the pier. Southern Water has been trying to remedy this situation by building a new treatment works, but getting planning permission has proved problematic. No-one wants the county's waste treated in their backyard.

It is particularly unfitting that Brighton should be so careless with its sewage because the success of the town was built upon the curative properties of its water. The storms and floods of the early part of the 18th century had ruined Brighton's fishing feet and sent the town into a downward economic spiral – it needed a miracle to get it back on its feet. Instead it got a miracle cure. A local physician Dr Russell wrote a bestselling book, *Dissertation on the use of sea water in the diseases of the glands*. It promoted the beneficial effects of bathing in and drinking seawater claiming it would cure a vast range of diseases. Such was the book's popularity that people began travelling to the town to take the saltwater cure. Bottles of this magical 'oceanic fluid' were sold in London and what had until then been a poor fishing village reinvented itself as a fashionable spa resort. Russell's ideas were developed further by a Doctor

Awsiter, who built an indoor bathhouse at the mouth of the
Wellsbourne with an impressive classical facade that bore the
inscription 'Hygea Devota' – a devotion to the Greek goddess
of health and sanitation, Hygea. Awsiter realised the problem
with drinking seawater was that it tasted horrible, 'there are
many constitutions too delicate, and stomachs too weak to
bear the nausea and sickness it produces, and even when the
inconvenience is overcome by daily struggles, it makes the
party thirsty for the remainder of the day'. His answer was to
promote mixing it with milk. He also claimed it cured infertil-
ity, 'to stand before all other remedies. There is remarkable

fecundity in sea water, beyond even the much-famed mud of the Nile'.

Inspired by the success of Aswiter's Baths, similar establishments sprung up nearby. Brill's Baths boasted the largest circular swimming pool in Europe, overlooked by a balcony that could seat 400 people. There were first and second-class baths for men and women, a barber's, a reading room, a billiard room and vapour baths. Swimming in the sea was experienced via bathing machines, little caravan-like changing rooms on gigantic wooden wheels that were pulled into the water. For the first half of the 19th century, men often bathed naked, while women wore long dresses and were led into the sea with help from formidable ladies known as 'dippers'. For those who didn't want to venture to the beach, salt water was piped into hotels and homes. In the early years of the 20th century there were still dozens of houses that received salt water.

An Indian Sake, Deen Mahomed, introduced 'shampooing', the original term for massage, to the town and was appointed Shampooing Surgeon to his majesty King George IV. This put him in charge of arrangements in the King's marble plunge bath at the Pavillion. The king was lowered into the bath in a chair by a complicated set of pulleys and levers.

It was Brighton's attraction as a health resort that first brought the Prince Regent to the town, and ultimately led to the Wellsbourne's demise. The Prince arrived in Brighton for the first time on 7th September, 1783. The Sussex Advertiser reported the event: 'at half past six His Royal Highness's arrival was announced by the ringing of the bells and a royal salute from the battery, when unhappily, through some indiscretion in reloading one of the pieces, it went off and wounded the undergunner mortally'.

The Prince soon became a regular summer visitor to Brighton and built himself a house – the Royal Pavillion. Designed by John Nash, the architect best known for the more sober terraces around Regent's Park, it is a fantastical eruption of domes and minarets styled on an Indian palace. The Chinese interior is even more over the top: the banqueting hall is topped by a dome 45 feet high painted like an eastern sky framed with palm trees. In the middle, a gigantic chandelier hangs from the claws of a silver dragon. The Regency period became known for its excess and decadence – not only in relation to its architecture: the menu for a banquet served at the Pavillion in 1817 lists 116 separate dishes.

———•◦•———

The Wellsbourne, at this point, was little more than a trickle that gathered into a stagnant, and unwelcome, pond just outside The Prince's front door on the Pavillion lawns. It frequently overflowed. On the 20th August, 1792, the *Sussex Advertiser* reported: 'last Saturday morning we had a very heavy fall of rain which has again completely flooded our northern brooks. At Brighton is caused a torrent that washed away a considerable part of the little channel between the Steine and the Prince's Pavillion. Had the work resisted the water, "tis thought a part of the Steine must have been overflowed'. The following year, the Prince and his neighbour, the Duke of Marlborough, built a brick sewer to contain the Wellsbourne. In return for this service to the town they were given permission to enclose a portion of land in front of their houses on the condition that they never build on it.

<hr/>

By the middle of the 19th century, Brighton had swelled to a population of 60,000 and it desperately required a new drainage system. The intercepting sewer was to be the new home of the Wellsbourne. An extraordinary feat of Victorian architecture, it ran seven and a quarter miles from Hove to Telescombe. But the Wellsbourne had grown in its underground home. The first contractor had to stop work because of the amount of water they encountered. Thirteen pumps driven by nine engines pumped out 68 million litres of water every day so work could continue.

The purpose of the sewer was to move the outfall further away from the town. To disperse the smell, sixty ventilator shafts were built. At Rottingdean, one was disguised as a coast-guard's cottage, and at Roedan, a coke furnace was kept alight twenty-four hours a day to draw a continous flow of air. The sewer worked by gravity, falling approxiamately one yard every mile. Built with glazed engineering bricks these glassy tunnels, a patchwork in hundreds of shades of red, are beautiful to behold. Each summer they are opened to the public and have proved to be one of the town's most popular tourist attractions.

We like to think of rivers as single entities but they are like more like trees with many small branches leading to a central trunk. Just like trees they bend, change course, adapting to the weather. The Wellsbourne's branches now include the 300 miles of sewer that zigzag back forth under the streets. Bubbling under Brighton patiently waiting for another wet summer followed by an even wetter autumn, and another chance to escape and run free.

Mathew Clayton grew up near the village Clayton, just outside Brighton. He has a wife called Gemma and a son called Laurie.

SOURCED
IN THE
WEST

BY
KURT JACKSON

Over the last few years I've completed several projects about rivers – in this country and on the continent as well. To follow a river from its source as it grows and changes, erodes and meanders, evolving itself and the land, this is not just a journey, getting to know the river itself, but is also about discovering and understanding the host country[side] – her history, people, culture, topography and wildlife. The river becomes a metaphor for life itself. Here I have tried to describe my personal experience of five different rivers, all by coincidence in the southwest of the UK, each having been the focus of a recent series of paintings.

THE THAMES... NEAR KELMSCOTT

It's December, it's a cold morning, I sit on the towpath or is it a footpath, anyway part of the Thames Way, on a knackered deck chair. I'm trying to paint looking downstream whilst at the same time trying to keep warm. Moving backwards and forwards in front of my canvas, wrapping and unwrapping my arms around my swaddled body whilst holding my paintbrushes and trying not to fall into the river: the edge of the bank is hidden in the undergrowth – docks, water mint, hogweed and teasels, the dry winter skeletal remains of those lush plants of summer. The river is wide here, and deep, not as large as it gets in its tidal reaches but still a big body of moving water – dark in the shade beneath the overhanging pollarded willows, their sprouting stumps inverted as reflected shadows through which the last of the autumn's leaves drift. The open stretches of water – the midstream shines and glows in the winter sunlight – glinting and dancing with the highlights on the sailing flotsam – passengers from upstream. Somewhere in the river's younger days, a breeze carried sycamore leaves onto the river or did they just fall with that autumnal gravity from a bankside tree to land without a splash and drift away?

The vapour trails above me from a nearby airbase are echoed in this surface and amongst them the odd splash lets me know there are fish out there: they're hidden, in their own world. Apart from that and the lingering stink of a fox it's all still and silent. I'm all alone. The Thames drifts slowly and quietly by, observed only by myself and maybe the fox behind and the fish below.

I'm excited by this winter palette in front of me – subdued umbers and dark greys, plum and deep mauve, ochres and Indian reds; naked trees against a ragged skyline and teasel heads silhouetted against a shiny Thames. Did William Morris enjoy it as much on his strolls down from his nearby manor?

I pour the reflections onto my canvas. I fling the seed heads as globules of paint, the cold shiver and shake of hands forms the scribbles of vegetation. I claw the surface with frozen fingernails which in turn animates the river's own surface to glint and sparkle in the low morning's radiance.

THE AVON BETWEEN BATH AND BRISTOL

I've plonked myself down on this bank, having stomped the vegetation down first, to sit with my legs dangling over the edge, facing upstream. For five years, I've been following and tracking this river through Gloucestershire, Wiltshire, and Somerset watching her grow and change, shaping her lands as they shape her. All because of a lingering memory of the early morning strolls I'd take with my father across dew-drenched fields to Bradford-on-Avon from my Grandmother's house... the first time I met this river.

Here the Avon is wide, green, slow and dark, full of life. A rural Eden close to the suburbs. This is a reserve – Eastwood Farm Nature Reserve with its mown paths and signboards about the residents for the neighbours. Between two cities on the edge of one city, the interface between the rural and the urban – but not a suburbia; the river takes the green idyll into the streets and the young men coupled under the trees take the edginess of the town into the country. There's huge colourful swirling graffiti tags on the bankside pipe opposite and distant traffic with its pumping bass and sirens and train rumblings but it's all accompanied by the serene cerulean flash of mister kingfisher.

I've spread my paints out around me and I stare into the verdant tunnel, into the distant depths where the river first appears to me, reflecting the wooded banks of autumn willow, hazel and sycamore. A glassy surface disturbed only by fish ripples and floating leaves. I'm laying down layers of deep green, dark almost black with seasonal orange-yellows and lime and lemon with leaves ready to fall. Picking out the glints and sparkles of Dace, Chubb, Perch, Trout, Roach, Carp, Pike, Tench and Bream (according to the sign). Bees rattle and buzz inside the Himalayan Balsam flower heads – pink and purple, like anatomical specimens with pungent nettles

and teasel heads to catch the light or be silhouetted against the sky.

A bloke appears on the opposite riverbank, a traveller, a woodsman – a chap who lives in the woods with his three big dogs and his trolley. He proceeds to remove and move his home piece-by-piece along the towpath from under one secret shady tree to another; first the tarpaulins then the hazel frames then a mattress. It goes on and on all through my painting. Towards the end as the afternoon is drawing to a close, I see him dragging an entire three-piece suite along the path with his patient canine mates still following along behind.

Another person, a middle-aged woman, stops and stares at me crouched in my nettles, surrounded by my paraphernalia, unable to understand what I'm doing – there's no fishing rod or picnic. I try to ignore her gaze and pretend she's not there, to concentrate on the work in hand.

A barge appears from out of that distance, a movement amongst the leafy reflections that gradually takes shape to become the decorative and rustic. It's that romantic and nostalgic craft we all love – the gypsy caravan of the waterways. Freedom in black and red; a turbine, a decked bicycle, a tub of herbs, a puff of rollie smoke, "alright?" and he's gone.

The reflections return when the ripples settle down: the mirror is reformed, the trees with their echoes. A heron screeches – the heronry is above the heavily-limed forest floor just up river. You always take their call personally as if they're affronted by your presence, your intrusion into their own private arcadia.

The painting is not working – it'll never work. Frustration, angst and desperation lead to desperate measures; paint is flung, swearing occurs, the water pot is emptied over the mess. The surface is scraped and scratched with fingernails and plant stems; rubbed and gouged. Then a magic occurs, slowly something happens and there, evolving from all these marks is an emergence, a transformation, an interesting bit here, a fine splash of colour there. The painting emerges from the chaos.

A painting or a picture? Only later will I know. Relief leads to reflection: I can sit back and relax a little. My hands are stained and nettle-stung, my palette is empty, my lap is lagged but there's something working in front of me – something to do with the capture or celebration of this river in front of me, next to me, under me, inside me.

THE DORSET STOUR

I was born in Blandford on my Grandparents' smallholding, a place I don't know. I went to live in Africa when I was one month old and never returned; the house and land has long gone, built over under a modern estate. I decided to visit Blandford and follow the nearby river down to the sea; a means of exploring and discovering my birthplace I suppose, looking for those proverbial and elusive roots.

So now I'm sitting at the water's edge – the river at my feet is quite broad and shallow and fast-flowing. The water looks clear and clean and, I suppose, how you would hope and expect a rural Dorset stretch of river to be. There's orange and cream shingle, or is it gravel, on the bed with large shoals of minnows moving busily above it – all trying to face the same direction but now and again loosing their poise in the current or nipping off to feed; a darting, tail-wiggling waggling dance. Vivid green rafts of coarse weed are anchored to the bottom; lazily-waving clumps, growing up to and floating just below the surface, looking invitingly like bathers' submarine cushions. A few alder trees opposite and behind me catch the breeze, which makes them shiver and shimmer.

Sketching and scribbling I face downstream where the water rolls and rushes towards a meander to disappear out of my sight about half a mile away. The late summer sun catches the riffles and ripples to glint and glare and the water-weeds' heads and shoulders break the surface to form clusters of diamonds – concentrations of intense sunlight, like patches of silver scales. All this demands my attention: those strong contrasts in light and dark, the stiller areas with their perfect reflections – how do I respond to that? Tentatively I mark the path of the river, the skyline, the land divided in two. I'm loath to paint every stick and leaf, and their twinned forms echoed below; I prefer to aim for an overall feel where you know the reflections are there with the water moving through. How to show that movement? The river's visible bed, the surface and the water in between. I lay down fields of colour and tone and then, with gestural marks and bits and bobs and splatters and accidents, smudges and drops, it begins. Trickles echo rivulets, scratches catch sticks and the whole clump and chunk of life and the world in front of me starts to unravel itself on the surface of the paper under my hands.

A woodpecker yaffles, laughing at my efforts. The mallards' quack seems to be taking the piss.

There's a warm breeze, the sun moves slowly in its arc, demoiselles, damsels and dragonflies all come and go, and the summer feels to be drawing to a close. The minnows remain in front of me doing their own thing in their club land in the shallows. I was fearful of the Blandford fly, that dipteran parasite, but apart from on the label of a Badger beer bottle they've been absent. A drunken jogging teenage girl assured me they did exist and did bite visitors to the Stour but only earlier in the year.

A flock of cygnets fly over in cliché formation – noisy wing beats, each stroke a cry heading to the west, to a preferable river beat.

The sun disappears behind a cloud, the river's sparkles vanish but then, all returns again, my continuity, my relief. Only one cloud.

Cows moo and low in the fields behind. A wagtail bobs and struts on the bank opposite – the model in front of her mirror.

It can't all be in my painting – there isn't room, but maybe it is and I just can't see it.

Reeds spear the sun.

Bubbles of pure sunshine drift away.

Birds take the piss.

I remember my mother's description of bathing in the Stour in her teens, in the late forties and decide I have to repeat the exercise, sixty years or so later, before this summer ends. I make the last few marks, the final punctuation, a full stop or two and then pack up, stuff my gear away. I insert the wet laden lagged sheet of paper into its portfolio to dry; enveloped away and protected from further accidental mark making.

I strip off, casting my clothes aside and plunge naked into the Stour. I panic the minnows and break the water's own particular subdued sighs and murmurs with my harsh screams and gasps as I submerge into that coldness to lie and be massaged by river, weed and current, pebble and minnow.

THE TAMAR... NEAR SALTASH/KINGSMILL

This is the place I've set my sights on – to find and see my first Cornish Avocets. Those exotic, elusive almost unbelievably pretty waders are the emblem of the RSPB, a symbol of beauty and rarity to me. I'd seen them as a young teenager on the coast of Suffolk but I'd never found them in Cornwall, my home. So here I am on the banks of the estuarine Tamar at low water with England (Devon) over there, the city of Plymouth down there and a rather suburban golf course behind me. The tide has retreated to leave a huge expanse of exposed golden glistening mud. Its surface mirrors the late afternoon sky: a playground for the multitudes of birds to feed, flirt, stroll and amble about on and in. I'm crouched under a tangle of wiggly wobbly mossy oak limbs with brambly briars trying to claw my clothes from me while I scribble on a tiny piece of board and battle with the approaching dusk. The light is dropping rapidly and the stillness and vastness of the estuary seems to exaggerate the widgeons whistling, amplifying their calls of surprise and sex, or maybe the mud has fine acoustics or is it just the time of day? And there they are – the avocets, in pairs or fours wondering across the mud doodling with their fine beaks and leggy legs, minding their own business and unaware of my excitement. There are also curlews sounding sad with the redshank, as well as ridiculously white egrets punctuating the shiny foreshore. They're all picking their way through this soupy larder eager to eat their fill before the tide rises once again to hide this place.

It's packed with wild beasties and living up to its nature reserve status. And then at high water it will be the home to another incredible tribe – with salmon, sea trout, shad, eels and sea lamprey all moving up or down the Tamar, that endless innate migration of emigration and immigration. To think they move past the doorstep and under the noses of all that urban life in Plymouth and Saltash; under Brunel's Bridge and under the warships and nuclear submarines largely unseen and unthought of.

This is what strikes me as extraordinary – this contrast between the primeval and wild continuum within the river and the busy urban sprawling activity of the twenty-first century, chugging and buzzing with engine and electric at the mouth of the river Tamar.

Nightfall sends me home away from the Tamar with my painty souvenir in hand, my head full of that riparian world and my ears still full of those birdcalls of the foreshore.

THE VALENCY, NORTH CORNWALL

I returned here by request of Radio Four to speak about the already much-reported flood – the outcome of the Valency turning into a raging torrent that tore the heart out of the valley and Boscastle. All the other interviewees had poured out their grief and despair at this tragedy and, of course, it couldn't be denied that there was a terrible side to the event with the destruction of homes and the temporary lost of livelihoods (but no loss of life), but I also felt there was another side to it.

I'd lived in the village for six years or so. It was our first home, it was here we had our first taste of married life, our first children were born here and it was where I really started to try and live as an 'artist'. The Valency and her valley behind the village became my playground and work place – I had an affair daily with the river for six years. It was an intimate affair; I knew every rock and pool, meander and cascade. I knew where the trout were easy to see, where the sun caught the water's surface in the morning, where the foliage of each season was mirrored at its finest. I even dreamt of the river. I also became familiar with the wider valley: I could expect certain flowers in the spring in certain places, I knew where the birds nested and I gathered wild fruits and wine-making flowers and saps along the Valency's banks. I think I felt that I was as au fait with this river as Mr Hardy and his blue eyes trotting daily along by the river en route to the village or even those people of long ago that had hidden their treasures – those golden lunulae in the Valency's bogs and marshes in the sources above St Juliot. Not even taking into account the farmers that had grown and raised their families for generations from the Valency's alluvium and in the shelter of her valley.

I hid under those trees along the river's banks scribbling and experimenting with new materials, discovering how to make new marks, how to respond to this paradise. I attempted huge oils on pallets and skip-scavenged boards; I spread the river's waters with dissolved pigments across sheet after sheet of watercolour paper, collages of paint on recycled wrappers and the local paper, playing with the first light of the day and the last. I attempted to capture that ultimate of subjects: the movement of water and all the life within it and around it; but not just any water, that of the Valency in North Cornwall.

However throughout this process of familiarisation (argu-ably an apprenticeship) the land owners, the National Trust, were gradually trimming and tidying the river's route, with neat paths on the banks, painted signs, benches, and kissing gates – the place was being tamed and loosing its wildness. It was only at dusk and in the night that the edginess and a nature in-charge feel returned. I gradually lost my feeling of attach-ment to the place and we moved west further down Cornwall. It was the end of my relationship with the Valency, a separation and ultimately a divorce!

Just before the radio interview I revisited the valley and was stunned. Although the topography was still familiar with its recognisable valley sides and skyline, the river had changed course completely – different meanders from one side of the valley floor to the other. There was driftwood and flotsam snagged and trapped halfway up the trees. Many trees had fallen, huge boulders were strewn around and new 'beaches' created from the recently-exposed rubble and earth. Just as dramatically all those manmade features of a park land had vanished along with the paths and tracks – washed away into Boscastle Harbour and out onto the Atlantic seabed. The river had re-established herself, reinstated herself as a force to respect, a powerful force of nature, a slap in the face to all our complacency, and this was what I was delighted about. It wasn't all a tragedy.

It reminded me of those continental watercourses. Every time I revisit them in the summer they've had their annual winter's rage and flung themselves around, had a tantrum and got stroppy before settling down again for a nice summer.

On this warm day there were butterflies floating and gliding above the river, birdsong and the blueness of the sky between the leaves was reflected here and there below, all very continental and exotic. I jumped into the Valency, naked and white and splashed and sploshed around, a few strokes in the deepest almost waste-deep stretch, with bruised knees and gasped from the cold – a real delight.

Then I painted and experienced a sort of déjà vu – there was a familiarity about the river, even after all the change that had occurred as a result of this tempestuous episode in the Valency's life.

NANCHERROW, WEST CORNWALL

One watercourse that I methodically followed from its source to the sea was the Tregaseal stream running just below where I live near St Just in Penwith. It bubbles out of the ground in a number of springs on the Carnyorth Common moorland, flows down the valley and into the sea. It seems a short distance when you look on the map but an epic journey of its own when you follow it in real life and that's what I did. I followed the route from the downs to the Atlantic with my paints and a series of sketchbooks. I did a painting every ten paces and produced one hundred and forty paintings over three weeks and gave myself a bad case of tennis elbow to match. A mad semi-conceptual idea, as much about doing the walk and discovering and exploring the place as just creating something to look at afterwards.

This stream or river, depending who you speak to, is possibly worthy of the title of the most westerly stream in Britain (south of Scotland, that is), rushing through this most Cornish area of Cornwall with its Kernewek names – Bostraze, Tregaseal, Nancherrow, Kenidjack, Porth Ledden, Zawn Buzz.

The water seeps out of the peaty downs with the three types of heather next to the stone circle and then collects itself amongst the cotton grass and yellow flag before choosing to flow away west down towards the Atlantic in Porth Ledden. Squeezing between granite boulders to form miniature falls and miniature rapids: only big enough to maybe dwarf the brown trout and bull-heads lurking there but not too deep for Trembath's or Rowe's cattle to wade in. Sandwiched between pocket-sized bronze-age fields and enclosed by the ever-present archaic granite hedging, it meanders a little. It leans against a valley side here or over-flows onto a flood plain of water meadows there.

Doorsteps the terraces of miners' cottages with their rhubarb gardens and scratchy scratching hens, undercuts a few cars nervously parked on the banks, a few sycamores and willows and then trying, not to notice, it passes the sewage works with their slight niff and whiff and their liquid addition. Under the lanes beneath listing granite bridges with Japanese knotweed roots trailing downstream and water dropwort crowd-ing and jostling for a position on the bank, it then journeys past gorse-strewn ruined mine engine houses and silent stationary waterwheels with the occasional dipper or grey wagtail sexily flashing and bobbing.

This was the real location of the industrial revolution but it is now empty of commerce and business: only the ruins show the past's business. A few cattle graze the edge of the valley and gaze upon the visiting rambler, the twitcher, the dog walker.

The water wiggles in the valley depths, glints amongst the spoil heaps and then speeds up with the anticipation of meeting the sea. There's eroded and polished stone banks with a plethora of flora; choughs and ravens above and darting troutforms amongst casserite-rich shingle below.

Eventually the river streams out of this most perfect of natural water features into the surf where the seal bottles and the basking sharks cruise and I can relax to sit back and reflect on all that I have seen and painted in those few miles.

Kurt Jackson has a distinguished career spanning almost thirty years as an artist and environmentalist.

Dart

BY
ALICE OSWALD

there goes the afternoon, faster than the rowers
breathe, they lever and spring
and a skiff flies through like
a needle worked loose from
its compass
under the arch where Mick luvs Trudi
and Jud's heart
has the arrow locked through it

From 'Dart', (Faber & Faber, 2002). In 2004, Alice Oswald was named one of the Poetry Book Society's 'Next Generation' poets. Her latest collection, Woods etc. *(2005), was shortlisted for the Forward Poetry Prize (Best Poetry Collection of the Year) and the T. S. Eliot Prize. In 2007, her poem 'Dunt' won the Forward Poetry Prize (Best Single Poem).*